THE BRONX

Rivergate Regionals

Rivergate Regionals is a collection of books published by Rutgers University Press focusing on New Jersey and the surrounding area. Since its founding in 1936, Rutgers University Press has been devoted to serving the people of New Jersey and this collection solidifies that tradition. The books in the Rivergate Regionals Collection explore history, politics, nature and the environment, recreation, sports, health and medicine, and the arts. By incorporating the collection within the larger Rutgers University Press editorial program, the Rivergate Regionals Collection enhances our commitment to publishing the best books about our great state and the surrounding region.

The Bronx

THE ULTIMATE GUIDE TO NEW YORK CITY'S BEAUTIFUL BOROUGH

LLOYD ULTAN & SHELLEY OLSON

Rutgers University Press

NEW BRUNSWICK, NEW JERSEY, AND LONDON

Library of Congress Cataloging-in-Publication Data
Ultan, Lloyd.
The Bronx : the ultimate guide to New York City's beautiful borough /
Lloyd Ultan and Shelley Olson.
pages   cm. — (Rivergate regionals)
Includes index.
ISBN 978-0-8135-7319-9 (pbk. : alk. paper) — ISBN 978-0-8135-7320-5
(e-book: epub) — ISBN 978-0-8135-7321-2 (e-book: web pdf)
1. Bronx (New York, N.Y.)—Guidebooks. 2. New York (N.Y.)—Guidebooks.
I. Olson, Shelley, 1951– II. Title.
F128.68.B8U578 2015
917.47'27504—dc23   2014035924

A British Cataloging-in-Publication record for this book is available from the
British Library.

Visit our website: http://rutgerspress.rutgers.edu

Manufactured in the United States of America

Contents

List of Maps   vii

Acknowledgments   ix

Why Visit The Bronx?   1

PART I: ATTRACTIONS

The New York Botanical Garden   5

The Bronx Zoo   12

Yankee Stadium   18

Wave Hill and the Mansions of Riverdale   23

Van Cortlandt Park and the Van Cortlandt House   31

The Bronx County Building: The Art of Democracy   42

The Edgar Allan Poe Cottage: Poverty and Poetry   50

Woodlawn Cemetery: Beauty for Eternity   54

The Valentine-Varian House: A Legacy of the Revolution   59

Pelham Bay Park: The Riviera of New York City   64

The Hall of Fame for Great Americans   76

The Bronx Museum of the Arts   92

PART II: WALKING TOURS

City Island: New England in The Bronx   97

Belmont: New York's Real Little Italy   111

The Grand Concourse Historic District: Art Deco Delights   117

Valentine to Poe: A Tour of Cultural Discovery   131

In the Footsteps of Edgar Allan Poe   144

Marvelous Mott Haven   153

PART III: PLACES TO GO, THINGS TO SEE

Museums in The Bronx	171
Art Galleries in The Bronx	177
Professional Musical and Theatrical Performance Venues	183
Tours and Events	186
Where to Stay	188
Index	193

Maps

1. The Bronx   xii
2. Wave Hill and the Mansions of Riverdale   28
3. City Island Walking Tour   101
4. Belmont Walking Tour   113
5. The Grand Concourse Historic District Walking Tour   119
6. Valentine to Poe Walking Tour   132
7. In the Footsteps of Edgar Allan Poe Walking Tour   145
8. Marvelous Mott Haven Walking Tour   157

Acknowledgments

The authors wish to express their sincere thanks to Michael Siegel for his invaluable assistance with the maps and to Dilip Kondepudi for his insightful advice.

In addition, the authors wish to give credit to the artists whose work can be seen in the photograph of an exhibition in the Bronx Museum of the Arts. Seen there are:

David Hammons, *Pray for America*, 1974. Body print, silkscreen, 91 × 37 in. framed. Collection of the Hudgins Family, New York; Courtesy of Tilton Gallery, New York.

Martha Rosler, *First Lady (Pat Nixon) from Bringing the War Home: House Beautiful*, 1967–1972. Photomontage, 20 × 24 in. Courtesy of the artist and Mitchell-Innes & Nash, New York.

Suzanne Lacy, *Anatomy Lesson (Floating)* and *Anatomy Lesson (After Montegna)*, 1973–76/2011. Four color digital prints (exhibition copies), one 20 × 60 in., three 11 × 17 in. Courtesy of the artist, Los Angeles.

THE BRONX

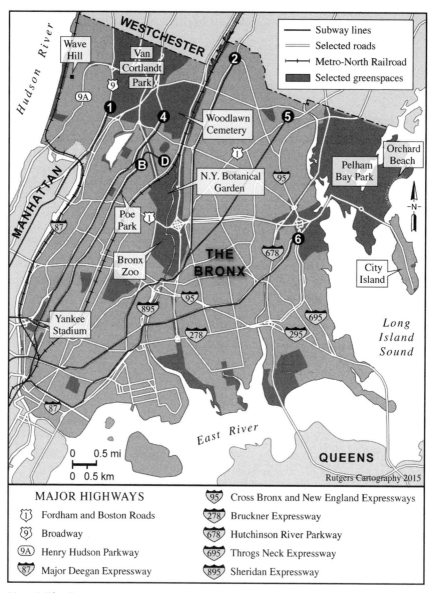

Map 1. The Bronx

Why Visit The Bronx?

The Bronx! Of the fifty million visitors coming to New York City every year, only a small fraction explores the areas outside the borough of Manhattan. By neglecting fully to experience all aspects of this throbbing and vital city, tourists overlook many sites that make the metropolis unique and they fail to witness the daily life of the majority of its eight million residents.

The Bronx! It is one of the city's five boroughs and the only one connected to the mainland. Alone, it has the same geographical area as Paris or San Francisco. Its almost 1.4 million diverse residents originate from every continent on Earth. A full 25 percent of its landmass is devoted to parkland, making it New York City's beautiful borough.

The Bronx! Here is where the visitor can find historic houses and sites that were battlegrounds during the American Revolution. Here is where the final home of poverty-stricken Edgar Allan Poe is preserved, and where historic nineteenth-century mansions of the wealthy can be visited. Here is where many famous industrialists, merchants, statesmen, authors, musicians, and artists are interred in landscaped splendor. Here is where the nation's first Hall of Fame, its most successful baseball team, the country's largest urban zoo and most magnificent botanical garden are found.

The Bronx! Here is where two of the nation's Founding Fathers lived and are buried. Here is where authors, playwrights, poets, composers, and musicians find inspiration that has enriched and still enriches the country's cultural life.

The Bronx! Its variety and its cultural riches beckon visitors to utilize the city's efficient subway and bus system to whisk them to the wonders of the city's beautiful mainland borough. Use this visitor's guide to take you on your journey of discovery.

PART I

Attractions

The New York Botanical Garden

With fifty majestic gardens and over one million plants, the New York Botanical Garden is a National Historic Landmark. This world-class oasis of natural beauty is only a twenty-minute train ride from Grand Central Station.

Within the garden, stroll amid uplifting colors of seasonal flower-beds, go bird-watching with a friendly guide during a Saturday morning walk, commune with ancient trees and extraordinary glacier-deposited boulders that appear as old as time, marvel at a chorus of breathtaking April cherry blossoms, or find solace in the soothing paths and whispering water of the Rock Garden in spring, summer, and autumn. Winter transforms the garden into a snowy wonderland.

Music and dance concerts as well as other events throughout the year are offered in this beautiful setting and are usually included with the price of admission.

The All-Garden Pass includes a tram tour that circles the property, with an auditory guide that will introduce you to the garden's history and the scope of diverse plant life.

A stroll by the beautiful Bronx River awaits the visitor where the refreshing waterfall, just steps from the newly restored Stone Mill, which originally manufactured snuff, feels a world away from the bustle of midtown New York City.

INFORMATION

2900 Southern Boulevard (Dr. Theodore Kazimiroff Boulevard), Bronx, NY 10458

HOURS: From March 1 to January 14, Tuesday to Sunday 10:00 A.M. to 6:00 P.M. From January 15 to February 28, Tuesday to Sunday 10:00 A.M. to 5:00 P.M. Closed most Mondays, Thanksgiving, and Christmas Day. The Garden is open on some holiday Mondays.

ADMISSION: Grounds only, Adults $10.00, Seniors $5.00, Students with valid ID, $5.00, Children 2–12, $2.00, Children under 2, free. Grounds are admission free all day Wednesday and from 10:00 A.M. to 11:00 A.M. on Saturday. Additional admission fee for All-Garden Pass includes admission to the Enid A. Haupt Conservatory, Everett Children's Adventure Garden, Rock Garden (April to October), and the Tram Tour.

CONTACTS: For general inquiries, telephone: 718-817-8700; website: www .nybg.org/plan_your_visit/. For special events, telephone: 718-817-8664. For customized group tours, telephone: 718-812-8687. For comprehensive directions, telephone: 718-817-8779; website: www.nybg.org/visit/ directions.php.

DIRECTIONS

BY PUBLIC TRANSPORTATION: Take the Metro-North Railroad's Harlem local line from Grand Central Station to the Botanical Garden station. The Garden's Mosholu Gate entrance is across the street on Southern Boulevard.

Alternatively, take the letter D or number 4 subway train to the Bedford Park Boulevard station. From the station transfer to the eastbound Bx26 bus to the Garden's Mosholu Gate entrance.

BY CAR OR TAXI: Take Major Deegan Expressway north to the Van Cortlandt Park South exit. Take the left fork on the exit ramp to Van Cortlandt Park South. Turn left and go up the winding hill that is Van Cortlandt Avenue West. At the top of the hill at Sedgwick Avenue, turn left. Just past Dickinson Avenue continue right, then making a left onto Mosholu Parkway, turn right and later turn right again onto Southern Boulevard. Shortly thereafter, turn left into the Mosholu entrance to enter the Botanical Garden. There is on-site parking.

About the New York Botanical Garden

The New York Botanical Garden occupies 250 acres in the northern half of Bronx Park bisected by the magnificent gorge of the Bronx River. The 40-acre forest on the grounds, open to visitors, is reputedly the last remnant of the forest that once covered all of New York City.

From the colonial times until the end of the nineteenth century, most of the site was farmland. In 1840, the Lorillard family erected a fieldstone snuff mill in the gorge, powered by the falls of the Bronx River, to produce tobacco products. Located on the east bank of the river, the mill is the oldest surviving factory building in New York City. It now has an outdoor terrace equipped with picnic tables and chairs overlooking the gorge with a view of the forest on the opposite bank.

In the 1880s, Nathaniel Lord Britton, one of the nation's earliest botanists, taught at Columbia University. On a trip to the Royal Botanic Gardens at Kew, England, his wife asked him why there was no such institution in New York City. Britton then began a movement to establish the New York Botanical Garden. Getting the backing of the university's botanical club and financial and political support from patrons Cornelius Vanderbilt, Andrew Carnegie, and J. P. Morgan, the newly founded New York Botanical Garden was given control of the northern half of Bronx Park. Britton became the garden's first director and supervised the landscaping and construction of the grounds in time for its opening in 1896.

Today, the garden has international recognition for its horticultural excellence, its educational programs, and its scientific research. It is a National Historic Landmark with twenty-seven outdoor gardens and plant collections and a Victorian-style conservatory (glasshouse) modeled after the one at Kew. Its library houses the most extensive collection of botanical and horticultural material in America and its Herbarium, with 5.6 million items, is the largest collection of preserved plant specimens in the Western Hemisphere.

Visitors can walk around the many gardens, see the special displays, stroll through the Bronx River gorge with its waterfall, and go bird-watching.

Attractions and Amenities

At the entrance, ask for a map of the Botanical Garden and a calendar of events to discover what will be going on that day that may be of interest to you.

TOURS

The Tram Tour is a delightful, twenty-five-minute, informative introduction to the 250 acres of the Botanical Garden. Included in the All-Garden Pass, it features a narrated introduction to the history, buildings, gardens, forest, and information on programs available as you are driven through the garden. Nine convenient stops provide areas to hop on or hop off to explore at your own pace. The tour is also an excellent way for visitors who cannot do a lot of walking to be able to see the garden. The tram is wheelchair accessible and equipped with a T-coil compatible induction loop. Headsets are found at the Visitor Center. Large-print written copies of the Tram Tour are available from the tram attendant.

Guided tours of the gardens, forest, and Enid A. Haupt Conservatory are available on specified days. Check the schedule of daily activities available at the entry gate for the time and meeting place of free guided tours on the day of your visit.

Audio tours are available through your personal cell phone: 718-362-9561. Enter the prompt number for the item you wish to hear followed by the # sign. Walking through the grounds, find the audio tour icon signs at select points of interest or on your map. These phone tours may also be accessed from home. iTunes U Audio Tours of permanent or changing exhibits are also available. Access the New York Botanical Garden website and enter the keyword "Audio Tours," to check on current iTunes U Audio Tours.

ENID A. HAUPT CONSERVATORY

This magnificent Victorian building, inspired by the impressive glasshouses in the Royal Botanic Gardens in Kew, England, was designed by Lord and Burnham Company, a leading firm known for its designs of greenhouses. Completed in 1902 at a cost of $177,000, time took its toll and the glasshouse faced the prospect of demolition. It was saved in 1978 by the generosity of Enid Annenberg Haupt, who contributed five million dollars toward its renovation and endowed it with an additional five million dollars for maintenance. Significant improvements and repairs were also made in 1998.

In this spacious glasshouse, eleven different habitats are reproduced—from the humid tropical rain forests filled with large-leafed, verdant vegetation to the arid habitats found in American deserts with a wide variety of hardy, sculpture-like cacti.

Special exhibits are held in the Conservatory throughout the year, for example, the annual Orchid Show in March and April. From mid-November through mid-January there is the holiday exhibit in which highly accurate model trains wind around miniature cityscapes of New York traveling from the Empire State Building through the Brooklyn Bridge and beyond, all built using plant material.

OUTDOOR SEASONAL DISPLAYS

Azalea Garden (early May to mid-June and beyond) consists of nearly one mile of wooded paths greeting a vast profusion of azaleas and rhododendrons from around the world. The Azalea Garden contains about 3,000 trees and shrubs, 28,000 ferns and forest-loving perennials, 40,000 bulbs, and 70,000 plants.

In Cherry Valley (spring) pink and white flowers adorn more than 200 blossoming cherry trees. Some trees are over sixty years old.

The Benenson Ornamental Conifers (all year) display the sculptural, green, four-season beauty of 400 conifer specimens growing on fifteen acres of rolling landscape.

Daffodil Hill (spring) has tens of thousands of glorious yellow and white daffodils comprising about 350 varieties, bringing joy to early spring.

The T. A. Havemeyer Lilac Collection (spring) contains about 90 varieties of lilacs with colors ranging from intense purple to delicate blue and white.

The Kobus magnolia located near the Visitor Center bears white blossoms reaching down to touch the ground (mid-March to mid-April). The grove of mature trees, Magnolia Way, greets the stroller with stunning silver-pink and white bursts of color and fragrance.

OUTDOOR THEMED GARDENS

The Rock Garden (April through November). This garden is adorned with delicate, jewel-like alpine flowers and woodland plants including sun-loving crocuses, delicate daffodils, and tiny tulips as well as a gently cascading waterfall. Thousands of woodland flowers along winding pathways display their beauty next to a refreshing stream leading to a calm pond. This 2.5-acre destination is considered one of the most magnificent rock gardens in the world.

Native Plant Garden. Housing over 100,000 native plants, this 3.5-acre section is striking. The 230-foot-long body of water at its center blends modernism in design with unhindered growth. Water gently flows through the three major segments, cascading from one segment to the next. This is an all-season garden with such plants as aromatic aster, New York aster, yellow trillium, and Indian grass, resplendent in the spring and gracefully asleep in the winter.

Peggy Rockefeller Rose Garden (May through October). A rose by every name—from Abraham Darby to Zéphirine Drouhin—is here, and each one of the 600 varieties of roses was carefully bred by award-winning rose enthusiasts. Designed in 1916 and completed in 1988, the garden contains around 4,000 rose plants beautifully arranged in their well-proportioned spaces framed by walkways that radiate out from a gazebo and circular center.

Everett Children's Adventure Garden (all year). This garden of exploration and discovery encourages children of all ages to interact with nature through a world of mazes and hands-on nature activities that use all five senses. Beautiful water birds will greet young visitors. Bring children to the Boulder Maze to climb and the Touch Tank to see and feel water-loving plants; young eyes meet microscopes as children explore and experiment. Halloween is a special time as pumpkins become magical faces and costumed guides greet visitors.

Ruth Rea Howell Family Garden (April through October). Gardening for the whole family occurs here for those with plots to cultivate. Resident children plant seeds, cultivate food they will eat, dig for worms, and enjoy hands-on activities every day. Come to the garden to learn about foods grown around the world.

Thain Family Forest (all year). This fifty-acre forest carries the unbroken heritage of the original, old-growth forest that was familiar to American Indians. Some trees are over two hundred years old. The forest is a major sanctuary for both migrating and resident birds. Enquire about guided tours before you visit.

SPECIAL EVENTS

Music Performances. From cocktail evenings to exhibit-themed afternoon concerts in both indoor and outdoor spaces, the Botanical Garden is a cultural destination.

Dance Performances. Enjoy the world's diversity in dance concerts themed around current exhibits.

Educational Offerings. The garden offers lectures, workshops, and courses to the public about plants in their scientific, functional, aesthetic, and global diversity.

DINING AND PICNICKING

The Garden Café, southwest of the Mosholu Gate, offers healthy salads and soups as well as hot meals and snacks. Similar fare is available at the Pine Tree Café in the Leon Levy Visitor Center near the Conservatory Gate. Picnic tables are located on the Clay Family Picnic Pavilion.

GIFT SHOP

The garden's gift shop, Shop in the Garden, between the Leon Levy Visitor Center and the Reflecting Pool, sells plants and gardening supplies as well as plant-themed jewelry, clothing, posters, gifts, books, and more.

The Bronx Zoo

From lions, tigers, bears, giraffes, exotic birds, snakes, and crocodiles to penguins flying through water, feel the extraordinary power and wonder of life around the globe with just a swipe of a Metro card and a short ride to the largest urban zoo in the world. The American bison was saved from extinction at the Bronx Zoo; wildlife conservation is a core mission of this institution. With 265 acres of habitats and exhibits and over 600 species of mammals, birds, reptiles, fish, and insects from around the globe, the zoo is the flagship of the Wildlife Conservation Society's multi-borough collection of wildlife parks. Don't miss the Congo Gorilla Forest, the ride on the Wild Asia Monorail, Tiger Mountain, and the zoo's newest exhibit, Madagascar!

As an unexpected bonus, the zoo is an excellent location for watching local and migrating birds that enjoy the wetlands and Bronx River, which runs through the zoo, not to mention the food and protected spaces meant for the wildlife housed there. The Bronx Zoo is one of New York's most beautiful and fascinating places to take long walks while appreciating the natural world and to support wildlife conservation. Repeat visitors might consider membership.

INFORMATION

2300 Southern Boulevard, Bronx, NY 10460

HOURS: Summer (April 3–November 1), 10:00 A.M. to 5:00 P.M. (to 5:30 P.M. on weekends and holidays). Winter (November 2–April 2), 10:00 A.M. to 4:30 P.M. Closed on Thanksgiving Day, Christmas Day, New Year's Day, and Martin Luther King Day.

ADMISSION: General Admission, Adults $16.95, Seniors (65+) $14.95, Children (3–12) $12.95, Children under 2, free. Pay-what-you-wish admission on Wednesdays, and always free for members. The Total Experience Ticket includes admission plus unlimited access to all rides and attractions. Adults $33.95, Seniors (65+) $28.95, Children (3–12) $23.95, Children under 2, free.

CONTACTS: Telephone: 718-367-1010; website: www.bronxzoo.com. Website for directions: www.bronxzoo.com/plan-your-trip/directions .aspx.

DIRECTIONS

Because of its large size, the Bronx Zoo has four entrances: Bronx River Gate, Southern Boulevard Gate, Fordham Road Gate, and Asia Gate.

BY PUBLIC TRANSPORTATION: To Southern Boulevard Gate, take either number 4 or letter D subway train to Kingsbridge Road, transfer on Kingsbridge Road to eastbound Bx9 bus to Southern Boulevard and 184th Street, and cross Southern Boulevard to entrance opposite 185th Street.

To Bronx River Gate, take subway train number 2 to Pelham Parkway, walk to Pelham Parkway South, walk one block west to Bronx Park East, turn south and walk one block to Bronx River Gate.

To Asia Gate, take either subway train number 2 or number 5 to Tremont Avenue (West Farms Square), and walk north on Boston Road three blocks to Bronx Park South and the Asia Gate.

To Fordham Road Gate, take either subway train number 4 or letter D to Fordham Road, transfer to the Fordham Road eastbound Bx12 or Bx12 Select bus to Southern Boulevard and continue walking eastward along Fordham Road to the Fordham Road Gate.

Alternatively, the BxM11 express bus from Manhattan stops along Madison Avenue, between 26th and 99th Streets, and goes directly to the Bronx River Gate (Gate B). (For schedule information and for pick-up and drop-off points, telephone 511 and say MTA, or visit the website: www.mta.info/ busco/schedules/.)

BY CAR OR TAXI: Take the Major Deegan Expressway north to Fordham Road, turn right onto Fordham Road to Southern Boulevard, and turn right onto Southern Boulevard to the parking lot entrance to your left on Southern Boulevard and Bronx Park South at the corner. Parking is available at all the gates, and the two largest parking lots are at the Southern Boulevard Gate and the Bronx River Gate. GPS addresses: Bronx River Gate (Parking B): Intersection of Bronx River Parkway and Boston Road. Southern Boulevard Gate (Parking C): 2300 Southern Boulevard. Fordham Road (Rainey Memorial) Gate (Parking F): Fordham Road. Asia Gate (Parking A): Bronx Park South.

About the Bronx Zoo

The Bronx Zoo, operated by the Wildlife Conservation Society (formerly the New York Zoological Society), occupies 265 acres of the southern end of Bronx Park. Its rocky, rolling meadowlands house 4,000 animals of more than 600 species from every continent on Earth. It is the largest urban zoo in the world. Almost all of the animals roam or fly in simulated natural habitats.

The idea for a zoo was sparked when a member of New York's Boone and Crockett hunting club noted that the wild game in the western plains of the United States was dying out. The member urged the club's president, Theodore Roosevelt, to take steps to establish a zoo so that the game could be preserved for future hunters. Roosevelt appointed a committee that became the New York Zoological Society. The committee appointed William Hornaday as its first director, and he chose the southern half of Bronx Park as an ideal site to display animals. The Bronx Zoo opened to the public in 1899.

A few years later, under Hornaday's leadership, American bison (buffalo) were gathered at the zoo. These bison were used to repropagate herds throughout the West, including in Yellowstone National Park. The bison at the zoo are called "the Mother Herd." Throughout the years, the zoo has led the effort to rescue many species all over the world from extinction. Critically endangered species, such as the Bali Mynah bird, now have a home at the Bronx Zoo. The zoo's recent change of name to "Wildlife Conservation Society" emphasizes its role in the rescue effort.

Early in its existence, the Bronx Zoo also encouraged artists to use its animals as models. Noted American sculptor Anna Hyatt Huntington studied at the Bronx Zoo. She carved the sleek lionesses gliding down the grassy slope on either side of the stairs leading from the fountain inside the Rainey Gate entrance to the Astor Court. One of the zoo's bison became the model for the American buffalo sculpted on the back of the Indian head nickel. The massive bronze Art Deco Rainey Memorial Gate that marks the entrance at Fordham Road depicts many types of animals in its decorative motifs. It was designed in 1934 by Paul Manship, the sculptor who is also known for the statue of Prometheus in Rockefeller Center.

The earliest animal exhibits were placed in cages located both inside and outside buildings dedicated to specific species. Beautiful buildings and enclosures, designed by Heins and LaFarge, originally housed animal exhibits. Because of the current enlightened concepts of caring for animals in as normal a habitat as possible, these structures, on which you can still see the animal names, no longer house the large animals for which they were intended. Yet, the sculptures of roaring big cats, playful primates, and massive elephant heads decorating these old buildings still delight the eye.

Attractions and Amenities

On entering, pick up the Bronx Zoo map. It is useful as you walk around the grounds and view the exhibits. Note the specific times for animal feeding or other special events. Baby strollers and wheelchairs for the handicapped are available.

TOURS

Zoo Shuttle has tickets for unlimited rides and pick-up and drop-off stations throughout the entire zoo. It affords views of many exhibits as it passes by. The shuttle is free to senior citizens. The shuttle does not run on Wednesdays during July and August.

Bengali Express Monorail is a guided tour through the Wild Asia exhibit.

ACTIVITIES

Camel ride (seasonal).

Zucker Bug Carousel offers rides for children.

The 4D Theater exhibits high-definition 3D movies with added sensory experiences.

OUTDOOR EXHIBITS OF ANIMALS IN THEIR HABITATS

Congo Gorilla Forest features about twenty lowland gorillas separated from the visitor only by a large pane of glass. Also here are other primates and the rare okapi.

Tiger Mountain features Siberian tigers in a replica of their native Russian habitat.

Wild Asia features forty acres of freely roving Asian deer, gaur, rhinoceri, elephants, and antelope seen on a guided monorail tour, the Bengali Express.

African Plains features lions, storks, zebras, herds of gazelles, nyalas, African wild dogs, and giraffes roaming in a replica of their African homeland.

Himalayan Highlands features snow leopards, red pandas, and white-naped cranes. Note the award-winning graphic pylons designed by a Tibetan monk.

Baboon Reserve features Ethiopian Highland primates, gelades, a close relative of the baboons, Nubian ibexes, rock hyraxes, and African waterfowl.

Bear Den features grizzly, brown, and polar bears.

Sea Lion Pool features sea lions swimming and lounging in a large and deep pool with simulated crags of rock. They are fed from April to October at 11:00 A.M. and at 3:00 P.M., except Wednesdays; and from November to March at 10:30 A.M. and at 3:00 P.M., except Wednesdays.

Rare Animal Range features Mongolian wild horses, Pere David deer, and other rare animals, many now extinct in the wild.

The Children's Zoo, which adults can enter only if accompanied by a child, introduces the world and science of animals to the young. Here children can touch and feed the animals, see the world from the point of view of animals and insects, negotiate a spider web, or crawl through a prairie dog's tunnel.

Other exhibits feature antelope, giraffes, wolves, wildfowl, bison, elk, mice, reptiles, flamingos, and many varieties of bird species.

INDOOR EXHIBITS

Jungle World features creatures from the world's tropical rain forests indoors in exhibits closely resembling their native habitats. There are no bars separating the visitor from the gibbons, otters, brightly colored birds, caymans, turtles, frogs, and other animals.

World of Birds features many species, such as the white-throated bee eater, parrots, hummingbirds—about sixty species in total flying within habitats with no screen or glass between them and onlookers.

The Aquatic Bird House features penguins and other aquatic birds in their own environments.

Madagascar! features many species of lemurs found only on this island off the coast of Africa, as well as hissing cockroaches, crocodiles, and other animals unique to Madagascar.

Reptile House features snakes, alligators, turtles, lizards, and other species.

Butterfly Zone features a wide variety of colorful butterflies flitting about with nothing between them and visitors.

Mouse House includes such rodents as chinchillas and gerbils as well as mice. Also included are species that prey on rodents, such as mongooses and snakes.

DINING AND PICNICKING

Casual dining is available at the Dancing Crane Cafe and other seasonal cafes found in the zoo, or bring a picnic lunch to some locations.

After your visit to the Bronx Zoo, you may also wish to partake of a delicious meal of Italian fare at any one of the fine restaurants along nearby Arthur Avenue. Cross Southern Boulevard and walk to 187th Street. Walk west along 187th Street to Arthur Avenue. For further information, consult the walking tour "Belmont: New York's Real Little Italy" in part II.

GIFT SHOPS

Gift shops are found at various sites throughout the zoo.

Yankee Stadium

Come and join in the excitement cheering prodigiously long hits, unbelievable running speed, precision pitching, cunning strategy, and incredible defensive athleticism displayed by professional athletes at a baseball game played at the highest level observed from the stands of the most famous sporting facility in the country. Revel in the storied history of the famed New York Yankees franchise at a museum and at monuments dedicated to their players' exploits. Tour the stadium's facilities and witness the behind-the-scenes venues normally closed to the general public. All this can be found at Yankee Stadium.

INFORMATION

1 East 161st Street, Bronx, NY 10452 (between Jerome and River Avenues).

HOURS: Baseball games and other athletic events are scheduled for different days and times throughout the year. This will affect the times tours are offered.

ADMISSION: The cost of seats at any sporting event depends on the location. The cost of a tour depends upon the type of tour purchased.

CONTACTS: For general inquiries, telephone: 212-YANKEES. For tickets to events, telephone: 718-293-6000. For group tours, telephone: 718-579-4531. Website: www.yankees.com.

DIRECTIONS

BY PUBLIC TRANSPORTATION: Take either the number 4 or the letter D subway train (or letter B train in rush hours only) to the 161st Street/ Yankee Stadium station. Trains of the Metro-North Hudson division run from Grand Central Station in Manhattan to the Yankee Stadium station. The station is a short walk from the stadium.

BY CAR OR TAXI: Take the Major Deegan Expressway to the 161st Street/ Yankee Stadium exit. There is ample parking in several parking garages and lots in the vicinity.

About Yankee Stadium

The current Yankee Stadium opened to the public in 2009, but its storied history and tradition makes it the most famous baseball venue in the world. The first "Cathedral of Baseball" was constructed in 1923. The American League Yankees had been sharing the old Polo Grounds in Manhattan on the west bank of the Harlem River as tenants of the National League New York Giants. With the acquisition of Babe Ruth by the Yankees, many Giants fans flocked to Yankee games to witness the spectacle of that phenomenal home-run hitter. In retaliation, the Giants evicted the Yankees from the Polo Grounds.

Quickly, the Yankee team's owners purchased land south of 161st Street at the corner of River Avenue in The Bronx across the Harlem River from the Polo Grounds. There they erected the new Yankee Stadium, a ballpark that had three tiers of seats instead of the standard two. Moreover, this structure was the first one to be designated a baseball stadium, rather than a park, grounds, or field. On opening day, April 18, 1923, the crowd saw Babe Ruth hit the first home run in the new venue and that gave rise to its nickname as "The House That Ruth Built." The Yankees also won their first World Series that year. It began a tradition that made the New York Yankees the winner of more world championships than any team playing any sport anywhere in the world. Through the years, such accomplished players as Lou Gehrig, Joe DiMaggio, Mickey Mantle, Roger Maris, Yogi Berra, Thurman Munson, and Derek Jeter joined Babe Ruth in making their mark on the history of baseball in Yankee Stadium.

Through the years, the stadium was also the venue for several historic boxing matches. Perhaps the most significant occurred in 1938 when Joe Louis, "the Brown Bomber," knocked out the German Max Schmeling in a world heavyweight championship fight. The bout had wider significance than its sporting aspect. Schmeling was backed by German Nazi leader Adolf Hitler who expected him to easily best Louis. The actual results brought joy to both Blacks and Jews as it definitively contradicted Nazi racial ideology.

The stadium was also used for college football games. The one that had the most lasting cultural impact occurred in 1928 when Notre Dame played Army. With no score recorded at halftime, Notre Dame coach Knute Rockne fired up his team in the Yankee Stadium locker room by telling them to "win one for the Gipper," a reference to the college's former halfback George Gipp who had died in 1920. When the film *Knute Rockne: All American* was made, the part of Gipp was played by young Ronald Reagan, who later used that line campaigning for the presidency.

Several professional football games were played at Yankee Stadium as well. From 1956 to 1973, the New York Football Giants called the stadium home. What is probably the most important football game ever played occurred on December 28, 1958—the National Football League championship game between the Giants and the Baltimore Colts. At the end of regulation time, the score was tied. In sudden and dramatic fashion, the Colts won in overtime. It is often called the greatest game ever played. Because the game was televised and attracted a wide national audience, this game elevated professional football to one of the nation's major sports.

Yankee Stadium was also used for soccer games. It was also the site for religious gatherings by Jehovah's Witnesses and Billy Graham, and of Masses celebrated by Popes Paul VI, John Paul II, and Benedict XVI. Rock concerts were held at the stadium, too.

In 1974 and 1975, Yankee Stadium was renovated by New York City because the original structure had deteriorated. Meanwhile, the Yankees played their games at Shea Stadium in Queens. Although much of the exterior remained intact, the renovations did change the dimensions of the field and some of the interior aspects. The first game played at the reopened stadium occurred on April 15, 1976.

By the beginning of the twenty-first century, it was clear that a facility with more modern amenities for both the fans and the team was needed. Construction began on the new Yankee Stadium on a site across the street from the original on the northern side of 161st Street. The new facility was also designed to evoke the design of the original structure without being an exact copy. Much of the exterior was taken from the 1923 design, while the field inside the stadium has the same dimensions as the one in the mid-1970s renovation. When the new Yankee Stadium opened in 2009, it was not really surprising that the

Yankees won the world championship, just as they had done when the original stadium opened in 1923.

Across 161st Street, on the site of the original stadium, New York City has created Heritage Field. It might be worth a look. A few of the artifacts from the original stadium form part of its design, and home plate used for the main ball field is on the site of the original. On the walkway, bricks are incised with significant dates and events that occurred in the original stadium.

Attractions and Amenities

The New York Yankees play their home games at Yankee Stadium throughout the baseball season. Special events, such as football, soccer, and hockey games, boxing matches, and concerts, also occur in this venue. The exact days and times of these events change from year to year.

Behind the grandstands can be found the New York Yankees Museum. It features uniforms, signed baseballs, photographs, and artifacts illustrating the glorious records of the most successful team in baseball and its most accomplished players.

Monument Park beyond the outfield wall and in front of the bleachers displays plaques honoring the great Yankee baseball players and managers, two of the team's owners, a general manager, a Yankee team radio and television broadcaster, and a Yankee Stadium announcer. In addition, there are plaques commemorating the visit of each of the three Roman Catholic popes who had celebrated Mass in Yankee Stadium and one that memorializes the first responders on September 11, 2001, at the time of the attack on the World Trade Center.

TOURS

Tours of Yankee Stadium are given regularly on a first-come, first-served basis and depend on availability. Arrive at least twenty minutes prior to tour time. All tours begin and end at Gate 6 at 161st Street and River Avenue. There are three types of tours available:

1. The Classic Individual Tour consists of eleven people or fewer and begins every twenty minutes from noon to 1:40 P.M., although increased demand could lead to scheduling for other times.

2. The Classic Group Tour consists of twelve to thirty people and is given from 9:00 A.M. to 11:40 A.M. and 2:00 P.M to 4:00 P.M daily and must be reserved in advance. No tours are given after 11:40 A.M. on game days.

3. The Party City Birthday Bash Tour includes all the Classic Tour sites plus a birthday party celebration at the Hard Rock Café. This tour is for twelve to thirty people and requires booking at least two weeks in advance.

Subject to availability, tours during the season include the New York Yankees Museum, Monument Park, the Dugout, the Clubhouse, and the Batting Cage. In offseason, the tour includes the New York Yankees Museum, Monument Park, the Press Box, and the Mohegan Sun Café.

DINING AND SOUVENIRS

Outside the stadium, vendors sell souvenirs and snacks. Souvenirs and meals can also be had at the many shops across River Avenue from the stadium and along 161st Street. Inside the stadium, there are several locations for obtaining both food and souvenirs. Branches of the Hard Rock Café and NYY Steak offer complete meals. The Mohegan Sports Bar, flanked by the bleachers in the outfield, affords a view of the games from behind a massive glass wall.

This visit can be combined with the Grand Concourse walking tour (see part II, "The Grand Concourse Historic District: Art Deco Delights") or with a visit to the nearby Bronx County Building (see part I, "The Bronx County Building: The Art of Democracy") or to the nearby art museum (part I, "The Bronx Museum of the Arts"). To get to the beginning of the Grand Concourse walking tour on 167th Street, take the northbound subway letter D train (B train in rush hours only) one stop to the 167th Street station. To get to the Bronx County Building, walk east, up 161st Street, three blocks to the Grand Concourse. To get to the Bronx Museum of the Arts, take any of the buses across the Grand Concourse at 161st Street north to 165th Street, or walk to 165th Street and the Grand Concourse.

Wave Hill and the Mansions of Riverdale

Visit one of the wealthiest neighborhoods in New York City. Filled with upscale single-family homes and dotted with magnificent nineteenth-century mansions, many of which are still privately owned, Riverdale does not look as if it is part of the great metropolis. But it is! Walk along the quiet asphalt streets, many of which still lack sidewalks, and drink in the atmosphere of tree-lined lanes, manicured lawns, and comfortable living. One of its treasures, Wave Hill, a large estate with two mansions and spectacular views, is open to the public. Come and be lifted spiritually and emotionally to a higher plane.

The high plateau overlooking the Hudson River tucked into the northwest corner of The Bronx is called Riverdale. Until the middle of the nineteenth century, farmers in the area shunned it. The rocky soil and the steep climb to reach the top made it among the least desirable locations to cultivate the soil. Residents used it as pastureland to graze cattle and sheep.

This view changed dramatically by the mid-nineteenth century. Wealthy New York City merchants and industrialists sought country homes to escape the dust, pollution, and noise of the growing metropolis. At the same time, there was a growing appreciation of picturesque and spectacular natural views, such as could be seen across the wide Hudson. Moreover, the cooling breeze wafting over high ground was an asset during hot summers in the days before air conditioning.

Two groups of developers purchased the farms, divided the land into estate lots, and sold the properties to New York City wealthy families who had to erect their own mansions. They called the developments Riverdale Park and The Park, Riverdale. The two soon became known simply as Riverdale. In the late 1920s, Joseph P. Kennedy, then head of 20th Century Fox, lived with his family, including young John F. Kennedy, in a substantial home on the southeast corner of West 252nd Street and Independence Avenue that has since been enlarged and altered. During World War II and afterward, classical composer Béla Bartók lived in a house on Cambridge Avenue near Ewen Park. U Thant of Burma also resided in Riverdale in the later 1960s and early 1970s while serving as the third secretary general of the United Nations. Several of the mansions the original families built still stand. Two are open to the public; others remain privately owned, but can be viewed from outside.

Since the opening of the Henry Hudson Parkway in the 1930s, Riverdale has become fully part of the city with luxury high-rise cooperative, condominium, and rental apartment houses sharing the neighborhood with single-family homes, garden apartments, shopping streets, and restaurants. Today, many of the inhabitants are Jewish, with a significant admixture of Irish and other ethnic groups. Some of the ambassadors to the United Nations have their homes and embassies here, notably the Russians, who occupy a massive white brick high-rise residence on Mosholu Avenue near West 256th Street. It is not unusual to see automobiles on the streets bearing diplomatic license plates.

INFORMATION

675 West 252nd Street, Bronx, NY 10471

HOURS: 9:00 A.M. to 5:30 P.M. from March 15 to October 31; 9:00 A.M. to 4:30 P.M. from November 1 to March 14, Tuesday through Sunday, closed Monday.

ADMISSION: $8.00 for adults, $4.00 for students and seniors 65 and older, $2.00 for children 6 and older, free to members and children under 6. Free Tuesdays and Saturday mornings from 9:00 A.M. until noon.

CONTACTS: Telephone: 718-549-3200; website: www.wavehill.org/visit/. For school group registration or additional information, e-mail: schoolgroups@wavehill.org.

DIRECTIONS

BY PUBLIC TRANSPORTATION: Take subway train number 1 northbound to 231st Street. Transfer to westbound and northbound bus Bx7 or Bx10 at West 231st Street and Broadway near the Chase Bank to West 252nd Street and Henry Hudson Parkway East. Walk west over the highway four blocks to Independence Avenue; turn left and walk one long block to the Wave Hill entrance at West 249th Street.

Alternatively, take the BxM1 Express bus on Third Avenue or the BxM2 Express bus on Sixth Avenue to West 252nd Street and Henry Hudson Parkway East. (For schedule information and for pick-up and drop-off points, telephone 511 and say MTA, or visit the MTA website: www.mta.info/busco/schedules/.) Walk west over the highway four blocks to Independence Avenue; turn left and walk one long block to the Wave Hill entrance at West 249th Street.

Visitors may also take subway train number 1 to 242nd Street. Board a free Wave Hill van on the west side of Broadway in front of the Burger King restaurant that leaves Tuesday through Sunday ten minutes after each hour from 9:10 A.M. to 4:10 P.M. taking visitors directly to the entrance. The van returns to 242nd Street and Broadway departing from the Wave Hill entrance on the hour from noon to 5:00 P.M.

BY CAR OR TAXI: Take the Henry Hudson Parkway northbound to 246th Street exit. Continue north on Henry Hudson Parkway East to West 252nd Street. Turn left over the highway to Henry Hudson Parkway West. Turn left onto West 249th Street. Turn right to Independence Avenue and the Wave Hill entrance.

About Wave Hill

A grand twenty-eight-acre estate with stunning gardens and the Glyndor Art Gallery, Wave Hill greets the visitor with breathtaking views of the Hudson River and the sweeping New Jersey Palisades, lifting the spirit and nourishing the soul. No wonder former residents include writer Mark Twain, young Theodore Roosevelt, who developed his love of nature here culminating in the expansion of the national parks during his presidency, and world-renowned conductor Arturo Toscanini. Charles Darwin and Thomas Huxley also visited here to relish its beauty and nature. The British mission to the United Nations had its home at Wave Hill, and the Queen Mother spent time here.

The Wave Hill estate is the site of two mansions. The mansion at the northern end is called Wave Hill. It was erected in sections over several years in varying styles. What is today the center portion that contains the mansion's entrance was built in 1844. Perhaps the most noted owner was publisher Thomas H. Appleton who invited some of his famous authors as his guests. These included William Makepeace Thackeray, John Tyndall, T. H. Huxley, and Herbert Spencer. In the summers of 1871 and 1872, young Theodore Roosevelt vacationed here with his parents. Mark Twain resided at Wave Hill for a few years in the early twentieth century, attracted by the spacious dining room that spanned the width of the house and the river views.

George Walbridge Perkins, a partner of banker J. P. Morgan who served as Theodore Roosevelt's campaign manager during his failed 1912 "Bull Moose" campaign to recapture the presidency, owned the house next. In 1928, tenant Bashford Dean, a professor at Columbia University, erected the Gothic north wing, called the Armor Hall, designed by noted architect Dwight James Baum. Dean placed his large medieval armor collection in the new wing. That collection became the heart of the medieval armor now on exhibit in the Metropolitan Museum of Art.

After 1933, the Perkins-Freeman family added the south wing to the mansion. Arturo Toscanini lived in the mansion while serving as conductor of the NBC Symphony Orchestra. Following World War II, the family leased Wave Hill to the British mission to the United Nations. In that capacity it hosted Prime Minister Anthony Eden and Queen Mother Elizabeth.

In the early twentieth century, Perkins erected a red brick Georgian-style mansion at the southern end of the estate. Called Glyndor II, it replaced a larger mansion on the site that had been destroyed by fire. Whenever Wave Hill was rented out, the family resided at Glyndor II. In 1960, the Perkins-Freeman family donated the estate with its two mansions to New York City.

Today, the site is open to the public serving as a botanical garden with outdoor horticultural displays and plants growing in the greenhouses. The grounds are also used from time to time for concerts, dance performances, and sculpture exhibits. Artworks are displayed in both mansions. Concerts are also given inside the Armor Hall. The public is permitted to wander around to enjoy the beauty of the grounds and its scenery.

TOURS AND SPECIAL EVENTS

Courteous guides, experts in New York history and horticulture, lead free walking tours, sharing knowledge of Wave Hill's past and the rich geology of the Palisades. Walking tours include the Monocot Garden, the Aquatic Garden, the Wild Garden, the woodland, the Marco Polo Stufano Conservatory, and the historic buildings.

Weekend family art activities related to nature will delight children. Occasional chamber concerts are also performed. Contemporary poets and writers, informally discussing new works in the Café or on the sweeping green lawns, may inspire your own creativity.

Innovative learning programs, integrating art and science, expand Wave Hill's offerings to children, adolescents, and educators. Wave Hill's grounds become the inspiring laboratory of hands-on natural science exploration, ecological learning experiences, internships, and more. Programs available include camp groups, school programs, Forest Project Summer Collaborative, internships, professional development, and Woodland Ecology Research Mentorship.

DINING AND PICNICKING

Outdoor picnic areas are available year round. The Café at Wave Hill, located in Wave Hill House, was recently enlarged during restoration of the historic mansion. The visitor will find a selection of gourmet sandwiches, salads, desserts, and beverages to be enjoyed indoors or outdoors on the magnificent stone patio overlooking the Hudson River.

Mansions and Other Notable Buildings

Christ Church, Riverdale, is at the West 252nd Street bus stop. This picturesque Episcopal church made of brick and local stone was designed by Richard M. Upjohn in 1866. It was the site of the funerals of both Yankee baseball Hall of Famer Lou Gehrig and former New York City mayor Fiorello LaGuardia.

The Kennedy House, at the southeast corner of West 252nd Street and Independence Avenue, was inhabited by Joseph P. Kennedy, then the head of the 20th Century Fox film studio, and his family from 1927 to 1929. Young John F. Kennedy grew up there, attending nearby Riverdale Country School and graduating from it. The boy never forgot his stay in Riverdale. When he was running for the presidency in 1960, at a rally in The Bronx, he stated, "You know, I'm from The Bronx; albeit Riverdale, but it is The Bronx!" Since the time of that family's residence, the house has been altered and enlarged from its original appearance.

The Anthony Campagna Estate is on the southeast corner of West 249th Street and Independence Avenue, just across the street from the

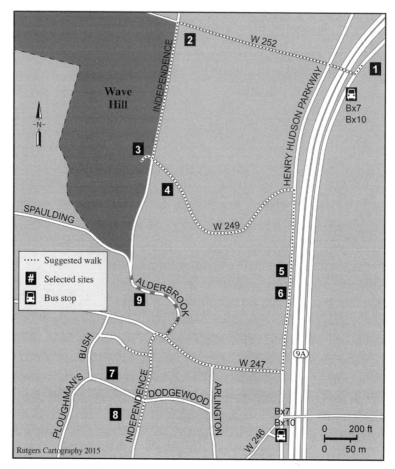

Map 2. Wave Hill and the Mansions of Riverdale

1. Christ Church, Riverdale
2. Kennedy House
3. Wave Hill
4. Anthony Campagna Estate
5. Riverdale Presbyterian Church
6. Duff House (Manse)
7. Greyston (Dodge Mansion)
8. Naumkeag
9. Alderbrook

entrance to Wave Hill. Located on a hill overlooking the Wave Hill estate with views of the Hudson River, this mansion was erected in 1922 and designed by Dwight James Baum for Anthony Campagna. Campagna was an Italian immigrant who amassed a fortune developing luxury apartment houses that still flank much of Park Avenue in Manhattan. The hill is paved with Belgian block with parallel stone slabs designed to form a smooth path for vehicles to reach the top. Sited just beyond a circular driveway, the mansion has stucco exterior walls and a tile roof. The house was once used for a series of scenes in

Contract on Cherry Street (1977), the only made-for-television movie starring Frank Sinatra. Today, it serves the ultra-Orthodox Jewish community as an educational facility. The site is still privately owned and can be admired only from the street.

The Riverdale Presbyterian Church, on Henry Hudson Parkway West just south of West 249th Street between the two high-rise red brick apartment houses, was designed in 1863 by James Renwick Jr. He was also the architect of Saint Patrick's Cathedral in Manhattan. Both are in the Gothic Revival style, but this church is more modest in scale, reflecting English country churches. At the time, Riverdale, with its mansions and estates, resembled the nineteenth-century English countryside.

The Duff House, on Henry Hudson Parkway just to the south side of the Riverdale Presbyterian Church, is the Manse, or residence, of the church's minister. Also designed by James Renwick Jr., it is an unusual architectural combination. The stone lower section is in the Gothic Revival style, but it is topped by a mansard roof, an element that was beginning to come into favor at the time.

Greyston, on West 247th Street and Independence Avenue, is located west of Henry Hudson Parkway West. Here, Independence Avenue has the aspect of a driveway coming into 247th Street. The Greyston mansion is located just south of the roadway and just west of the driveway. One of the earliest Riverdale mansions erected, Greyston was designed by James Renwick Jr. in 1864 for William E. Dodge. Dodge was the co-owner of the Phelps-Dodge Copper Company. Made of gray stone, with the date of its completion placed above its main doorway, the house boasts of many gables and chimneys. The family was always interested in education, and helped found Teachers College, Columbia, in 1887. Dodge's daughter, Grace Dodge, who lived in the mansion her entire life, championed vocational education. The mansion is still privately owned, but can be approached and viewed from the outside. The estate grounds behind it are now filled with single-family homes.

Naumkeag is located a short distance behind Greyston positioned on a right angle to it facing Independence Avenue (the driveway coming in from West 247th Street). An orange brick mansion with limestone trim, it was built for Cleveland Dodge, the son of William E. Dodge and the brother of Grace Dodge. The house, still privately owned and closed to the public, has a light and airy feeling about it. Cleveland Dodge graduated from Princeton University and was deeply involved in its development, serving for many years on its board of trustees. He was instrumental in making Woodrow Wilson president of Princeton. On October 12, 1918, President Wilson and Dodge were reviewing a World War I Liberty Bond parade in Manhattan when a telegram was thrust into the president's hand. It was from the Imperial German government asking for Wilson's peace terms. Dodge took Wilson back with him to Naumkeag where they discussed what to do. Wilson then penned a reply in the mansion's library. One month later, on November 11, 1918, the Armistice ending the fighting in World War I went into effect, an event that had its origins in Naumkeag.

Alderbrook, while located on Independence Avenue south of West 248th Street, is best seen from West 247th Street and Independence Avenue. There is a private pedestrian road, called Alderbrook Road, leading down the hill to the mansion itself, which is accessed from the north side of West 247th Street just to the east of Independence Avenue. Alderbrook was erected about 1880 for Percy Pyne, then the head of the National City Bank, today Citibank. Inspired by the designs of Andrew Jackson Dowling, it is a brick house in a Gothic Revival style with gables and spires carved with foliage. In the twentieth century, Alderbrook served as the home and studio of the sculptor Elie Nadelman, who died in 1946. Nadelman was known for his unique and often eccentric works. The mansion is still privately owned and its interior closed to the public. Its grounds are now filled with single-family homes that form a private community taking its name from the mansion.

Van Cortlandt Park and the Van Cortlandt House

Field and forest, horseback riding, world-class running trails, free summer concerts, barefoot dancing to global music on the lawn of historic Van Cortlandt House (where General George Washington had his headquarters in 1776 while his troops were encamped on the adjoining Parade Ground)—this is Van Cortlandt Park. Bird-watching and nature hikes with Urban Park Rangers and Audubon guides, New York City's home of the Urban Arbor Conservation Program and the Van Cortlandt Park Conservancy, ball fields, including weekend cricket with South Asians and West Indians at the bat, tennis competitions, facilities for baseball, softball, soccer, and seasonal ice skating—this is Van Cortlandt Park. Come for free summer swimming in a huge outdoor pool surrounded by birdsong, enjoy lunch on a landmarked golf clubhouse porch directly overlooking Van Cortlandt Lake, bring your clubs to the first municipal golf course in America, or enjoy summer barbecue and picnics on the lawns.

Van Cortlandt Park is larger than Central Park. About half of Van Cortlandt Park is a protected nature preserve with well-marked, scenic trails for hiking. Sitting quietly on the banks of Van Cortlandt Lake amid diverse ducks, geese, and occasional wild swans refreshes the spirit.

INFORMATION

This vast park extends from Broadway on its western boundary to Jerome Avenue and Van Cortlandt Park East on the eastern boundary, from the New York City line on its north to Van Cortlandt Park South and Gun Hill

Road on its south. The historic house, Parade Ground, and pool are located near Broadway and 242nd Street.

Visitors are urged to stop first at the Van Cortlandt Park Visitor Center located off Broadway east of West 246th Street on the asphalt path leading to a point beyond the rear of the Van Cortlandt House to pick up a park map. The Nature Center also provides a calendar of daily events with locations and times. Hours and fees for specific activities are given below in the Attractions and Amenities section.

CONTACTS: For general inquiries, telephone: 718-430-1890. Website for current park activities, on-line maps, comprehensive travel directions, and additional information: www.nycgovparks.org/parks/VanCortlandtPark.

DIRECTIONS

BY PUBLIC TRANSPORTATION: Take the northbound number 1 subway train to 242nd Street/Van Cortlandt Park.

Alternatively, take the northbound express bus BxM3 on Madison Avenue to 246th Street and Broadway at Van Cortlandt Park. (For schedule information and for pick-up and drop-off points, telephone 511 and say MTA, or visit the MTA website: www.mta.info/busco/schedules/.)

BY CAR OR TAXI: Take the Major Deegan Expressway north to the Van Cortlandt Park South exit. Take the right fork on the exit ramp onto Van Cortlandt Park South (westbound). Turn right (north) on Broadway. Street parking is available on Broadway. There is free parking available at the Van Cortlandt Park Golf House (accessed from the northbound entrance to the Major Deegan Expressway on Van Cortlandt Park South at the north end of Bailey Avenue) and the Shandler Ballfield (accessed on Jerome Avenue north of the end of the Woodlawn-Jerome line [number 4 subway]).

About Van Cortlandt Park

Van Cortlandt Park, at 1,146 acres, the third largest park in New York City, is in the northwest Bronx. It abounds in attractions, both natural and constructed, that make a trip there filled with wonder and variety.

The rocky ridges within the park are 375 million years old, the oldest bedrock in the city. The American Indians called the stream that wends its way through the park from the north *Mosholu*, meaning "smooth stones." The European colonial settlers called it Tibbett's Brook after a local landowner.

In 1699, New York City merchant Jacobus Van Cortlandt purchased much of the land in today's park from his father-in-law, Frederick Philipse. He dammed Tibbett's Brook to form the lake now in the park. Water rushing over the lake's spillway powered gristmills and sawmills that stood on the site until 1911 when they were hit by lightning and burned down. Today, visitors can relax on the side of the lake watching ducks, geese, and perhaps an occasional swan glide over the water.

In 1748, Jacobus's son, Frederick Van Cortlandt, erected a stone house made of cut fieldstone. The windows are framed in red brick with faces carved over each lintel. The Van Cortlandt family occupied the house for the next 140 years. When the American Revolution broke out and British forces threatened to occupy New York City, Augustus Van Cortlandt was the city's clerk. For safekeeping, he placed the city's records beneath the arch of his father's vault in the family cemetery on Vault Hill, a rocky ridge behind the house some distance away.

During the American Revolution, George Washington used the house as his headquarters in October 1776 until he was ejected in November by British general Sir William Howe, who used it briefly for the same purpose. During the conflict, Hessian troops, German mercenaries paid by the British, and Tories, Americans supporting the British cause, encamped on the grounds.

Several battles and skirmishes were fought in and around the house. In one of these, in 1778, a band of Stockbridge Indians fighting for the American cause were ambushed by Hessian and Tory units in what is now the northeast section of the park. The Indians were chased as far as the Van Cortlandt family fields (today's Parade Ground) north of the house. Indians killed in the battle were buried in the northeastern section of the park still called Indian Field. Washington returned to the Van Cortlandt House in July 1781 to conduct a reconnaissance of British fortifications in Manhattan with an eye to a possible invasion of the city from the north. Washington's final visit came in November 1783 when he led his army, the state's first governor, and civil officials from the Van Cortlandt House to Manhattan to take possession of New York City from the evacuating British in the last act of the American Revolution. Today, the Van Cortlandt House, the oldest structure in The Bronx, is furnished with period furniture and paintings. It is open to the public as a historic house museum.

In the 1840s, the Croton Aqueduct providing a water supply to an expanding New York City was built through the land that would become Van Cortlandt Park. Placed underground, its route later became part of one of the many nature and hiking trails within the parkland where visitors can enjoy the natural woods and plants and view many species of birds.

In the 1880s, John Mullaly, an Irish immigrant who edited an Irish ethnic newspaper, agitated for the purchase of parkland on the mainland for the people of the city. He argued that the purchase would not cost much because a sparse population then kept land values low, a condition that could not last as the city's population expanded northward. Moreover, the natural topography meant that much of the land needed no landscaping, thus making the creation of parkland still less expensive. In 1888, a commission guided by Mullaly purchased Van Cortlandt Park, along with Bronx Park, Pelham Bay Park, Crotona Park, Claremont Park, St. Mary's Park, and the routes of Mosholu Parkway, Pelham Parkway, and Crotona Parkway. These purchases laid the foundation of the Bronx park system that now covers 25 percent of the borough's land.

In 1895, in response to a petition, a golf course was laid out in the park. At the time, it was a grand experiment. This was the first municipally owned golf course in the nation. Other cities watched the result. When the Van Cortlandt Golf Course proved to be overwhelmingly popular, other cities followed suit and built their own municipally operated golf courses. The city later constructed the Mosholu Golf Course in the park near Jerome Avenue at its juncture with Bainbridge Avenue in the early twentieth century.

Mullaly envisioned the family cornfield north of the Van Cortlandt House as a Parade Ground for the New York City units of the state's National Guard. For decades thereafter, guardsmen marched over the field and performed sham battles watched by local residents. In the 1930s, Robert Moses, New York City's first citywide parks commissioner, redesigned the Parade Ground as athletic fields. Today, baseball, soccer, and other games are played on what is still called the Parade Ground. Moses also erected the stadium on Broadway north of 240th Street where track and field contests are held, and whose exterior walls are used as handball courts.

When the New York Central Railroad planned to erect a new Grand Central Station on 42nd Street and Park Avenue in Manhattan, its officials wanted to know what various types of stone that were being considered for the station's walls would look like after years of exposure to the elements. Since the 1880s, the Putnam Division of the New York Central Railroad had its line running through Van Cortlandt Park. The Central's officials transported thirteen massive slabs of each type of stone to Van Cortlandt Park and placed them along the west side of the railroad's tracks to observe how they would weather. The Putnam Division has since been shut down, its tracks have been taken up, and the route has become today's Putnam Trail with wonderful views of Van Cortlandt Lake. The massive slabs alongside the trail are still there, forming the "Stonehenge of The Bronx."

In the second decade of the twentieth century, a cross-country race course was laid out. Its starting and finishing point is at the western end of the Parade Ground, but it forces runners to traverse a challenging course atop Vault Hill and through wooded areas. It is considered the premier cross-country track in the nation. Many championship collegiate and secondary school meets are held at this cross-country course throughout the year.

For those who wish to go horseback riding, there is an equestrian center in the park. Located along Broadway at West 256th Street south of Mosholu Avenue, it boasts of an Olympic-sized indoor arena, four outdoor riding rings, and miles of bridle trails throughout the natural woodlands of Van Cortlandt Park.

Robert Moses, who was also the city's highway commissioner, routed both the Henry Hudson Parkway and the Major Deegan Expressway through Van Cortlandt Park. He did provide a means to walk from one area of the park to another and still enjoy the quiet and the natural landscape.

In the 1970s, utilizing a federal grant, the city built a large swimming pool complex southwest of the Van Cortlandt House. It attracts thousands of users every summer.

Since 2012, an ice skating rink is installed alongside Broadway near the stadium every winter.

Attractions and Amenities

Visitors to Van Cortlandt Park have the opportunity to partake in the varied available activities from outdoor fitness equipment to free nature walks with the Urban Park Rangers. In addition, one can see how the many and diverse residents of New York City, especially of The Bronx, relax, just being themselves.

The attractions and facilities in Van Cortlandt Park include:

Baseball fields number twenty and are located throughout the park. There are two turf fields at the Allen Shandler Recreation Area at Jerome Avenue south of 233rd Street, six turf fields at West 242nd Street and Broadway, one turf field at Caryl Field at West 263rd Street and Broadway, two Little League fields at Frank Kelly Field at West 259th Street and Broadway, one Little League field at Kepler Field at Van Cortlandt Park East and East 240th Street, four regulation fields inside the Van Cortlandt Park Stadium, and four turf fields at East 233rd Street and Van Cortlandt Park East. Permits are needed for organized events and for leagues. They are free for youth under the age of eighteen; those eighteen and over must pay a fee for the permit. For permit information, telephone: 718-430-1840.

Basketball courts are located in Van Cortlandt Stadium and in the playground at Van Cortlandt Park South and Gouverneur Avenue.

Bird-watching enthusiasts have spotted 230 different species in the park. Every Saturday at 8:00 A.M., a free bird walk is led by an expert. Bring binoculars and wear comfortable shoes. For information, telephone: 718-430-1890; or check the website at www.nycgovparks.org/parks/VanCortlandtPark.

Bicycling can be enjoyed on the 1.7-mile bicycle path circling the Parade Ground.

Bocce courts are available on a first-come, first-served basis, since no permits are required to use them, except for tournaments. Visitors may observe those using the facility to play the Italian game at the northern end of the Parade Ground.

Cricket fields are concentrated near Broadway on the Parade Ground and near the stable area north of Henry Hudson Parkway. South Asians and West Indians play cricket on warm weekends. Permits are required to reserve a cricket field. Telephone 718-430-1840 for permit information.

Dog walking and running is allowed. Dogs must be on a leash at all times, except in the Van Cortlandt Park Dog Run at Broadway and West 252nd Street. See the website www.nycgovparks.org/facilities/dogareas for the rules and regulations for canines.

Fishing is permitted in Van Cortlandt Lake inside the park accessed at Van Cortlandt Park South at the north end of Bailey Avenue. The use of barbed hooks and lead weights is prohibited, and all fish caught must be immediately released. Discarded fishing line and other refuse must be placed in the trash bins. All New York City and New York State fishing regulations must be followed. See the website www.nycgovparks.org/facilities/fishing for additional information.

Football fields are found in the park at West 246th Street and Broadway and at East 233rd Street and Van Cortlandt Park East.

There are two **golf facilities** in Van Cortlandt Park. The Van Cortlandt Golf Course is on Van Cortlandt Park South off Bailey Avenue and the entrance to the northbound Major Deegan Expressway. The Mosholu Golf Center and Driving Range is at Jerome Avenue near Bainbridge Avenue. Tee times can be reserved by telephone or on-line. New York City residents can play golf with a valid residential permit. For information about Van Cortlandt Golf Course or to reserve a tee time, telephone 718-543-4595. For information about the Mosholu Golf Center and Driving Range, telephone 718-655-9164. For both courses, the website is www.golfnyc.com/request_tt.

Handball courts are found in different sections of the park. Nine are at Van Cortlandt Stadium at West 242nd Street and Broadway, three are in the Classic Playground at Van Cortlandt Park South and Gouverneur Avenue, and two more are at East 239th Street and Van Cortlandt Park East.

Hiking trails in Van Cortlandt Park are wonderful. Surround yourself with forest choosing either lake views, wooded hills, or open areas filled with Revolutionary War history. Obtain a map of the trails at the Nature Center near the rear of the Van Cortlandt House or on-line at the Van Cortlandt Park website.

The Cass Gallagher Nature Trail, named for a local activist and champion of Van Cortlandt Park, is a 1.4-mile moderately difficult hike beginning near the horse stables, a short walk from Broadway and Mosholu Avenue.

The John Kieran Trail, named after the famed naturalist and *New York Times* sportswriter who resided nearby, is an easy 1.25-mile walk beginning near the Van Cortlandt Golf Course in from Van Cortlandt Park South. The trail travels through areas around the lake and through wetlands, crosses Tibbett's Brook using a wooden bridge, and connects to the Parade Ground. There are great areas for bird-watching.

The John Muir Trail, bearing the name of the famed crusading American naturalist, is a 1.5-mile trail of moderate difficulty and is the only trail that traverses the park from east to west. The hiker can begin at one end at Broadway and Mosholu Avenue or the other end at Van Cortlandt Park East and Oneida Avenue. At the eastern end of the trail are Indian Field and a small stone monument commemorating the 1778 Revolutionary War battle when a band of Stockbridge Indians, fighting for the Americans, were ambushed by Hessian and Tory troops, fighting for the British, and massacred and buried on the site. There are three ecologically different forests on this route. In the Northeast Forest, the hiker finds tulip trees, sweet gum, red oak, and a marsh that is the home to frogs. In the second area, the Croton Woods, there are sugar maples and hickory trees, as well as the Old Croton Aqueduct. The third area, the Northwest Forest, has tall tulip, hickory, and majestic oak trees.

The Old Croton Aqueduct Trail is an easy-to-moderate 1.1-mile hike. It begins either at Van Cortlandt Park South and Dickinson Avenue or nearby at Mosholu Parkway and Gun Hill Road. Built in the 1840s, the Croton Aqueduct was a major engineering project that brought water from northern Westchester County (north of The Bronx) to New York City, then confined only to Manhattan Island. This trail is part of the scenic forty-one-mile route of the aqueduct.

The Putnam Trail is an easy 1.5-mile walk beginning at Van Cortlandt Park South and Bailey Avenue, and may be accessed through the Van Cortlandt Park Golf Course parking lot. The trail follows the path of the former Putnam Division of the New York Central Railroad that originated in Brewster, New York, fifteen miles to the north, and which operated from the 1870s to the 1980s. The trail takes the hiker through a beautiful oak and hickory forest native to the region. It also passes by the massive stone slabs erected by the railroad to determine which stone would look best as the walls of the new Grand Central Station after exposure to the elements. They are sometimes referred to as the "Stonehenge of The Bronx."

Horseback riding is available at the Riverdale Equestrian Center on Broadway between the Henry Hudson Parkway and Mosholu Avenue. Situated on twenty-one beautiful acres, it has an indoor Olympic-sized ring, four outdoor rings, and access to many miles of wooded trails for riding in Van Cortlandt Park. For a horseback trail riding guide, telephone: 718-548-4848; website: nycgovparks.org/parks/VanCortlandtPark/facilities/horseback.

Ice skating (seasonal) is located at a rink at Broadway and West 242nd Street at the stadium. Hours: November through March, Monday to Thursday, noon to 8:00 P.M.; Friday to Sunday, noon to 10:00 P.M. Admission: Adults, Seniors, and Children, $5.00 on weekdays, $8.00 on weekends. Skate rental: $5.00. Contacts: Telephone: 718-780-9001; website: www.nycgovparks.org/parks/VanCortlandtPark/facilities/iceskating.

Outdoor fitness equipment is interspersed along the track circling the Parade Ground.

Playgrounds in the park have facilities suitable for children of varied ages, three of which are accessible to those with handicaps. Classic Playground at Van Cortlandt Park South and Gouverneur Avenue is level 4 accessible with transfer platforms and ground-level play features, but no adaptive swing. Woodlawn Playground at 239th Street and Van Cortlandt Park East is level 3 accessible with universally accessible swings. Southwest Playground at West 240th Street and Broadway is level 4 accessible with transfer platforms and ground-level play features, but no adaptive swing. Sachkerah Woods Playground is at Jerome Avenue and Gun Hill Road.

Rest rooms are scattered throughout Van Cortlandt Park and are open all year. All are handicapped accessible.

The **running tracks** in the park are widely different and vary in use. The one near Van Cortlandt House is 1.25 miles long. It may be the most inspirational in New York City. This track circles the area where the local American Indians once planted corn and was later a site for battles and skirmishes during the American Revolution.

The Cross-Country Track extending from West 246th Street near Broadway to the city line is three miles long. It is considered one of the preeminent tracks in America and is used for national scholastic and college track meets. North of its Parade Ground start and finish lines, this challenging track travels through forest, hills, and wetland.

The running track inside the Stadium is rubberized.

Soccer fields are in two locations—near West 240th Street and Broadway and at East 233rd Street and Van Cortlandt Park East. Since they are well used, permits are needed for teams. Contact the website www.nycgovparks.org/permits/field-and-court/request.

The **swimming pool** (seasonal) is huge, free, and outdoors. It is located at Broadway and West 242nd Street. With no deep end, diving is prohibited. You must bring a sturdy combination lock to secure your belongings. Swimwear is required. Glass bottles, electronic devices, and newspapers are not allowed. Free swimming classes are available. Hours: Late June to early September: 11:00 A.M. to 3:00 P.M.; 4:00 P.M. to 7.00 P.M. Contacts: Telephone: 718-548-2415; website: www .nycgovparks.org/parks/VanCortlandtPark/facilities/outdoor-pools/ van-cortlandt-pool.

Tennis courts number eighteen. Ten outdoor hard courts are located near West 242nd Street and Broadway. Eight outdoor hard courts can be found near 233rd Street and Jerome Avenue. Permits and reservations are necessary. For information telephone 718-549-6494 or consult the website: www.nycgovparks.org/parks/VanCortlandtPark/ facilities/tennis.

SPECIAL PROGRAMS

The Nature Center is located behind and just east of the rear of the Van Cortlandt House in from West 246th Street and is open from April 1 to October 31. Step inside and learn about the local natural habitat. Observe living turtles and look closely at preserved species that inhabit the park. Pick up a Van Cortlandt Park map, chat with knowledgeable Urban Park Rangers, and join them on their scheduled guided tours. Telephone 718-548-0912 for further information.

Urban Park Ranger free programs for the public enable the visitor to connect with the natural world of New York City, to explore the ecosystem, to learn to identify birds, plants, and animals, and to make new friends. Available to both children and adults, these family-friendly programs add depth to your view of the natural world within the metropolis. For most programs, simply show up at a designated location, usually the Nature Center, a few minutes before they begin. Telephone 718-548-0912 for information.

Van Cortlandt House Museum

INFORMATION

Broadway near West 246th Street

HOURS: Tuesday to Friday, 10:00 A.M. to 4:00 P.M.; Saturday and Sunday, 11:00 A.M. to 4:00 P.M., Closed Mondays. Visitors should arrive at least thirty minutes before closing.

ADMISSION: Adults $5.00, Students and Seniors $3.00, Children under 12, free. Free admission to the museum on Wednesdays.

CONTACTS: For information and museum tours, telephone: 718-543-3344; website: www.historichousetrust.org/item.php?i_id=30.

ABOUT THE VAN CORTLANDT HOUSE MUSEUM

Erected in 1748, the Van Cortlandt House is the first historic house designated by New York City. It was the scene of many skirmishes and other action during the American Revolution, served as George Washington's headquarters three times, and British general Sir William Howe's headquarters once. The house remained inhabited until the creation of the park in 1888. Van Cortlandt family members donated some of their original heirlooms that form the wonderful collection of period furnishings and decorative arts that fill each room. The gift shop is located inside the museum.

Dining and Picnicking

Dining is available seasonally via food carts and food trucks at various locations throughout the park. The lovely Lake House is a great place to grab a sandwich or other light fare. Sit on the wide porch overlooking Van Cortlandt Lake and watch ducks, geese, and occasional swans gliding by framed by water and forest. For information telephone: 718-543-4595.

Barbecuing and picnic areas are found both at Broadway near the end of the elevated subway line at West 242nd Street in front of the pool and in the Allen Shandler Recreation Area at Jerome Avenue south of 233rd Street. There is a limited number of barbecue grills and picnic tables in each area. Barbecuing is not permitted near trees. Propane tanks are prohibited. Coals and all other litter must be placed in metal trash cans and the grills must be cleaned before departure.

The Bronx County Building

THE ART OF DEMOCRACY

Atop a high ridge overlooking the surrounding neighborhood stands the Bronx County Building, often referred to as the Bronx Civic Center. Not only is it the civic heart of The Bronx, but it and the area around it is also filled with art and sculpture by well-known artists that honor democracy and cultural diversity. Few sculptures have as colorful a past as the fountain located on the same ridge in Joyce Kilmer Park across 161st Street to the north. The Heinrich Heine–Lorelei Fountain was commissioned by an Austrian empress to honor a German-Jewish poet and his most beloved poem. It was rejected as her gift, however, by his German birthplace on anti-Semitic grounds, but welcomed by Bronx German Americans and placed in what later became a park named after Joyce Kilmer, an Irish American poet who had been killed in World War I. It stands as testament to the legacy of religious and artistic freedom that has defined The Bronx since its inception.

In the last quarter of the nineteenth century, civil engineer Louis A. Risse, an immigrant from Alsace-Lorraine, envisioned the ridge north of 161st Street as a site of a wide tree-lined boulevard called the Grand Concourse. He projected a triangular grand entrance called the Concourse Plaza at 161st Street. The plaza was redesigned as Joyce Kilmer Park in 1927.

The Bronx County Building south of the park was opened in 1934. Justice comes alive in the Bronx County Building where trials by the Bronx County Supreme Court are held. The beauty of its Art Deco–Neo-Classical façade adorned with striking bas-reliefs and statues surrounding it suggests the strength, grace, and magnificence of good government. The splendid works of art found at both the southern end of Joyce Kilmer Park and across 161st Street at the Bronx County Building celebrate American democracy and the ideals of justice.

INFORMATION

Grand Concourse and 161st Street

HOURS: The Bronx County Building is open Monday through Friday (except holidays) from 10:00 A.M. to 4:30 P.M.

ADMISSION: Free.

DIRECTIONS

BY PUBLIC TRANSPORTATION: Take subway letter D train (B train in rush hours only) to the 161st Street/River Avenue station. Leave at the Walton Avenue exit. Walk along the north side of 161st Street and climb the decorative steps in the middle of the block to enter Joyce Kilmer Park.

Alternatively, take the BxM4 Express bus on Madison Avenue to 161st Street and the Grand Concourse. (For schedule information and for pick-up and drop-off points, telephone 511 and say MTA, or visit the MTA website: www.mta.info/busco/schedules/.) Cross the Grand Concourse and then cross 161st Street to Joyce Kilmer Park and climb the decorative stairs in the middle of the block to enter the park.

Joyce Kilmer Park

At the top of the staircase rising from the middle of the block on 161st Street is the *Heinrich Heine–Lorelei Fountain*. It commemorates the German nineteenth-century poet Heinrich Heine and his most beloved poem, "Die Lorelei." The poem, written in almost musical language, tells the story of a siren combing her hair atop a crag of rock overlooking the Rhine River. Her beautiful song lures passing sailors to steer toward the rock and their doom by crashing their boats and drowning.

The Empress Elizabeth of Austria (the consort of Emperor Franz Josef) commissioned sculptor Ernst Herter to design the fountain in 1888 as her gift to the city of Düsseldorf, Germany, Heine's birthplace. According to the *New York Times*, the city refused the gift in 1893 because Heine was born Jewish and because of "dislike of the

Jews, which in some Germans amounts to a mania and causes frequent outbursts of Judenhetze (Jew baiting)." On hearing this, the German American community in New York asked for the fountain, intending to put it at Fifth Avenue and 59th Street in Manhattan. When it was uncrated, they were shocked at the bare-breasted mermaids at the fountain's base. They also refused the gift.

At that time, the area around the planned Grand Concourse was heavily German, and the people there loved Heine's poem. Moreover, the plans for the Concourse Plaza entrance to the boulevard called for some fountain to be placed in the center of the triangle. Since the newly arrived fountain was available, it was installed at this spot in 1899.

On the fountain, the siren combs her hair sitting on top of a base bearing a bas-relief portrait of Heinrich Heine. Walk around the fountain and find near the base pieces of boat and fishnets, and even a skull or two.

Behind and slightly to the west of the fountain, standing on a granite base, is a statue of Louis J. Heintz. Heintz was a nineteenth-century brewery executive who was popular with his fellow businessmen and political leaders. Because the city neglected to build or repair streets, or even to plan new ones, after it annexed the western half of today's Bronx in 1874, he led a movement to create a commissioner of street improvements elected by the residents of the mainland area. After the State Legislature approved the office's creation, Heintz won the election held in 1890 to become the first commissioner. He immediately began paving all the dirt roads and approved Louis A. Risse's plan for the Grand Concourse. Unfortunately, Heintz suddenly died in office in 1893, but what he began was continued under his successor. When New York created the five-borough city, The Bronx became one of the five, and its commissioner of street improvements was used as the model for the new office of borough president in each of the boroughs. To honor Heintz and his achievements, his friends and supporters erected this statue in his honor. Their names can be found on the plaque on the rear of the statue's base.

The Bronx County Building

The entire square block between the Grand Concourse and Walton Avenue south of 161st Street to 158th Street is occupied by the massive ten-story Bronx County Building. This is the seat of the local Bronx government. The Bronx borough president's offices, the Bronx county clerk's office, the Bronx surrogate (who presides over cases involving wills and estates), the Bronx public administrator (who administers estates of those who died without a will and finds their heirs), and the courtrooms of the Bronx County Supreme Court (trying major criminal and civil cases) are all found within this mostly limestone structure. It was designed by Joseph H. Friedlander and Max Hausle in the late 1920s. Construction began in 1932 and the building opened in 1934. Looking at its Art Deco design, many believe at first glance that it must have been one of the federal New Deal projects of the 1930s, but it was financed entirely through New York State and New York City funds long before the New Deal began. As a building design, it was ahead of its time.

Enter at the building's grounds at the corner entrance through the wall from the sidewalk on the Grand Concourse at 161st Street. Inside, on the lawn area, resting on a granite base, is an artifact from World War I. It is the keystone arch of the stone bridge at Château-Thierry, where the American army met the oncoming Imperial German army and, for the first time, caused the invader to retreat. It was the beginning of the end of the war. In 1938, the French government feared the intentions of Nazi Germany and gave the keystone as a gift to the United States in an attempt to gain American sympathy. Using the auspices of a New York City American Legion post, this was ultimately decided to be the site of the gift. It was installed with parade, pomp, and ceremony in 1940, but by that time, World War II had begun and the French Republic was in great jeopardy.

Climb the few steps facing the keystone leading to the upper platform. The building itself is marked by Art Deco design elements with Neo-Classical touches. Note the Art Deco abstract designs on the metal elements separating the windows of one floor from the other. The four entrances to the building are marked by fluted columns. Atop each of them rests a huge slab. On the front façade of each of the slabs are carved the seal of the State of New York and the seal of the City of New York. On each slab between the carved seals is incised an inscription extolling the high purposes of government or of justice. The massive carved high-relief blocks flanking each of the staircases leading to an entrance bear allegorical sculpture related to each inscription. These massive blocks were carved by noted sculptor Adolph Weinman assisted by Edward F. Sanford, George Snowden, and Joseph Kis-selewski. On the building's façade along the third floor are bas-relief figures carved by the famed Art Deco sculptor Charles Keck.

Walk around the building to see the sculptural elements. Of the blocks flanking the staircase leading to the entrances from the Grand Concourse, the one nearest 158th Street is called *Spirit of Progress*, while the one nearest 161st Street is entitled *Civic Fame*. They are meant to complement the inscription above the columned entrance-way that reads: "Government is a contrivance of human wisdom to provide for human wants. Men have a right that these wants should be provided for by this wisdom." The bas-relief sculptural panels on the third floor (except at the corners) illustrate the *Triumph of Good Government*. At the corner of the Grand Concourse and 161st Street, the panel depicts the *Wisdom of the Law*.

Of the blocks flanking the 161st Street side staircase, the one closest to the Grand Concourse is named the *Majesty of the Law*. The figure of Moses holding the Ten Commandments faces the staircase. Oddly, the commandments are depicted only as Roman numerals. The carved block closest to Walton Avenue bears the name of *Civic Government*. Here the figure facing the staircase is Justice, but she is not blindfolded. The inscription over the entrance reads: "The administration of justice presents the noblest field for the exercise of human capacity. It forms the ligaments that bind society together. Upon its broad foundations is erected the edifice of public liberty." The third-story frieze, except for the corners, continues depicting the *Triumph of Good Government*. The panel on the corner of 161st Street and Walton Avenue shows the *Punishment of Law*. The staircase leading to the 161st Street entrance appeared in scenes in two motion pictures—the black-and-white *Naked City* and the color *The Bonfire of the Vanities*.

On the Walton Avenue side, there is no staircase or entrance. The slope of the site dictated that a more modest entrance appear below the platform. Thus the grand columned façade is a false one, leading only to the windows of some offices inside. Nevertheless, the allegorical blocks found at the edge of the platform still reflect the inscription incised above the columns. That inscription reads: "Let it be remembered finally that it has been the pride and boast of America that the rights for which she contended were the rights of human nature." The block closest to 161st Street is called *Loyalty, Valor, and Sacrifice*, while the one nearest 158th Street bears the title *Victory, Peace, and Love of*

Country. The four panels flanking the false entrance on the third-floor frieze pick up on these themes. The two on the side nearest 161st Street are depictions of the *Revolutionary War* and the *Civil War*, while on the two on the other side of the false entrance are illustrated the *Spanish-American War* and the *World War* (now called *World War I*). The rest of the frieze (except for the corners) continues showing the *Triumph of Good Government*. On the corner of Walton Avenue and 158th Street can be found *Moral Law*.

On the 158th Street side, the staircase block closest to Walton Avenue shows the *Triumph of Civic Administration*, while its counterpart nearest the Grand Concourse illustrates the *Effect of Good Administration*. The inscription over the entranceway reads: "Law and order enforced with justice and by strength lie at the foundation of civilization. Law must be based on justice else it cannot stand and it must be enforced with resolute firmness." The third-floor frieze (except for the corners) continues to depict the *Triumph of Good Government*. On the corner of 158th Street and the Grand Concourse is shown the *Protection of Law*. On the 158th Street side of this corner panel on the unfolded scroll near the bottom held by a figure, if the angle of the sun is right causing shadows to be cast on the scroll, a building clearly labeled Bronx County Courthouse is revealed.

Standing on each of the four corners of the building are two flagpoles. Two of them fly the American flag next to the dark blue New York State flag. Two others display the orange, white, and blue vertical-striped New York City flag and the same colored horizontally striped flag of the Borough of The Bronx.

If the visitor is there at the hours the Bronx County Building is open to the public, enter through the Grand Concourse entrance. Note the doors themselves are made of elaborately decorated bronze and glass. Visitors must pass through metal detectors and empty their pockets to go beyond the entrance doors. Public restrooms are located on either side in the corridor beyond the detectors.

Inside, beyond the metal detectors, is a bay with a bank of four elevators. Note the decorative metal Art Deco style bas-relief sculptures on the door of each elevator. At the far end of the bay is a bronze and glass doorway. Here is the coat of arms of the Borough of The Bronx just over the doorway. Inside is the Veterans' Memorial Hall. It is open only when a public meeting or event is happening. If you can, step inside, and read the quotations on plaques from great Americans, including Abraham Lincoln and Woodrow Wilson, throughout the hall.

Most notable in Veterans' Memorial Hall are four huge murals depicting events in the history of The Bronx. They were all painted by James Monroe Hewlett, a major muralist of his day who later became the head of the American Academy in Rome. The first mural depicts the arrival of Jonas Bronck, the first European settler. He is shown clean-shaven, even though men in the 1600s sported moustaches and Van Dyke beards. The second mural shows the opening of the first court on Bronx soil with Justice John Pell presiding, although no courtroom in colonial days would be as large as the one painted. The third mural, the 1776 Battle of Pell's Point, where 750 Americans fought 4,000 British troops to a standstill in today's Pelham Bay Park, is the most historically accurate. The final mural shows George Washington leaving the Van Cortlandt House in 1783 in what is now Van Cortlandt Park to begin the march to take possession of New York City in the final act of the American Revolution. This painting is the most controversial. The historic incident happened in November and Hewlett depicts the scene with trees in full leaf and spring flowers everywhere. He insisted it had a more interesting look that way.

Visitors have the opportunity to visit a courtroom when a trial is in session. The Supreme Court, despite its name, is the court of original jurisdiction handling major criminal and civil cases over $25,000 involving medical malpractice, labor law, motor vehicle accidents, and other cases seeking relief caused by the wrongful action of others. A guard or court officer can direct visitors to the floors where trials are held. Quiet and decorum must be observed. At the end of a trial, when the judge is charging a jury before it deliberates on a verdict as to the law that applies in the case, no visitor is permitted to enter or leave that courtroom until the judge has completed the task. Here the visitor can see real lawyers and genuine judges conduct a case. The visitor will note that reality is slightly different from dramatic depiction of trials in movies or on television. However, this is democratic justice in action.

This visit can be combined with a visit to nearby Yankee Stadium (see part I, "Yankee Stadium") or with the Grand Concourse walking tour (see part II, "The Grand Concourse Historic District: Art Deco Delights") or to the nearby art museum (see part I, "The Bronx

Museum of the Arts"). To get to Yankee Stadium, walk west, down 161st Street, three blocks to River Avenue. To get to the start of the Grand Concourse walking tour on 167th Street, take the northbound Bx1, Bx1 Limited, or Bx2 bus on the Grand Concourse at 161st Street across the street from the Bronx County Building to 167th Street where the tour begins. To get to the Bronx Museum of the Arts, take any of the buses across the Grand Concourse north to 165th Street, or walk to 165th Street and the Grand Concourse.

The Edgar Allan Poe Cottage

POVERTY AND POETRY

Edgar Allan Poe, one of America's greatest authors and poets, the inventor of the detective story and master of mystery and horror, lived a life full of struggle and poverty. The only home in which he lived that survives today is the tiny cottage in The Bronx where he spent the last years of his life and where he witnessed his greatest sorrow. For over a century, the Edgar Allan Poe Cottage has been a Mecca for Poe devotees from around the world to make a pilgrimage to the place where he penned some of his greatest works and to see how he lived.

INFORMATION

Grand Concourse and Kingsbridge Road in Poe Park. Mailing address: Bronx County Historical Society, 3309 Bainbridge Avenue, Bronx, NY 10467.

HOURS: Saturday 10:00 A.M. to 4:00 P.M.; Sunday 1:00 P.M. to 5:00 P.M. Group tours at other times on request in advance.

ADMISSION: Adults: $5.00; Students, Seniors, and Children: $3.00.

CONTACTS: Telephone: 718-881-8900; website: www.bronxhistoricalsociety.org/poecottage.html.

DIRECTIONS

BY PUBLIC TRANSPORTATION: Take subway train letter D to Kingsbridge Road, exit at the back of the station, and climb up the steps to the street.

Alternatively, take the BxM4 Express bus on Madison Avenue to Kingsbridge Road and the Grand Concourse. (For schedule information and for pick-up and drop-off points, telephone 511 and say MTA, or visit website: www.mta.info/busco/schedules/.) Cross Kingsbridge Road to Poe Park and Poe Cottage.

BY CAR OR TAXI: Take the Major Deegan Expressway northbound to the West 230th Street exit. At the end of the ramp, turn right onto 230th Street, and then turn right onto Bailey Avenue to Kingsbridge Road. Turn left onto Kingsbridge Road to the Grand Concourse. Do not use the underpass. Street parking only.

About the Edgar Allan Poe Cottage

The small wooden farmhouse was erected in 1812 as one of several to house workers on the Valentine family farm. It is the only one of those cottages to have survived. Then, it had an unobstructed view of the rolling hills to the shores of Long Island Sound. The arrival of the New York and Harlem River Railroad (today's Metro-North Harlem Division) in 1841 with a station nearby called Fordham attracted settlers who formed a village around it named after the station.

Poe, born in 1809, spent much of his life moving from place to place searching for literary recognition and financial security. In the early nineteenth century, writers were not paid much for their published work, and most writers either were independently wealthy or held a full-time job. Poe insisted that he should be paid adequately for his poems and stories and that he should not need an additional job to make a living. Poe was not wealthy and he spent much of his working life editing literary magazines and writing often scathingly critical reviews of other authors' works. Because of this, he made many enemies among the literati who hated him for condemning their works as not worthy. As a result, he was often let go by those who controlled the magazines.

In April 1844, Poe, his beloved young wife, Virginia (who was also his cousin), and Maria Clemm, his mother-in-law (who was also his aunt), moved to New York City, a place he grew to dislike. Unfortunately, Virginia contracted tuberculosis, then almost always a fatal disease. In a desperate attempt to save her, he rented the cottage on a farm next to the old colonial Kingsbridge Road in Fordham from the Valentines for $100 a year. He moved there in the summer of 1846 hoping the fresh country air would improve his wife's ravaged lungs. It did not work. In January 1847, Virginia died.

Poe descended into a fit of melancholy, tended by the devoted Maria Clemm and the faculty at nearby Saint John's College (now Fordham University). After he recovered, Poe began to receive visits from his friends who arrived by railroad and he began to write again. While living at the cottage, his short story "The Cask of Amontillado" was published and he wrote the enduring poems "The Bells" and "Annabel Lee" plus the long philosophical prose poem "Eureka."

In 1849, Poe left on a lecture tour to raise money to begin a new literary magazine. He was on his way back to the cottage when he stopped at Baltimore where he died under mysterious circumstances. Maria Clemm wound up Poe's affairs in New York and closed the cottage.

In the years following, many people rented Poe's old cottage, but were increasingly bothered by Poe devotees who made the trip to Fordham wanting to see the residence of the famous author. By the 1890s, rapid urbanization threatened the very existence of the cottage. Kingsbridge Road, once a narrow dirt trail, was widened and paved in 1895 to become the urban street it is today. Poe Cottage was in its path, but an organized effort got the building moved the few feet eastward to save it. Shortly thereafter, the construction of apartment buildings abutting the cottage put it in jeopardy once again. This time, another campaign convinced New York City to purchase the apple orchard across Kingsbridge Road, convert it into Poe Park in 1902, and to move the cottage to its northern end in 1913. The Edgar Allan Poe Cottage then was opened to the public.

Visitors to the Edgar Allan Poe Cottage are treated to a guided tour. The main floor is furnished with Poe's rocking chair and the bed in which Virginia Poe died. Other items were not used by Poe, but fit the descriptions of the cottage's sparse furnishings and their placement written by Poe's admirers who visited him while he was in residence. Inside, on the outer wall, are exhibits illustrating Poe's life and the history of the cottage. In one corner is a bronze portrait bust of Poe by sculptor Edmond T. Quinn that was dedicated in 1909, the centennial of Poe's birth. A narrow staircase leads to the attic bedroom where the visitors may view a video production highlighting the history of the cottage and of Poe.

The Edgar Allan Poe Cottage is more than just a memorial to a great and influential writer. Because Poe was desperately poor in his lifetime, this modest cottage was all he could afford. Since it is associated with

Poe, the cottage is preserved. Unlike almost all historic houses open to the public, Poe Cottage is unique in that it preserves the dwelling and ambience of a poor man of his time. It is instructive to compare it with the Bartow-Pell Mansion in Pelham Bay Park, which was erected by a wealthy family in the 1840s, the same decade Poe resided here. See part I, "Pelham Bay Park: The Riviera of New York City," for information on the Bartow-Pell Mansion Museum.

Visitors may continue exploring Poe's stay at Fordham and today's modern neighborhood by taking the walking tour found in part II, "In the Footsteps of Edgar Allan Poe."

Woodlawn Cemetery

BEAUTY FOR ETERNITY

Woodlawn Cemetery is many things. Designed with delicate and beautiful landscaping, its 400 acres are filled with rolling hills, meadows, a wide variety of mature trees, a lake, streams, and gently curved pathways. Intended as a place where the wealthy of New York City's industrial age could find a final resting place, it is replete with grand and impressive mausoleums created by some of the great architects of the era—McKim, Mead & White, Carrière & Hastings, and John Russell Pope among them—in such styles as Art Nouveau, Egyptian Revival, Greek Revival, and Romanesque Revival, many adorned with Tiffany stained-glass windows. Memorial sculpture abounds with works by Daniel Chester French and Anna Hyatt Huntington among many others. Its imposing mausoleums and simple graves form a nonsectarian hall of fame ranging from such military leaders as Civil War hero and first admiral of the United States Navy David Farragut and Union general Franz Sigel; such composers as Irving Berlin, George M. Cohan, W. C. Handy, Victor Herbert, Fritz Kreisler, and Duke Ellington; performers embracing Nora Bayes, Gus Edwards, Harry Carey, Lionel Hampton, Miles Davis, Celia Cruz, Canada Lee, and Bert Williams; authors, poets, and journalists headed by Herman Melville, Countee Cullen, Finley Peter Dunne, Grantland Rice, Damon Runyon, and Elizabeth Cochran Seaman (Nelly Bly); artists, sculptors, illustrators, and cartoonists embracing Thomas Nast, George McManus, James Montgomery Flagg, J. C. Leyendecker, and Alexander Archipenko; such sports figures as Tex Richard, Dan Topping, Gertrude Ederle, and Frankie Frisch; industrialists and merchants, including Herman

Ossian Armour, Arde Bulova, John Wayne "Bet a Million" Gates, Jay Gould, Richard Hudnut, Sidney Dillon, William E. Dodge, Collis P. Huntington, James Cash Penney, Joseph Pulitzer, Louis Sherry, Isidor Straus, Madam C. J. Walker, and F. W. Woolworth; such leaders of the women's rights movement as Elizabeth Cady Stanton, Carrie Chapman Catt, and Alva Smith Vanderbilt Belmont; and such statesmen as Ralph Bunche, Christian Archibald Herter, William McAdoo, and Fiorello LaGuardia. And these names constitute only a mere fraction of Woodlawn's famous permanent residents.

INFORMATION

On 233rd Street and Webster Avenue with another entrance on Jerome Avenue near the north end of Bainbridge Avenue. Mailing address: Webster Avenue and East 233rd Street, Bronx, NY 10470.

HOURS: Open to visitors every day 8:30 A.M. to 5:00 P.M. Severe weather, such as heavy snow or extreme winds, may cause the cemetery to close for the day. The administration offices are closed on Sundays and major holidays.

ADMISSION: Free. Fees for tours are given below.

CONTACTS: Telephone: 718-920-1469; website: www.thewoodlawn cemetery.org/.

DIRECTIONS

BY PUBLIC TRANSPORTATION: For the 233rd Street and Webster Avenue gate, take number 2 subway train to the 233rd Street station, walk three blocks west down the hill, and then cross Webster Avenue to the entrance on 233rd Street at Webster Avenue.

Alternatively, take the BxM11 Express bus on Madison Avenue to 232nd Street and White Plains Road. Walk one block north to 233rd Street, then turn left and walk three blocks west down the hill, then cross Webster Avenue to the entrance on 233rd Street.

Visitors might wish to take Metro-North Harlem Division Line local train from Grand Central Station to the Woodlawn station, then walk about a half a block from the station and cross Webster Avenue to the entrance on 233rd Street at Webster Avenue.

To the Jerome Avenue entrance, take the number 4 subway train to the last stop, Woodlawn station. On exiting the station, cross Bainbridge Avenue, turn left, and walk a half a block to the entrance.

Alternatively, take the BxM4 Express bus on Madison Avenue to Bainbridge and Jerome Avenues (For schedule information and for pick-up and

drop-off points, telephone 511 and say MTA, or visit website: www.mta
.info/busco/schedules/.) Then walk a half block north to the entrance.

BY CAR OR TAXI: Take the Major Deegan Expressway to exit 13, East 233rd
Street. To get to the 233rd Street and Webster Avenue entrance, continue
straight along 233rd Street and enter at the 233rd Street entrance at Webster
Avenue to your right.

To get to the Jerome Avenue entrance, make a right at the end of the exit
ramp onto Jerome Avenue and ride for approximately one mile where a
grassy mall separates the roadway into two parts. At a break in the mall to
your left, turn left into the gate of the cemetery.

There is limited parking at each entrance.

About Woodlawn Cemetery

Woodlawn Cemetery began as an idea of a Presbyterian clergyman, the
Rev. Absalem Peters, in the 1850s. He was appalled that the residents
of upper New York City (today's midtown Manhattan) in a funeral
cortege on its way to Brooklyn's Greenwood Cemetery had to travel
through chaotic city commercial traffic, transfer to a ferry to cross the
East River, and then transfer again to a hearse and carriages in Brooklyn to reach their destination. He felt that this journey was undignified
and disturbed the grief-stricken families. He believed they would be
better served by a cemetery located on the mainland to the north of
Manhattan. He formed an association that purchased two large farms
in what is now The Bronx. The newly named Woodlawn Cemetery
opened in 1863.

The funeral and burial of Admiral David Farragut in 1870 put
Woodlawn on the map. Farragut was a personal friend of General
Ulysses S. Grant, then the president of the United States. Because of
this, the nation's president, vice president, and every member of the
cabinet marched behind Farragut's hearse to the burial in Woodlawn.
No other person in American history has received a similar honor. The
resulting publicity signaled that Woodlawn was the place for prominent people to be interred. Indeed, Farragut's grave and monument
was named a National Historic Landmark in 2013.

In the cemetery's early days, many visitors arrived who simply
wished to walk in the landscaped grounds and, perhaps, picnic. In
those days, there were few public parks, and cemeteries were regularly
used for genteel recreation. Over the years, a host of famous Ameri-

cans, along with many others from the locality and those who are not famous, have chosen to spend eternity among the beautiful landscaped grounds of Woodlawn. There are people who were involved in the 1912 sinking of the *Titanic* who are interred in Woodlawn. Their number is second only to those in the cemetery in Nova Scotia in Canada. Woodlawn is also the site of the Anna Bliss Titanic Memorial dedicated to those who perished in the disaster.

Today, there are over 300,000 people buried in Woodlawn Cemetery. They are interred in magnificent mausoleums, graves marked by imposing architecture and statuary, and those whose presence is recorded by a simple single gravestone. Most recently, the cemetery has constructed community mausoleums for the increasing number of people who wish to have above-ground burial but cannot afford to erect a mausoleum just for themselves.

Surprises abound. Visitors may come across Old West lawman William "Bat" Masterson, music education philanthropist August Juilliard, inventor of the Klieg light Anton Kliegl, clipper ship designer William Webb, Ziegfeld Follies star Bert Williams, the namesake of Broadway's Tony awards Antoinette Perry, Futurist artist Joseph Stella, famed actress Laurette Taylor, United States senator from Montana William A. Clark, author Clarence Day, publisher Frank Leslie, founder of General Motors William Durant, among many others well known for their contributions to their fields.

Because of its landscaping, important architecture and art, and its large and impressive gathering of famous people who helped make the country what it is today, Woodlawn Cemetery was declared a National Historic Landmark in 2011.

Tours

Group tours can be arranged any time of year and tailored to meet specific interests. Arrange a tour in advance by calling the Woodlawn Conservancy at 718-920-1469. Group rates are $15.00 per person, $10.00 for students and seniors, with a minimum amount of $150.00 per tour. There are special rates for student and senior groups.

A guided audio walking tour in either English or Spanish is available at the 233rd Street and Webster Avenue office for $5.00. The narration lasts sixty minutes and highlights forty important sights. Those entering on foot at the Jerome Avenue gate should ask the security guard for an automobile ride to the 233rd Street and Webster Avenue office where the visitor can obtain the narrated walking tour.

A map of the cemetery grounds is available for the asking at either of the two entrances. The map highlights the location of the resting places of some of the famous people in Woodlawn and a visitor may use this to wander around the delightful landscaped grounds to discover them.

Special Events

Tours, concerts, and lectures are scheduled throughout the year by the Woodlawn Conservancy. Telephone or visit the website for more information.

Dining and Picnicking

Spending long hours exploring the site may necessitate taking a box or bag lunch. There are no eating facilities within the cemetery. Recreational activities are limited out of respect for the site. Public restrooms are located near each of the two entrances.

The Valentine-Varian House

A LEGACY OF THE REVOLUTION

Visit the Valentine-Varian House and experience the effect the American Revolution had on the ordinary people caught up in the conflict. Here is a fieldstone farmhouse erected in the Georgian style by a blacksmith, Isaac Valentine, in 1758 along the original Boston Post Road, now Van Cortlandt Avenue East. Because of its strategic location on the main road to the King's Bridge, which connected the mainland to Manhattan, the stone house was caught up in six battles and was occupied by troops from both sides. The survival of the Valentine-Varian House makes it truly a legacy of the Revolution.

INFORMATION

3266 Bainbridge Avenue between Van Cortlandt Avenue East and 208th Street. Mailing address: Bronx County Historical Society, 3309 Bainbridge Avenue, Bronx, NY 10467.

HOURS: Saturday 10:00 A.M. to 4:00 P.M.; Sunday 1:00 P.M to 5:00 P.M. Group tours at other times on request in advance.

ADMISSION: Adults $5.00; Students, Seniors, and Children $3.00.

CONTACTS: Telephone: 718-881-8900; website: www.bronxhistorical society.org.

DIRECTIONS

BY PUBLIC TRANSPORTATION: Take subway train letter D to 205th Street station, exit at the middle of the station, and take the escalator up. Exit through the turnstiles, turn left, and climb up the steps to the street. On the street, turn around, walk to the corner, and turn right. Walk northward along Bainbridge Avenue just beyond Van Cortlandt Avenue East to the entrance of the Valentine-Varian House.

Alternatively, take the BxM4 Express bus on Madison Avenue to Van Cortlandt Avenue East and Rochambeau Avenue. (For schedule information and for pick-up and drop-off points, telephone 511 and say MTA, or visit website: www.mta.info/busco/schedules/.) Walk one block east to Bainbridge Avenue, turn left and walk half a block to the entrance of the Valentine-Varian House.

BY CAR OR TAXI: Take the Major Deegan Expressway to exit 13, East 233rd Street. Make a right at the end of the exit ramp onto Jerome Avenue and, bearing left, ride for approximately one mile to the second traffic light (where Jerome Avenue meets Bainbridge Avenue), then turn slightly left onto Bainbridge Avenue to 208th Street. The old stone house will be at your left. Street parking only.

About the Valentine-Varian House

In the growing controversy with Britain over taxation and liberty leading to the American Revolution, Paul Revere often passed by the house with letters from the Massachusetts Committee of Correspondence to the Patriots in New York City. In 1775, newly appointed general George Washington passed by on his way to Boston to take command of the troops besieging the British. In the fall of 1776, Valentine's house was in the middle of the Continental Army's defense of the area against the onslaught of the British Army. Starting in November, the British, with their German Hessian mercenaries and supported by Tories (Americans fighting for the British) took control of the region and occupied and fortified the stone farmhouse. Throughout the war, Isaac Valentine remained in the house to try to prevent the occupiers from destroying it.

Nevertheless, because it was located along a major roadway leading to the King's Bridge, the only crossing connecting the mainland to Manhattan, fierce fighting often broke out between American army and local militia forces on one side and the British, Hessians, and Tories in the vicinity. Valentine's house and his property was the scene of no less than six battles in the course of the war. In July 1781, the French army, allied with the Americans and commanded by the Comte de Rochambeau, encamped on the Valentine farm. Rochambeau himself slept in the house. One of his officers called it "a wretched farmhouse."

After the war, farmers in the area were faced with trying to repair their churned-up farms. It took a long time. Meanwhile, in 1789, John Adams passed by on his way to New York to be inaugurated the nation's first vice president. Shortly thereafter, President George Washington passed by a second time on his way to visit the New England states. He noted that the scars of the war were still evident, but that the crops seemed to be flourishing. Isaac Valentine, however, was impoverished by the war. Deeply in debt, in 1792 he was forced to sell the house and his farm.

The Valentine property was purchased by Isaac Varian of New York, who moved into the stone house. He was the father of a large family, and the Varians occupied the house and the farm for three generations. One of his grandsons, Isaac Leggett Varian, served as mayor of New York City from 1839 to 1841. By 1905, however, increasing urbanization led to a rise in property values and real estate taxes. It was no longer profitable to operate a farm in the area. Consequently, Jesse Huestis Varian sold it all at auction.

The house was purchased by William F. Beller, an official in the New York Customs House. He recognized the historic importance of the structure and he bought it just to preserve it. Through the years, he leased it at no or little rent to various people just to be sure the house remained occupied. By 1965, increasing costs made it impossible to continue this policy. His son, William C. Beller, sold the land to developers who constructed a light-colored brick apartment house now on the house's original site on Van Cortlandt Avenue East at Bainbridge Avenue. He then donated the Valentine-Varian House to the Bronx County Historical Society and paid the cost of moving it across the street to its new location on Bainbridge Avenue between Van Cortlandt Avenue East and 208th Street.

Inside the Valentine-Varian House

Visitors to the Valentine-Varian House are treated to a guided tour. Despite all of the tumult and changes that occurred during its existence, much of the original structure put in place in 1758 by Isaac Valentine can still be seen. The darker-colored wide floorboards are original. Look carefully at the nails that hold them in place. Note that the heads of the nails are not perfectly round. They were created by blacksmith Isaac Valentine on his forge. One room displays a section of the interior wall structure protected by glass. Here are hand-sawn chestnut laths, held in place by the same hand-forged nails with a mortar made of mud, lime, and cow hair. Rarely can such colonial construction be seen in such detail.

The Bronx County Historical Society operates the house as the Museum of Bronx History. It contains permanent and changing exhibits consisting of objects, photographs, paintings, drawings, etchings, lithographs, and maps that illustrate aspects of the growth and development of the borough over three centuries. Here it is still possible for the visitor to witness what this thriving, urban borough was like in days gone by. The society also presents special events in and around the museum from time to time.

On the Grounds of the Valentine-Varian House

On the north lawn of the house stands a stone statue identified by the legend on its base as the Bronx River Soldier. After the Civil War, the Oliver Tilden Post of the Grand Army of the Republic, the organization of Union veterans from the town of Morrisania (now part of The Bronx), purchased land in Woodlawn Cemetery to inter its dead. The GAR post hired John Grignola to carve a statue of a Civil War soldier to mark that plot. The post members rejected the final result, saying that it was marred by a chip. Grignola kept the statue in his studio until John B. Lazzeri, an official at Woodlawn Cemetery, visited. Grignola gave the statue to him. In 1898 Lazzari placed it on a granite pier in the Bronx River behind his house south of Gun Hill Road. It was held in place by metal L-bolts. Over six decades the L-bolts began to loosen until the statue fell over in the Bronx River. The New York City Parks Department stored it in a warehouse, and the Bronx County Historical Society found it there. Arrangements were made to restore the statue and to place the Bronx River Soldier on the lawn of the Valentine-Varian House for safekeeping. It has been standing there ever since 1970 as a reminder of the role The Bronx played in the Civil War.

On the south lawn of the Valentine-Varian House, toward the rear of the building, are two gardens such as might have existed when the house was new in colonial days. One is a vegetable garden; the other is an herb garden.

Also on the south lawn is a flagpole donated by the Neumann-Goldman Post of the Jewish War Veterans, an organization based in the neighborhood. It honors two servicemen of the Jewish faith who died during World War II. The post holds a ceremony of remembrance at this site every Memorial Day.

Visitors may continue exploring the surprising wonders of the area around the Valentine-Varian House, which includes another major historic house museum, by taking a walking tour in part II, "Valentine to Poe: A Tour of Cultural Discovery."

Pelham Bay Park

THE RIVIERA OF NEW YORK CITY

Three times the size of Manhattan's Central Park, Pelham Bay Park welcomes visitors with Orchard Beach on Long Island Sound, field and forest, salt marsh and freshwater pond, rich history and diverse wildlife. At 2,766 acres, it is the largest park in the five boroughs of New York City and a destination that should not be missed.

Spanning a spectacular thirteen-mile saltwater shoreline, including over one mile of glorious, white, crescent-shaped sandy beach with gently lapping waves, Orchard Beach is the Riviera of New York City. Take a swim or lie on a big towel under a bright beach umbrella, walk on the wide ocean promenade, or, beyond the sand, relax under a tree in Pelham Bay Park's green fields with water views, a perfect place for picnics or quiet contemplation. Play in ball fields or bring young children to playgrounds. Hike or bird-watch in an expansive wildlife preserve with diverse habitat ranging from tidal pools and wetlands to forest trails with history dating back to the Siwanoy Indians. Go horseback riding on miles of bridle trails or explore nature with the Urban Park Rangers who offer free, seasonal programs and guided tours. Free outdoor summer concerts are given on the large, beachfront stage. Join the thousands of visitors drawn to them each year. There are two challenging golf courses. Excellent, extensive biking trails winding through the diverse landscape extend an invitation to bicyclists.

Situated within the park is the beautiful Bartow-Pell Mansion, a historic house-museum complete with nineteenth-century period furniture, a carriage house, and landscaped gardens. It also offers chamber concerts and special events throughout the year.

INFORMATION

This very large park is situated in the northeastern corner of The Bronx between Interstate 95 and Long Island Sound. The park is divided into two parts by the Hutchinson River and Eastchester Bay. The larger part of the park is in the north. The northern part is more natural; the southern part is filled with more active play areas and caters mostly to the residents of the surrounding neighborhoods.

HOURS: Open every day; no official closing time.

ADMISSION: Free.

CONTACTS: For current park activities, on-line maps, and additional information, visit the Friends of Pelham Bay Park website: www.pelhambaypark .org or the Pelham Bay Park website: www.nycgovparks.org/parks/pelham -bay-park. For the Pelham Bay Park Administrator's Office, telephone: 718-430-1891 or e-mail: pbadministration@parks.nyc.gov. New York City Parks Department website: www.nycgovparks.org/.

DIRECTIONS

BY PUBLIC TRANSPORTATION: Take the number 6 subway train northbound to the Pelham Bay Park station or take the BxM6 Express bus on Madison Avenue to the Pelham Bay Park station. (For schedule information and for pick-up and drop-off points, telephone 511 and say MTA, or visit website: www.mta.info/busco/schedules/.) On leaving the station, walk along the sidewalk (not beneath the elevated subway line) southward beside the shops there to the corner of Wilkinson Avenue. For facilities in the northern part of the park, take the Bx12 bus with the destination "Orchard Beach" (Memorial Day to Labor Day). Alternatively, on the triangular traffic island across the street from the shops, take the Bx29 bus with the destination "City Island," and get off at either of the two stops located inside the park, one after the bus turns onto City Island Road near the Pelham stables or the other at the traffic circle near Rodman's Neck.

Another alternative is to take the Westchester County Bee-Line number 45 bus at the station and get off at the Bartow-Pell Mansion near the golf courses.

For the southern part of the park, take the walkway bridge directly from the subway station over the highway to the east side of the Bruckner Expressway/New England Thruway service road that forms the boundary of this section of the park.

From locations in The Bronx, in addition to the buses listed above, every other Bx5 Bruckner Boulevard/Story Avenue line bus terminates at the southern part of the park at the subway station until 10:50 P.M. On summer weekends, Bx5 bus service is extended to Orchard Beach in the northern part of the park.

BY CAR OR TAXI: For the northern part of the park, take the Bruckner Expressway/New England Thruway to the Orchard Beach/City Island exit. Free parking in the northern part of the park can be found at the small parking lot on Rodman's Neck off the City Island traffic circle and the Pelham/Split Rock Golf Course. The large parking lot at Orchard Beach is free in autumn, winter, and spring, but there is a fee for parking there in the summer.

For the southern part of the park, take the Bruckner Expressway/New England Thruway to the Country Club Road/Pelham Bay Park exit and continue on the service road until you come to the edge of the park on your right, or take the Hutchinson River Parkway to the Pelham Parkway East exit. Free parking is available at the Middletown Road lot.

About Pelham Bay Park

American Indians of the Algonquin Siwanoy tribe were the first to settle in the area, although the ground was also used for fishing and clamming by the neighboring Weckquasgeek tribe. In 1654, Thomas Pell, a self-taught physician from England and Fairfield, Connecticut, purchased a huge tract of land from them, of which Pelham Bay Park is merely a remnant. His estate was eventually named the manor of Pelham.

The area became a battleground during the American Revolution. On October 18, 1776, 4,000 British troops landed from British naval ships anchored in what is now Turtle Cove off Rodman's Neck and marched northward into the area just west of today's golf courses. There, they were confronted by 750 Continentals led by Colonel John Glover, a fisherman from Marblehead, Massachusetts. The artfully concealed Americans, protected by stone walls flanking the British route, managed to convince their enemy that the American force was stronger than the British. The action, called the Battle of Pell's Point, caused the British to pause in their tracks while the Americans secretly withdrew. This enabled George Washington and the main American army encamped in northern Manhattan and the western part of today's Bronx to escape entrapment and to safely withdraw to fight the Battle of White Plains and to continue the war to a victorious conclusion.

After the war, the Pell family gradually sold off their lands. By the mid-nineteenth century, several wealthy New York City merchants and industrialists purchased estates along the shores of Long Island Sound to erect elegant mansions. One of these, the Bartow-Pell Mansion, is the only one within the park's boundaries to have survived to this day.

In 1888, New York City purchased the land that became Pelham Bay Park. At the time, it was the only city park located on a seashore. Since Newport, Rhode Island, was then the playground of the wealthy, Pelham Bay Park was touted as the "Newport of the Masses." Today, it contains acres upon acres of natural plant and animal life and abounds in numerous varieties of recreational facilities.

Attractions and Amenities

Visitors to Pelham Bay Park have an extensive choice of recreational activities, both constructed, such as ballparks, playgrounds, and bicycle paths, as well as diverse natural habitats and spectacularly beautiful walks in the wild. Because of its size, the attractions are divided into the northern and southern sections of the park. It is suggested that you download a map of the park prior to your visit at www.pelhambay park.org/category/places-to-visit/. The map is at the bottom of the web page.

IN THE NORTHERN PART OF
PELHAM BAY PARK

Baseball fields are located on Rodman's Neck, near the traffic circle. For the required sports permits call 718-430-1840 or contact the New York City Parks Department website: www.nycgovparks.org/permits/sport-field.

The **basketball courts** at Orchard Beach have stunning ocean views. For special event or league permits for Orchard Beach courts telephone 718-430-1840 or contact the New York City Parks Department website: www.nycgovparks.org/permits/sport-field.

Five miles of **bicycle paths** weave through scenic Pelham Bay Park. Check the map for routes: www.nycbikemaps.com/maps/bronx-bike -map/.

Bird-watching: Pelham Bay Park is one of only four parks in New York City designated as a National Audubon Society Important Bird Area. The park is famous for its owls, colonies of herons and egrets, nesting wild turkeys, American woodcock, and fall migrant osprey. Two hundred and sixty-four species of birds and two distinct sub-species ("Eurasian" Green-Winged Teal and "Ipswitch" Savannah Sparrow) find refuge and have been sighted in Pelham Bay Park. Diverse habitats, each supporting its own wildlife, include 800 acres of mature and old-growth forest, 360 acres of salt marsh and salt flats, several freshwater ponds, and a thirteen-mile coastline hugging the Hutchinson River, Eastchester Bay, and Long Island Sound.

Because the park is located on the north-south flyway of migrating birds, a great diversity of species is found seasonally, as well as year-round residents. Late April, May, and early June are excellent months to spot migrating species. Notable summer residents include warbling vireos, who may travel as much as 13,000 miles, flying from South America and back each year, just to nest in Pelham Bay Park. Other birds include mute swans, wood ducks, blue-winged teals, ring-necked pheasants, American white pelicans, great blue herons, snowy egrets, bald eagles, peregrine falcons, solitary sandpipers, laughing gulls, snowy owls, belted kingfishers, downy woodpeckers, and many more. The Friends of Pelham Bay Park events page has information about seasonal birding opportunities and guided walks: www.pelhambay park.org/category/events/.

Fishing: Thirteen miles of coastline, including the waters of the Hutchinson River, Eastchester Bay, and Long Island Sound, provide numerous opportunities for the fisherman. Please note that fishing is not allowed on Orchard Beach during beach season. Discarded fishing lines and other refuse must be placed in trash bins and city and state fishing regulations must be followed. See the park website for details: www.nycgovparks.org/facilities/fishing.

Glover's Rock: The Siwanoy Indians used this rock as a lookout point for their trading routes. It is also believed to be the rock identified as Michow, having some religious significance. To visit Glover's Rock, follow Orchard Beach Road just north of Turtle Cove. Glover's Rock is located on the right of the road just before the turn-off to Orchard Beach.

Pelham and Split Rock Golf Courses are two beautiful public eighteen-hole golf links open to visitors. Pelham Course is quite challenging. Dining is available for lunch or dinner in the lovely restored Clubhouse restaurant. Telephone: 718-885-1258. Turtle Cove Golf Center, located at 1 City Island Road, features miniature golf, PGA instruction programs, grass tees, batting cages, and golf simulators. Event spaces are also available. Telephone: 718-885-1129.

Handball courts are found at Orchard Beach near sections 4 and 5 of the promenade. Telephone: 718-430-1840.

Hiking: The Kazimiroff Nature Trail, Siwanoy Trail, and Split Rock Trail wind through Pelham Bay Park. Each offers unique vistas and opportunities for the bird watcher, hiker, and nature lover. During summer months, heavy growth may make portions of the trails overgrown. The Kazimiroff Nature Trail may be entered at the north part of Orchard Beach at section 2 of the promenade. Wetland with wonderful high grasses and wading birds, shoreline, forest, and memorable views are found on this trail. The long loop is about a forty-five-minute walk; the short loop takes about thirty minutes walking; both circle Hunter Island. For a briefer walk, simply enter a short distance and observe the wildlife before retracing your steps. The trail is named after the conservationist and Bronx Borough Historian Theodore Kazimiroff (1914–1980), founder of the Bronx County Historical Society.

The Siwanoy Trail is about 3.5 miles long. Extending from its entrance near the bus stop on City Island Road at the Shore Road intersection, it travels through deep woodland and branches in the Bartow-Pell Woods and behind the Orchard Beach Meadow. Excellent birding opportunities are found in the forest and wetland. Check map for routes: www.pelhambaypark.org/wp-content/uploads/2012/02/Pelham-map-rev2005.pdf.

Split Rock Trail is about 1.5 miles long and begins at the Bartow traffic circle. Traversing Goose Creek Marsh and the Thomas Pell Wildlife Sanctuary, it brings the hiker to the glacier erratic, the Split Rock, an impressive boulder that has been broken by glacial forces.

For **horseback riding**, the Bronx Equestrian Center is a full-service facility in Pelham Bay Park. It offers English and Western riding lessons as well as trail rides, pony rides, hay wagon rides, and wedding events. It is open every day of the year, from 9:00 A.M. until dusk. It is located on Shore Road, north of Pelham Bridge. Five miles of bridle trails with views of salt marsh and verdant forest are available to riders in Pelham Bay Park, making it hard to believe that one is in New York City. Friends of Pelham Bay Park membership cardholders receive a

$5.00 discount on riding lessons. Bronx Equestrian Center telephone: 718-885-0551 or see website: www.bronxequestriancenter.com.

Hunter and Twin Islands: Nature speaks gently to the visitor in Hunter and Twin Islands, located north of Orchard Beach near section 1 of the promenade. Actually a group of islands joined by artificial formations, this area is now a protected wildlife refuge where walks with nature lift the spirit and free the soul. This 138-acre wildlife refuge, whose official name is Hunter Island Marine Zoology and Geology Sanctuary, includes Twin Islands, Cat Briar Island, Two Trees Island, and the northeastern shoreline of Hunter Island. The terrain is reminiscent of the New England coast with wonderful outcroppings of Hartland Schist, a durable rock typical of New England coastal areas. Huge boulders deposited during the retreat of the last ice age, nearly 15,000 years ago, adorn the landscape in ageless beauty. The ecosystem of the region is protected and is unusual in the state of New York.

Pelham Bay Park Lagoon is a wonderful place to **kayak or canoe.** The quiet waters are good for beginners; persons with experience may want to explore the small islands of Long Island Sound by boat. Paddlers must bring their own boats. Launch your boat at the northwest corner of Orchard Beach Parking Lot. Permits required for boaters: www .nycgovparks.org/sub_things_to_do/facilities/marinas/pdf/Kayak_ Launch_Permit.pdf.

Orchard Beach Nature Center, located at section 2 of the promenade, has fascinating exhibits that explore the ecosystem of the Orchard Beach area as well as programs for children and adults. Telephone: 718-885-3466 (summer only).

Orchard Beach: The crown jewel of Pelham Bay Park, Orchard Beach's calm waves and white sand leave a visual impression hard to match in a busy city. The visitor is welcomed with over a mile of beautiful crescent-shaped shoreline created by New York City's master builder Robert Moses in 1936 on the site of the Pelham Bay that gave the park its name. Two large curved Art Deco bathhouses marked by concrete colonnades and blue terra-cotta tiles flank the staircase forming the main entrance to the promenade and the beach.

Orchard Beach is enjoyed by 1.4 million people each summer. Mingle with the beachgoers coming from various sections of the borough who represent the variety of the people of the planet and form special memories of your own. The beach is wheelchair accessible, with mats on the sand near section 7. Two specially equipped wheelchairs are also available. Lifeguards are on duty from 10:00 A.M. to 6:00 P.M., Memorial Day to Labor Day. During that period, special buses marked Bx12 Orchard Beach will take you directly from the number 6 subway train (Pelham Bay Park stop at the end of the line) to the beach. Off-season, the beach is quiet and lovely for a gentle stroll near the calm Long Island Sound. Off-season, however, it is a longer walk to the beach northward from the bus stop at City Island Circle near Rodman's Neck (located in Pelham Bay Park) when taking the regular Bx29 bus (destination City Island). Swimming is prohibited when lifeguards are not on duty.

Playgrounds: Orchard Beach Playground, located in section 12 of the promenade, offers stunning ocean views while children play on the sand and enjoy colorful play equipment. Pelican Bay Playground, located near section 6 of the Orchard Beach promenade, has nautical-inspired play equipment and spray showers that will delight children.

Rest rooms: Several restrooms are located at Orchard Beach around the promenade.

Split Rock is a boulder that was broken by glacier movement in the region during the last ice age, fifteen thousand years ago. During the American Revolution, on October 18, 1776, Colonel John Glover, a fisherman from Marblehead, Massachusetts, commanding 750 Continental troops, fought four thousand seasoned British soldiers to a standstill in the Battle of Pell's Point. The battle began at this rock. Glover's action enabled George Washington to escape entrapment on Manhattan and in the western Bronx to regroup and fight at White Plains. Split Rock is located at the intersection of Hutchinson River Parkway and the New England Thruway.

Three **tennis courts** are found at Orchard Beach. Tennis courts close from the Sunday before Thanksgiving until the first Saturday in April. Permits are required for use. Information concerning permits may be obtained by telephoning 718-430-1840 or at the website: www.nycgov parks.org/permits/tennis-permits.

IN THE SOUTHERN PART OF PELHAM BAY PARK

The Aileen B. Ryan Recreational Complex: The complex, named for a popular and widely respected woman who served in the New York

State Assembly and then in the New York City Council, is located near Bruckner Boulevard and Middletown Road. Baseball, a quarter-mile running track, and the Playground for All Children, with special facilities for the physically challenged, expand access to all.

A monument to the sports-trained body, the **American Boy**, sculpted in 1923 by Louis St. Lanne, is made from a single, large block of Indiana limestone. It stands at the western edge of Pelham Track and Field.

There are six **baseball fields** in Pelham South. Two are located near the Playground for All Children, three are on the corner of Bruckner Boulevard and Middletown Road, and one is near the dog run. For the required sports permits call 718-430-1840 or contact the New York City Parks Department website: www.nycgovparks.org/permits/sport-field.

Basketball courts are available near Bruckner Boulevard and Middletown Road.

Bird-watching: A restricted landfill area attracts many species of birds; special birding expeditions are sometimes conducted by the Urban Park Rangers in this usually closed area. These special expeditions are open to the public upon registration. See the Friends of Pelham Bay Park website events page for information about seasonal birding opportunities and guided walks: www.pelhambaypark.org/category/events/.

Two **bocce courts**, located inside the Playground for All Children, are available and do not require permits.

Bronx Victory Garden and Memorial Grove: *Golden Winged Victory*, sculpted by Belle Kinney, stands proud on a seventy-five-foot-high classical column; she is considered one of the most beautiful landmarked monuments in New York City. *Winged Victory* is located on Crimi Road, just north of the number 6 subway station. Architect John H. Sheridan designed the monument to honor World War I soldiers from The Bronx who served and lost their lives. The lovely grove near the monument has hundreds of linden trees and Norway maples that were transplanted from the Grand Concourse during its 1927 reconstruction.

The **dog run** is located near Middletown Road and Stadium Avenue.

The forty-one-acre **Huntington Woods** is named after Archer Milton Huntington, who purchased the property in 1896 and built an estate. Archer Huntington began the Hispanic Society of New York and co-founded the Museum of the American Indian, which became part of Audubon Terrace in Upper Manhattan. He also built and funded art museums and libraries across America and in Spain. His second wife, Anna Hyatt Huntington, was a noted sculptor. Her equestrian sculpture of José Martí, liberator of Cuba, stands at the Avenue of the Americas entrance to Central Park. Other of her works can be found in the Bronx Zoo and Woodlawn Cemetery. Huntington Woods is now tended by Wild Metro, an environmental organization that combines its efforts with Friends of Pelham Bay Park to maintain the natural beauty of the area and to remove invasive species from the Woods and South Meadow. Visitors, including schoolchildren studying ecology, enjoy the forest, marshland, and shore regions of Huntington Woods.

Pelham Bay Nature Center in the south part of the park is reached through the entrance at Bruckner Boulevard and Wilkinson Avenue. Join the Urban Park Rangers for birding and winter owl watches, hikes, and photography of the natural world throughout the year. Maps and information about ongoing programs may also be obtained in the Nature Center. Telephone: 718-319-7258 (all year).

Pelham Track and Field: This quarter-mile running track includes a rubberized surface, synthetic turf for football, and a long-jump area.

Playgrounds: Sweetgum Playground is located near Bruckner Boulevard and Wilkinson Avenue. It has modern play equipment and is close to the north picnic area.

Playground for All Children includes fully accessible play equipment. Children with special needs will find Braille signs, textured pavement, accessible swings, and handrails that can be reached by children on crutches or in wheelchairs. A lovely Sensory Garden, sponsored by Friends of Pelham Bay Park, gives all children the chance to explore the color, scent, and texture of plants in raised beds accessible to everyone, including those who are in wheelchairs.

Restrooms are located in Pelham South Park Headquarters Building and at the Playground for All Children.

There are nine **tennis courts** in the southern part of the park. Tennis courts close from the Sunday before Thanksgiving until the first Saturday in April. Permits are required for use. Information concerning permits may be obtained by telephoning 718-430-1840 or at the website: www.nycgovparks.org/permits/tennis-permits.

The Bartow-Pell Mansion Museum

The Bartow-Pell Mansion Museum, erected about 1840, is the last remaining mansion of the nearly two dozen which once stood in the northeast Bronx taking advantage of spectacular water views and the impressive landscape. The cut stone mansion is built in Greek Revival style and has beautifully furnished rooms with nineteenth-century period furniture. The winding staircase in the center of the home is stunningly beautiful. The restored Carriage House nearby is not to be missed. Guided tours are available with historical explanations of the time when the Bartow family lived in the house. Concerts, lectures, and numerous other activities are scheduled at various times.

INFORMATION

Mailing address: 895 Shore Road, Bronx, NY 10464

HOURS: Mansion and Carriage House: Wednesday, Saturday, and Sunday, noon to 4:00 P.M.; gardens and grounds: Daily, 8:30 A.M. to dusk.

ADMISSION: Adults $5.00; Seniors and Students $3.00; Children under six, free; gardens and grounds, free.

CONTACTS: Telephone: 718-885-1461; website: bpmm.org; website for tours and programs: www.bartowpellmansionmuseum.org/events/calendar.php.

DIRECTIONS

BY PUBLIC TRANSPORTATION: Take the Westchester Bee-Line Bus number 45 from the Pelham Bay Park subway station to the Bartow-Pell Mansion entrance. The line accepts New York City Metrocards. This bus leaves the subway station at 11:20 A.M., 12:20 P.M., 1:20 P.M., and 2:20 P.M. Ask to get off at the Pelham Bay / Split Rock Golf Course / Bartow-Pell Mansion stop. To return to the Pelham Bay Park subway stop, the number 45 bus stops across from the Bartow-Pell Mansion's entrance nearer the golf course just after the hour from noon to 5:00 P.M. The bus trip is about ten to fifteen minutes each way. For additional information contact the Westchester Bee-Line Bus website or call 914-813-7777.

BY CAR OR TAXI: For detailed driving instructions, visit the Bartow-Pell Mansion website: www.bartowpellmansionmuseum.org/visit/directions.php.

Dining and Picnicking

Food is available to the public at the Clubhouse of Pelham-Split Rock Golf Course. Call 718-885-1258 for details. The Turtle Cove Golf Center also has food. During beach season, from Memorial Day through Labor Day, Havana Café, at Orchard Beach, has Cuban food, fast food, and some healthy options. Pushcarts along the beach provide snacks. On Rodman's Neck, food carts are available seasonally.

Surrounding Orchard Beach on the north and south lawns are wonderful picnic areas with trees dotting the landscape with ocean views. In the southern part of the park, picnic areas are located near the Park Headquarters and just past the tennis courts. There is a limited number of barbecue grills and picnic tables. No barbecuing is allowed near trees; propane tanks are prohibited; coals must be placed in fireproof cans and litter must be cleaned and placed in trash cans. Groups of twenty or more require permits. For more information, see the website: https://nyceventpermits.nyc.gov/Parks/.

After exploring the vast expanse of Pelham Bay Park, you may wish to have a delicious meal at any of the fish and seafood restaurants that abound in nearby City Island, easily reached from a bridge that connects the island to the park. Take the Bx29 bus with the destination City Island along City Island Road in the park. You may also wish to stay and enjoy exploring this nautical island itself. For a walking tour, consult part II, "City Island: New England in The Bronx."

The Hall of Fame for Great Americans

Today, several people in various categories are enshrined in halls of fame. They exist for sports figures, musicians, and actors, among others. The one that started it all is the Hall of Fame for Great Americans, which opened its doors in 1900 on what is now the campus of the Bronx Community College. Here are enshrined the Americans who are deemed to have achieved the highest level of excellence. Walk among the greats. See them face-to-face in the busts fashioned by some of the most accomplished sculptors. Contemplate their accomplishments and what they did to advance the nation and the world.

INFORMATION

100 Hall of Fame Terrace between Sedgwick Avenue and University Avenue (Dr. Martin Luther King Jr. Boulevard), Bronx, NY. Mailing address: Bronx Community College, 2155 University Avenue, Bronx, NY 10453.

HOURS: Every day, sunup to sundown.

ADMISSION: Free.

CONTACTS: Telephone: 718-289-5100 for the college; 718-289-5910 for Hall of Fame director. Website: www.bcc.cuny.edu/HallOfFame/.

DIRECTIONS

BY PUBLIC TRANSPORTATION: Take the subway number 1 train to 238th Street station. At the southeast corner of the intersection of Broadway and 238th Street, take the eastbound number Bx3 bus to the Bronx Community College campus on University Avenue. Walk north past the stairway entrance. Do not go up the stairway, but continue walking to the corner. Turn left and go up the slight hill that is Hall of Fame Terrace. Near the summit of the hill is the entrance to the campus that leads to the Hall of Fame. Turn left onto the campus. You may obtain further guidance from the security guard at the entrance.

Alternatively, take subway number 4 train to Burnside Avenue. At the northwest corner of Burnside Avenue and Jerome Avenue, take the westbound bus number Bx40 or Bx42 up the winding steep hill to University Avenue. Walk north on the west side of University Avenue past the stairway entrance to Bronx Community College. Do not go up the stairway, but continue walking to the corner. Turn left and go up the slight hill that is Hall of Fame Terrace. Near the summit of the hill is the entrance to the campus on your left that leads to the Hall of Fame. You may obtain further guidance from the security guard at the entrance.

BY CAR OR TAXI: Take the Major Deegan Expressway to the West 179th Street exit. Go up the steep, winding ramp to Sedgwick Avenue. At Sedgwick Avenue turn left and continue along one long block to the first intersection on your right (Hall of Fame Terrace). Turn right to the entrance to the campus near the top of the hill to your right. You may obtain further guidance and parking information from the security guard at the entrance.

About the Hall of Fame for Great Americans

The idea for the Hall of Fame for Great Americans began in the last decade of the nineteenth century with Henry Mitchell MacCracken, then the chancellor of New York University. He saw the institution's neighborhood near Washington Square in Manhattan becoming increasingly industrialized. Believing that this was no environment for a student body in which to learn and to contemplate, he searched The Bronx for a suitable site for a new and larger campus with grass and trees. He found it in an area that overlooked the Harlem River that he immediately dubbed University Heights. He purchased the property of several wealthy estate owners and then hired an architect to design the first academic buildings.

The man whom MacCracken hired was Stanford White, the leading American architect of the day. White appropriated elements of the works of leading European architects of the Classical, Renaissance, and Baroque eras in creating his own buildings, and he did so for New York University.

The first three academic buildings on the campus were the Hall of Languages (completed in 1894) and the Hall of Philosophy (completed in 1912) that flanked the columned Gould Memorial Library (completed in 1899) marked by its high rotunda. The library was donated by Helen Gould, the daughter of nineteenth-century robber baron Jay Gould, and named in his honor. The buildings were sited at the edge of a steep slope leading down to the Harlem River. To prevent the entire ensemble from slipping downward in the future, White buttressed it with a retaining wall that snaked behind the structures. When Mac-Cracken saw that retaining wall, he determined that it be put to some educational use, and thought of using it as a Hall of Fame for Great Americans. He persuaded White to change the retaining wall into a 630-foot-long limestone and granite open-air colonnade topped by a vaulted ceiling of Guastavino tiles.

To allow as many people to be involved in the selection process as possible, MacCracken encouraged any American or American organization to nominate candidates for inclusion in the Hall of Fame. An electoral college of more than 100 prominent citizens coming from each state in the Union in the fields of higher education, science, jurisprudence, business, and public life would then select the finalists for that year. The person chosen had to have been dead for at least twenty-five years to assure that his or her fame was not fleeting. Elections were first held every five years, later changed to every three. At first each person chosen was honored by the installation of a bronze plaque placed below a space between the columns that bore his or her name, birth and death dates, and a quotation. Only later were bronze portrait busts of those honored placed in the spaces above the plaques. Many of the sculptors of the busts are among the most distinguished in the country. They include Daniel Chester French (designer of the Lincoln statue in the Lincoln Memorial), James Earl Fraser (who sculpted the statues of Justice and Law for the U.S. Supreme Court building), and Frederick MacMonnies (who sculpted the reliefs on the Washington Square arch). Those elected to the Hall of Fame include authors, educators, architects, inventors, military leaders, judges, theologians, philanthropists, humanitarians, scientists, statesmen, artists, musicians, actors, and explorers.

In the period between elections, national attention was aroused with the announcement of the names of those chosen. Later, with great ceremony and fanfare, the bust would be unveiled near the place where the honoree had lived or worked, or where those who had nominated the honoree were headquartered. After another interval, the bust would be installed in the Hall of Fame with music and lectures. Each step of the process was followed avidly in the press, and this spread interest in the Hall of Fame far and wide in the first half of the twentieth century. In fact, it is even mentioned in the 1939 movie version of *The Wizard of Oz*. In the scene where the Munchkins sing and dance around Dorothy after her house had fallen on and killed the Wicked Witch, they promise her that she would be a bust in the Hall of Fame! (Unfortunately, Dorothy never made it.)

By 1973, New York University faced serious financial problems and decided to sell their University Heights campus in The Bronx and consolidate their operations at Washington Square. The New York State Dormitory Authority purchased it and gave it to the Bronx Community College of the City University of New York, which occupies the grounds today. The last election to the Hall of Fame for Great Americans occurred in 1976. Following that, a dispute between the two academic institutions has prevented any subsequent elections from happening. Nevertheless, there have been several plans proposed to revive the election process. In the meantime, the Hall of Fame for Great Americans remains on the campus and is open to the public.

Visit to the Hall of Fame

Enter the Hall of Fame from the northern entrance to the colonnade. As you continue walking through the arcade, you will encounter on either side the following busts of those who were honored in the following order:

1. Elias Howe (1819–1867), inventor of the sewing machine, elected in 1915, sculpted by Charles Keck.
2. Alexander Graham Bell (1847–1922), inventor of the telephone, elected in 1950, sculpted by Stanley Martineau.
3. John James Audubon (1789–1851), observer and painter of American birds, elected in 1900, sculpted by A. Stirling Calder.
4. Eli Whitney (1765–1825), inventor of the cotton gin and the idea of using interchangeable parts in industry, elected in 1900, sculpted by Chester Beach.
5. Samuel Finley Breese Morse (1791–1872), artist and inventor of the telegraph, elected in 1900, sculpted by Chester Beach.

6. Robert Fulton (1765–1815), inventor of the lock system and the commercial steamboat, elected in 1900, sculpture a replica of one by Jean-Antoine Houdon.

7. Asa Gray (1810–1888), renowned botanist and founder of the National Academy of Science, elected in 1900, sculpted by Chester Beach.

8. Matthew Fontaine Maury (1805–1873), naval officer who charted ocean currents, thus improving navigation, elected 1930, sculpted by F. William Sievers.

9. James Buchanan Eads (1820–1887), engineer who designed the Mississippi levee system, elected 1920, sculpted by Charles Grafly.

10. Simon Newcomb (1839–1909), astronomer who calculated orbits of planets and the Moon's motions, elected 1935, sculpted by Frederick MacMonnies.

11. Maria Mitchell (1818–1889), Vassar's first professor of astronomy, with a lunar crater named for her, elected 1905, sculpted by Emma S. Bingham.

12. George Westinghouse (1846–1914), inventor of the railroad train airbrake and electrically controlled signals, elected in 1955, sculpted by Edmondo Quattrocchi.

13. Louis Agassiz (1807–1873), leading zoologist and geologist, elected in 1915, sculpted by Anna Hyatt Huntington.

14. William Crawford Gorgas (1854–1920), physician who eradicated yellow fever in Cuba and Panama, elected in 1950, sculpted by Bryant Baker.

15. William Thomas Green Morton (1819–1868), dentist who first used ether as a general anesthetic, elected in 1920, sculpted by Helen Farnsworth Mears.

16. Walter Reed (1851–1902), army physician who discovered yellow fever was caused by mosquito bites, elected in 1945, sculpted by Cecil Howard.

17. Joseph Henry (1797–1879), physicist who discovered induced current and built the first electromagnetic motor, elected in 1915, sculpted by John Flanagan.

18. Josiah Willard Gibbs (1839–1903), physicist with theories of thermodynamics and statistical mechanics, elected in 1950, sculpted by Stanley Martineau.

19. This space is still vacant.

20. Wilbur Wright (1867–1912), co-inventor of the airplane, elected in 1965, sculpted by Vincent Glinsky.
21. Orville Wright (1871–1948), co-inventor of the airplane, elected in 1955, sculpted by Paul Fjelde.
22. Thomas Alva Edison (1847–1931), inventor of the electric light, the phonograph, and the motion picture camera, elected in 1960, sculpted by Bryant Baker.
23. Albert Abraham Michelson (1852–1931), physicist who measured the speed of light, elected in 1970, sculpted by Elizabeth Gordon Chandler.
24. George Washington Carver (1864–1943), discoverer of new uses for peanuts, soybeans, and sweet potatoes, elected in 1973, sculpted by Richmond Barthe.
25. Thomas Paine (1737–1809), writer who roused Americans to declare independence, elected in 1945, sculpted by Malvina Hoffman.
26. Benjamin Franklin (1706–1790), writer, statesman, diplomat, and inventor of bifocals, elected in 1900, sculpted by Robert Aitkin.
27. George Washington (1732–1799), Continental Army general and president, elected unanimously in 1900, sculpture a replica of one by Jean-Antoine Houdon.
28. John Adams (1735–1826), first vice president and second president, elected in 1900, sculpted by John Francis Paramino.
29. Henry Clay (1777–1852), statesman and legislator, known for forging compromises in Congress, elected in 1900, sculpted by Robert Aitkin.
30. Thomas Jefferson (1743–1826), statesman, philosopher, president, author of the Declaration of Independence, elected in 1900, sculpted by Robert Aitkin.
31. Abraham Lincoln (1803–1865), president who restored the Union and ended slavery, elected in 1900, sculpted by Augustus Saint-Gaudens.
32. Daniel Webster (1782–1852), legislator, statesman, and orator, elected in 1900, sculpted by Robert Aitkin.
33. James Madison (1751–1836), Father of the Constitution and the Bill of Rights and president, elected in 1905, sculpted by Charles Keck.

34. John Quincy Adams (1767–1848), statesman, diplomat, and president, elected in 1905, sculpted by Edmond T. Quinn.

35. Andrew Jackson (1767–1845), successful general, first "common man" president who upheld Union supremacy, elected in 1910, sculpted by Belle Kinney.

36. Alexander Hamilton (1755–1804), Treasury secretary, founder of the *New York Post* and the Coast Guard, elected in 1915, sculpted by Giussepi Ceracchi.

37. James Monroe (1758–1831), president and author of the Monroe Doctrine, which closed the Western Hemisphere to colonization, elected in 1930, sculpted by Hermon A. MacNeil.

38. Patrick Henry (1736–1799), statesman and orator who argued for American independence, elected in 1920, sculpted by Charles Keck.

39. Grover Cleveland (1837–1908), president who fought for government reform and financial honesty, elected 1935, sculpted by Rudolph Evans.

40. William Penn (1644–1718), Quaker leader and statesman who founded Pennsylvania, elected 1935, sculpted by A. Stirling Calder.

41. Theodore Roosevelt (1858–1919), president and statesman who regulated big business and spearheaded the conservation movement, elected in 1950, sculpted by Georg Lober.

42. Woodrow Wilson (1856–1924), president who regulated business, banking, and labor, and supported world peace, elected in 1950, sculpted by Walter Kirtland Hancock.

43. John Marshall (1755–1835), chief justice who established the Supreme Court's right to declare laws unconstitutional, elected in 1900, sculpted by Herbert Adams.

44. Joseph Story (1779–1845), Supreme Court justice who upheld federal authority and opposed slavery, elected in 1900, sculpted by Herbert Adams.

45. James Kent (1763–1847), law professor whose commentaries became the standard for law education, elected in 1900, sculpted by Edmond T. Quinn.

46. Rufus Choate (1799–1859), orator and foremost trial lawyer of his era, elected in 1915, sculpted by Hermon A. MacNeil.

47. This space is still vacant.

48. Oliver Wendell Holmes Jr. (1841–1945), Supreme Court justice whose dissents often were accepted later, elected in 1965, sculpted by Joseph Kiselewski.
49. This space is still vacant.
50. William Tecumseh Sherman (1820–1891), general who brought total war to the Confederacy, elected in 1905, sculpted by Augustus Saint-Gaudens.
51. Franklin Delano Roosevelt (1882–1945), president during the Great Depression and World War II, elected in 1973, sculpted by Jo Davidson.
52. John Philip Sousa (1854–1932), band leader and composer of marches, known as the March King, elected in 1973, sculpted by Karl H. Gruppe.
53. Ulysses Simpson Grant (1822–1885), victorious general in the Civil War and president, elected 1900, sculpted by James Earle Fraser with Thomas Hudson Jones.
54. Thomas Jonathan "Stonewall" Jackson (1824–1863), Confederate general and renowned strategist, elected 1955, sculpted by Bryant Baker.
55. John Paul Jones (1747–1792), Father of the United States Navy and Revolutionary War naval captain, elected in 1925, sculpted by Charles Grafly.
56. Robert Edward Lee (1807–1870), commanding Confederate general and university president, elected 1900, sculpted by George T. Brewster.
57. David Glasgow Farragut (1801–1870), naval commander in the Civil War, later the first United States admiral, elected 1900, sculpted by Charles Grafly.
58. Edward Alexander MacDowell (1861–1908), classical music composer and pianist, elected 1960, sculpted by C. Paul Jennewien.
59. Henry David Thoreau (1817–1862), essayist and philosopher who originated the concept of civil disobedience, elected in 1960, sculpted by Malvina Hoffman.
60. Daniel Boone (1734–1820), pioneer, opened up Kentucky and the West to settlement, elected in 1915, sculpted by Albin Polasek.
61. Stephen Collins Foster (1826–1864), composer of popular ballads and minstrel songs, elected in 1940, sculpted by Walter Kirtland Hancock.

62. George Peabody (1795–1869), merchant, financier, and philanthropist who pioneered foundation grants, elected in 1900, sculpted by Hans Schuler.

63. James Abbott McNeill Whistler (1834–1903), artist and portrait painter who experimented with color, elected in 1930, sculpted by Frederick MacMonnies.

64. Gilbert Charles Stuart (1755–1828), painter of portraits of the Founding Fathers, notably George Washington, elected in 1900, sculpted by Chester Beach.

65. Peter Cooper (1795–1883), builder of the first American locomotive, steel industry pioneer, and founder of Cooper Union, elected in 1900, sculpted by Chester Beach.

66. Augustus Saint-Gaudens (1846–1907), monumental sculptor who accented his subjects' personalities, elected in 1920, sculpted by James Earle Fraser.

67. Charlotte Saunders Cushman (1816–1876), opera singer and acclaimed actress in Shakespearean roles, elected in 1915, sculpted by Frances Grimes.

68. Edwin Booth (1833–1893), popular and acclaimed dramatic actor in Shakespearean roles, elected in 1925, sculpted by Edmond T. Quinn.

69. Frances Elizabeth Willard (1839–1898), educator, reformer, and feminist, advocate of woman suffrage, elected in 1910, sculpted by Lorado Taft.

70. Susan B. Anthony (1820–1906), feminist reformer who worked for equal pay and votes for women, elected in 1950, sculpted by Brenda Putnam.

71. Lillian D. Wald (1867–1940), social worker who organized visiting nurse and public school nurse services, elected in 1970, sculpted by Eleanor Platt.

72. Jane Addams (1850–1935), social worker and pacifist who received the 1931 Nobel Peace Prize, elected in 1965, sculpted by Granville W. Carter.

73. This space is still vacant.

74. Mary Lyon (1797–1849), feminist who founded Mount Holyoke College for women, elected in 1905, sculpted by Laura Gardin Fraser.

75. Sylvanus Thayer (1785–1872), military engineer and educator

who revitalized West Point's curriculum, elected in 1965, sculpted by Joseph Kiselewski.

76. Booker T. Washington (1858–1915), educator, first president of Tuskegee Institute, elected in 1945, sculpted by Richmond Barthe.

77. Alice Freeman Palmer (1855–1902), educator, history scholar, president of Wellesley College, elected in 1920, sculpted by Evelyn Longman.

78. Emma Willard (1787–1870), promoter of equal education and higher education for women, elected in 1905, sculpted by Frances Grimes.

79. Roger Williams (1603–1683), religious leader, who favored religious toleration and church-state separation, elected in 1920, sculpted by Hermon A. MacNeil.

80. Mark Hopkins (1802–1887), educator, philosopher, and president of Williams College, elected in 1915, sculpted by Hans Hoerbst.

81. Phillips Brooks (1835–1893), orator and preacher, Episcopal bishop of Massachusetts, elected in 1910, sculpted by Daniel Chester French.

82. Henry Ward Beecher (1813–1887), clergyman, preacher, and fervent abolitionist, elected in 1900, sculpted by Massey Rhind.

83. Horace Mann (1796–1859), leader in public education and founder of America's first teacher training school, elected in 1900, sculpted by Adolph A. Weinman.

84. William Ellery Channing (1790–1842), theologian, abolitionist, helped establish Unitarianism and an American literature, elected in 1900, sculpted by Herbert Adams.

85. Jonathan Edwards (1703–1758), religious leader, theologian, and president of Princeton, elected in 1900, sculpted by Charles Grafly.

86. Walt Whitman (1819–1892), poet of democracy and editor of the *Brooklyn Eagle*, elected in 1930, sculpted by Chester Beach.

87. Sidney Lanier (1842–1881), poet, musician, and literary critic in the South after the Civil War, elected in 1945, sculpted by Hans Schuler.

88. James Fenimore Cooper (1789–1851), internationally famed novelist of epic tales of the American frontier, elected in 1910, sculpted by Victor Salvatore.

89. Harriet Beecher Stowe (1811–1896), author of *Uncle Tom's Cabin*, the antislavery novel influencing public opinion in the North before the Civil War, elected in 1910, sculpted by Brenda Putnam.

90. John Lathrop Motley (1814–1877), author of multivolume narrative histories of the Dutch Republic, elected in 1910, sculpted by Frederick MacMonnies.

91. Samuel Langhorne Clemens (1835–1910), known as Mark Twain, writer, lecturer, and American humorist, elected in 1920, sculpted by Albert Humphreys.

92. Francis Parkman (1823–1893), botanist, historian of the American frontier, elected in 1915, sculpted by Hermon A. MacNeil.

93. Edgar Allan Poe (1809–1849), poet, critic, short story writer, inventor of the detective story, elected in 1910, sculpted by Daniel Chester French.

94. George Bancroft (1800–1891), historian, Father of American History, founder of the U.S. Naval Academy, elected in 1910, sculpted by Rudolph Evans.

95. William Cullen Bryant (1794–1878), poet and editor of the *New York Evening Post*, elected in 1910, sculpted by Herbert Adams.

96. John Greenleaf Whittier (1807–1892), poet, journalist, and ardent abolitionist, elected in 1905, sculpted by Rudolph Evans.

97. Oliver Wendell Holmes (1809–1894), poet, essayist, and physician who researched childbed fever, elected in 1910, sculpted by Edmond T. Quinn.

98. James Russell Lowell (1819–1891), poet, editor of *Atlantic Monthly*, teacher, diplomat, and political satirist, elected in 1905, sculpted by Allan Clark.

99. Ralph Waldo Emerson (1803–1882), philosopher, poet, essayist, lecturer, and Transcendentalist, elected in 1900, sculpted by Daniel Chester French.

100. Nathaniel Hawthorne (1804–1864), novelist and short story writer, elected in 1900, sculpted by Daniel Chester French.

101. Washington Irving (1782–1859), satirist, historian, travel writer, Father of American Letters, elected in 1900, sculpted by Edward McCartan.

102. Henry Wadsworth Longfellow (1807–1882), internationally renowned poet, elected in 1900, sculpted by Rudolph Evans.

The following persons were elected, but have not yet had busts installed:

A. Louis Dembits Brandeis (1856–1941), first Jewish Supreme Court justice, champion of economic, social, and political justice, elected in 1973.
B. Clara Barton (1821–1912), humanitarian who founded the American Red Cross, elected in 1976.
C. Luther Burbank (1849–1926), botanist, horticulturalist, and agricultural science pioneer who developed over 300 plant varieties, elected in 1976.
D. Andrew Carnegie (1836–1919), large-scale industrialist and philanthropist who founded public libraries across the country, elected in 1976.

Other Campus Attractions

The Bronx Community College campus is replete with attractions of unique historical and architectural interest that date from the period before it served higher education through the period when it was occupied by New York University to today.

The Gould Memorial Library, in the center of the Hall of Fame complex facing the quadrangle, was inspired by the Pantheon in Rome. Architect Stanford White used yellow Roman brick and limestone pilasters for the exterior wall. Six Indiana sandstone columns line the portico.

Stop at the entrance and note the massive bronze doors. Stanford White had been murdered and a sensational court case led to the conviction of his killer. His artist colleagues honored him with these memorial bronze doors designed by his son, Lawrence White. They feature eight symbolic relief sculptures as a tribute to their friend who opened doors for other artists.

Enter and climb the staircase. Note the large and unusual sconces illuminating the space and the arched ceiling. It is inspired by a staircase entrance to the Vatican in Rome.

At the top of the staircase enter the room straight ahead. Although this massive space is now used only occasionally for special ceremonies and receptions, it originally served as a circular reading room crowned by a soaring coffered dome. The rotunda is lined with sixteen Corinthian columns of rare Irish Connemara green marble. The floor is covered with marble mosaic tiles from Italy. Circling the rotunda at the mezzanine level are Tiffany stained-glass windows. Above, on the balcony at the base of the dome, are statues of the Greek Muses. Around the room, above the places where the book stacks were once located on each level, inscribed in gold are the names of the famous authors in each academic field whose works could be found there.

There are several attractions toward the south side of the Hall of Fame complex.

To the right of the south exit from the Hall of Fame, nearest the slope leading down to the Harlem River, is the Bergrisch Lecture Hall. Completed in 1964, it was designed by the noted mid-twentieth-century architect Marcel Breuer. Breuer was known for the style called Brutalism. Concrete was poured into a space created by wide wooden slats. When the concrete hardened, the wooden slats were removed, but the images of the grain in the wood remained preserved in the concrete. The wall thus created remained unadorned. The lecture hall is also made spectacular by its design that lifts the entire width of the structure up off its base in a huge cantilever to form the room inside. This building is the most distinct of the three that Breuer's architectural firm designed for the New York University campus.

Just to the west and north of the Bergrisch Lecture Hall is the Julius Silver Residence Center and Cafeteria, a large complex of buildings connected by covered walkway bridges now called Community Hall, Altschul House, and Colston Hall. It was also completed in 1964 and designed by Marcel Breuer & Associates, Robert F. Gatje, associate.

Just across the road from the southern exit of the Hall of Fame and slightly to the east of it is the old red brick building known today as Butler Hall. This is one of the three campus buildings that predates the arrival of New York University. Erected about 1859, this structure was originally the residence of Henri W. T. Mali, the Belgian consul general to the United States. His mansion and estate was one of several at the time that occupied the high lands that overlooked the Harlem River and northern Manhattan and the New Jersey Palisades beyond.

Along the walkway south of the Butler Hall entrance can be seen the tall flagpole located on a small eminence. The flagpole was originally the mast of Sir Thomas Lipton's yacht *Shamrock IV*, one of several the British tea merchant entered to try to win the famed America's

Cup yacht race, which he never did. Lipton donated the mast to New York University.

At the base of the flagpole are several old cannon. The largest one, with its barrel sticking out from behind the hedge surrounding the flagpole, is a German cannon captured by the French in the course of World War I. It was presented to New York University by French marshall Ferdinand Foch, the commander of the Allied troops in the war, on his visit to the campus in the early 1920s.

Near the south side of the flagpole rests a small boulder on which is carved the words "Fort Number Eight." The inscription refers to a Revolutionary War fort built on the campus site in 1775 by the Americans to protect the upper Harlem River valley. It was one of a series of fortifications, and this one was the eighth in a line that stretched from the mainline shore opposite the northernmost tip of Manhattan Island to here. The invading British captured Fort Number Eight when they advanced to this area in November 1776, and it remained in their hands throughout the rest of the war. The foundations of the fort were uncovered in the early 1960s with the construction of Bergrisch Hall, along with British military buttons, musket balls, and the remnants of a meal. Long after the fort had disappeared, the boulder was inscribed by Gustav H. Schwab, a German immigrant who was the American representative of the North German Lloyd steamship line and owned the site as part of his nineteenth-century estate. South of the flagpole is the red brick building today called South Hall. It was erected in 1857 as Schwab's mansion. He called the mansion and his estate Fort Number Eight, after the Revolutionary War fort that was once on the site.

Back on the quadrangle where the Hall of Fame complex is found, toward the middle of the southern side of the quadrangle, is Meister Hall. Originally erected for New York University, it was designed by Marcel Breuer and Associates, Hamilton Smith, associate, in the firm's signature Brutalist style. The building was originally called Technology II, and opened in 1972, one year before New York University sold the campus. Later, it was renamed to honor noted educator Morris Meister, the first president of Bronx Community College. Previously, Meister had championed and served as first principal of the Bronx High School of Science, which was founded to educate students of superior intellect. In the 1950s, Meister began to advocate the establishment of a higher education institution to meet the needs of high school graduates who required more practical teaching and training in a growing number of skilled professions, but who did not consider a full four-year college experience necessary. He also believed that those high school graduates who had just missed the cutoff for acceptance into four-year colleges could use the opportunity to take two years of college-level courses to provide them with the foundation that would enable them to transfer to a four-year college for their final two years of a complete college education. This led to the establishment of Bronx Community College of the City University of New York, which awards its graduates associate's degrees in professional and foundation college-level subjects.

There are also two attractions at the northern end of the campus.

At the northernmost edge of the campus, just to the east of the north entrance to the Hall of Fame and to the west of the entrance gate, is the North Hall and Library, designed by the noted contemporary architect, Robert A. M. Stern. The building was opened in 2012. Stern is noted for his attempts to blend in new buildings, with all their modern amenities, with nearby older, historic architectural styles. In this, the first structure on the campus erected under the auspices of the City University and Bronx Community College, he tried to harmonize the exterior with Stanford White's nearby Hall of Fame complex. The brickwork resembles the Roman brick used on the three Hall of Fame complex buildings. The ceiling of the portico leading to the library entrance is a vault made of Guastavino tile, echoing the vaulted ceiling of the Hall of Fame.

Normally, this building is open to students and faculty only. However, if you can gain permission to see the interior, the experience can be rewarding. The divided stairway straight ahead bears murals of contemporary artist Daniel Hauben on each of the two landings. They are part of a series of paintings commissioned for the library called *A Sense of Place*. Each depicts a scene of contemporary Bronx life.

On the second floor is the library reading room. It is modeled after the double-barreled Bibliothèque Ste. Geneviéve in Paris. The 40-foot-high ceiling has its barrels bordered in a hand stenciled Greek key pattern. Affixed to the 91-foot-long and 100-foot-wide balcony that borders the central part of the reading room are smaller murals from the series by Daniel Hauben illustrating Bronx life.

Outside of the campus entrance gate, but still a part of the campus, across from Hall of Fame Terrace, is the old mansion today called MacCracken Hall. It was originally built in the 1880s as the mansion of William Loring Andrews, a successful leather tanner and merchant. He had an interest in bookbinding and its history, collected many rare old books, and rebound them in uniform leather covers. His old estate constitutes most of today's college campus. Purchased by Henry Mitchell MacCracken, the house was used as his residence while he served as New York University's chancellor. It is still used by the Bronx Community College today.

Visitors may return to Manhattan by walking eastward on Hall of Fame Terrace to University Avenue (Dr. Martin Luther King Jr. Boulevard). Cross University Avenue to the northeast corner of the intersection near the Public Library building. Take the number Bx3 northbound bus to the last stop, West 238th Street and Broadway. Transfer to the downtown elevated subway number 1 train there to return to Times Square and beyond.

Or, walk along the east side of University Avenue (Dr. Martin Luther King Jr. Boulevard) to the southeast corner of Burnside Avenue. Take the north- and eastbound number Bx40 or Bx42 bus to Jerome Avenue. Transfer to the downtown elevated subway number 4 train there to Grand Central Station and beyond.

Those who come by car can turn west on Hall of Fame Terrace and, at the bottom of the hill, turn right onto Sedgwick Avenue. The first wide intersection is Fordham Road. Turn left onto Fordham Road for a comparatively short distance and make a left-hand turn onto the ramp leading to the southbound Major Deegan Expressway.

The Bronx Museum
of the Arts

Art and baseball are neighbors in The Bronx. Consider visiting the Bronx Museum of the Arts before or after a Yankee game to enjoy contemporary multicultural art in the calm and peaceful atmosphere of this lovely and unpretentious museum. It is located only a short walk from Yankee Stadium.

INFORMATION

1046 Grand Concourse between 165th and 166th Streets

HOURS: Thursday, Saturday, and Sunday, 11:00 A.M. to 6:00 P.M.; Friday, 11:00 A.M. to 8:00 P.M.

ADMISSION: Free.

CONTACTS: Telephone: 718-681-6000 or 718-681-6181. For tours: telephone: 718-681-6000, ext. 127. Website: www.bronxmuseum.org/ education@bronxmuseum.org.

DIRECTIONS

BY PUBLIC TRANSPORTATION: Take the letter D subway train (letter B train in rush hours only) to 167th Street. Use the McClellan Street exit at the rear of the train and walk one and a half blocks to the museum entrance; or take the number 4 train to 167th Street and River Avenue and walk three blocks eastward (up the hill) to the Grand Concourse (or transfer to the eastbound Bx35 bus to the Grand Concourse), then cross the Grand Concourse and turn right to walk southward two and a half blocks to the museum entrance.

Alternatively, take the BxM4 Express bus on Madison Avenue to 165th Street and the Grand Concourse at the museum. (For schedule information and for pick-up and drop-off points, telephone 511 and say MTA, or visit website: www.mta.info/busco/schedules/.)

BY CAR OR TAXI: Take the Major Deegan Expressway to eastbound Cross Bronx Expressway to Jerome Avenue exit. At Jerome Avenue, make a short right turn to Mount Eden Parkway, then turn left again onto Mount Eden Parkway to the Grand Concourse. Turn right on the Grand Concourse to 165th Street. Street parking only.

About the Bronx Museum of the Arts

Although the Bronx Museum of the Arts was founded in 1971, it did not occupy this site until 1982. It originally used the space known as the Veterans' Memorial Hall in the Bronx County Building on the Grand Concourse and 161st Street.

When the Young Israel of the Concourse synagogue on 165th Street closed, the museum set its sights upon the newly empty building as a perfect place for its exhibitions. The portion of the museum at the corner of 165th Street (officially 1040 Grand Concourse) was originally designed as a synagogue by Simon H. Zelnick in 1961. The interior was altered for museum use. An expansion was added in 1988 designed by the firm of Castro-Blanco, Piscioneri & Feder. In 2006, a larger addition to the museum with a new entrance opened at 1046 Grand Concourse in the middle of the block and attached to the original building. It was designed in a striking contemporary plan by Arquitectonica with Bernardo Fort Brescia and Laurenda Spar in charge. Its façade emulates fan folds made of aluminum and glass with dark masonry block.

The Bronx Museum of the Arts specializes in exhibitions of contemporary and twentieth-century paintings, sculpture, and drawings by Americans with an emphasis on works by Latin American artists and artists with a direct connection to The Bronx. The permanent collection includes over 600 contemporary works in diverse media. In 2012, the museum received a Ford Foundation grant that supported the purchase of over forty new works of art, including pieces by Vito Acconci, Alvin Baltrop, Elizabeth Catlett, Juan Downey, Oyvind Fahlstöm, Raphael Montañez Ortiz, and Martin Wong. On the lower level, there is a large space that is used for special events, performances, dynamic talks with exhibiting artists, family art activities, and more, which are scheduled at various times throughout the year. The museum also has a gift shop and rest rooms.

Visitors may wish to explore the neighborhood in which the Bronx Museum of the Arts is located by taking the walking tour found in part II, "The Grand Concourse Historic District: Art Deco Delights," or explore another nearby attraction, part I, "The Bronx County Building: The Art of Democracy," or go a bit farther to see the nearby attraction found in part I, "Yankee Stadium."

PART II

Walking Tours

City Island

NEW ENGLAND IN THE BRONX

City Island off the coast of the northeast Bronx provides the visitor with an easily accessible experience of a charming New England village with a spectacular array of fine seafood restaurants all within the confines of the city of New York. Watch the gulls, geese, and ducks flying over the blue waters of Long Island Sound as they search for food among mussels and fish. See local residents gliding over the water in boats under full sail or powered by outboard motors. This half-mile wide, one-and-a-half-mile long idyllic island is the home to 4,500 people who reside among the few modern townhouses and condominiums set amid the host of historic structures from the mid-nineteenth century, all found only twelve miles from Times Square.

DIRECTIONS

BY PUBLIC TRANSPORTATION: Take subway number 6 train northbound to the Pelham Bay Park station. Transfer to the Bx29 bus at the stop near the bus shelter on the triangular traffic island on the side of the Bruckner Expressway service road. Be sure the bus has the destination "City Island." Get off at the first stop on City Island.

BY CAR OR TAXI: Take the Bruckner Expressway northbound to the Orchard Beach/City Island exit. Follow the signs to City Island. Cross the Pelham Bridge and then turn right through Pelham Bay Park. At the traffic circle, continue following the signs to City Island and cross the City Island Bridge. Stop after turning right off the bridge. There is street parking, plus ample parking in lots for patrons at most restaurants.

Activities

FISHING TRIPS

Riptide III

701 Minnieford Avenue, Bronx, NY 10464

HOURS: All day from 8:00 A.M. to 4:00 P.M.

FARES: Adults $65.00, Seniors $60.00, Children under 12 $40.00. Save $3.00 on Adult or Senior tickets by purchasing in advance.

CONTACTS: Telephone: 718-885-0326; website: www.riptide3.com.

City Island Current Fleet

Sailing from Jack's Bait and Tackle, 551 City Island Avenue, Bronx, NY 10464

HOURS: All day.

FARES: Adults $65.00, Seniors $60.00, Children $40.00. Advance purchase is strongly recommended.

CONTACTS: For tickets, telephone Zerve at 212-209-3370; website: www .zerve.com/ICFleet.

BOAT RENTALS

Jack's Bait and Tackle

551 City Island Avenue, Bronx, NY 10464

HOURS: Four-person fiberglass boats with outboard motors available on a first-come, first-served basis every day 6:00 A.M. to 4:00 P.M.

FEES: $59.99 on weekdays, $69.99 on weekends, including taxes, gas, map, life jackets, floatation devices, operating instructions, and lessons. Driver's license and credit card required.

CONTACTS: Telephone: 718-885-2942; website: jacksbaitandtackle.com.

About City Island

The Dutch settlers of New Amsterdam first called the island Miniwitz, which was corrupted by the English who took over the Dutch colony in 1664 to Minneford, a name that still appears on places on the island. Thomas Pell of Fairfield, Connecticut, purchased the island and much of the nearby mainland from the local American Indians in 1654. It became part of his vast manor of Pelham in colonial times and of the town of Pelham after the American Revolution. Farmers began to use the land to raise crops and livestock.

In 1760, Benjamin Palmer and twenty-nine others formed a consortium to purchase the island to make it into a major commercial and maritime city. To promote the scheme, they changed its name to City Island. Its colonial charter allowed them to also own the rights beneath the waters around the island. Consequently, those who own land on the waterside today also own the land beneath the water, and this led to the creation of some private beaches on the shoreline.

The American Revolution dashed Palmer's scheme. The British anchored two warships in Long Island Sound and plundered the island's farmers during the day. After sundown, Americans arrived by canoe from the mainland and plundered them by night. Palmer and other consortium members were ruined.

In the nineteenth century, passenger steamboats plying the sea lanes between Manhattan and New England needed experienced pilots to navigate the treacherous, rock-filled waters of the East River and Hell Gate. Pilots resided on City Island where the ships picked them up on their way to New York City on the southern tip of Manhattan Island and dropped them off on the return journey. Sailors resided on the island and a flourishing fishing industry began. Starting in 1839, Orrin Fordham, a Connecticut shipbuilder, devised a system of planting oysters in the seabeds off City Island that could be harvested. Oysters and lobsters were caught right off shore. This led to the rise of a thriving seafood industry and of restaurants that served fresh shore dinners to ever increasing numbers of customers on day trips.

In 1862, David Carll established a shipyard on City Island and became its first major boat builder. After the Civil War, he built luxury and racing yachts. Other boat builders followed his lead. Many wealthy New Yorkers kept their yachts on City Island. During the world wars, City Island shipyards provided sub chasers, tugboats, PT boats, landing craft, and minesweepers for the navy. In peacetime, City Island shipyards created the yachts that won the prestigious America's Cup races in 1958, 1964, 1967, 1970, 1974, 1977, and 1980. No America's Cup yacht built on City Island ever lost the race. While the rise of fiberglass construction for boats led to the gradual demise of these shipyards, yacht clubs, sailing schools, marinas, sail makers, fishing and lobster boats, and marine supply and repair shops preserve the island's nautical heritage.

New York City annexed the southern portion of the town of Pelham, including City Island, in 1895. Despite being part of the great metropolis, island residents live a much more laid-back life than those in the midst of the hurly-burley of Manhattan. In fact, it is a distinction to boast that a person was born on City Island. Such people are called Clamdiggers. Anyone who was born elsewhere, even one day before arriving, can never achieve that distinction. That person is called a Musselsucker.

Today, City Island still retains the air of a nautical New England village. Because of this, houses and sections of the island have been used as sets in several Hollywood productions and television films and series. These motion pictures include *Long Day's Journey into Night* starring Katharine Hepburn, *Awakenings* starring Robert De Niro and Robin Williams, *Love Is All There Is* starring Lainie Kazan and Angelina Jolie, and the aptly named *City Island*. Included among the television productions are episodes of *Coronet Blue* and *Law and Order: Criminal Intent*. The island's nautical atmosphere also attracted silent film Western star Harry Carey, announcer Big Wilson, world-famous neurologist Oliver Sacks, and Judith Scheindlin (Judge Judy) to live there at various times.

City Island retains much of its quaint nineteenth-century atmosphere, while providing visitors the opportunity to dine on some of the finest fish and seafood dishes in New York.

Walking Tour

City Island Avenue, the main street, runs roughly in a north-south direction. This is where visitors can find such institutions as the four houses of worship, the public library, schools, shops, art galleries, and restaurants. There are over thirty restaurants on the island ranging in cuisine from Italian to Japanese, but the vast majority specializes in fish and seafood. Most of the side streets to the east and west of City Island Avenue are strictly residential filled with single-family homes, bungalows, and substantial residences made of wood, stucco, or brick dating from the nineteenth and twentieth centuries. Walk along these quiet streets. Each has its own charm, even quaintness, and some have surprises. Going from north to south, here are a few places of particular interest.

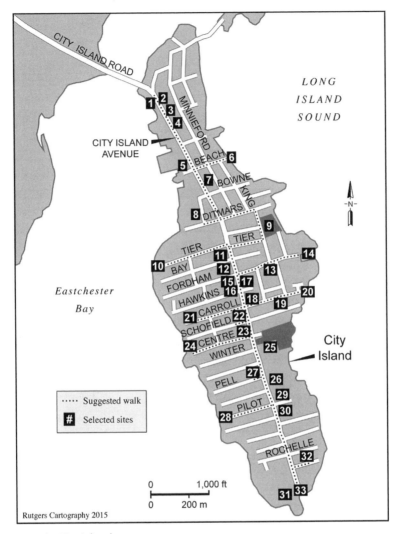

Map 3. City Island

1. Bridge Park
2. Home of former Bronx borough president
3. Saint Mary Star of the Sea Roman Catholic Church
4. Samuel Pell House
5. Jack's Bait and Tackle
6. Touring Kayak Club of New York
7. Temple Beth El of City Island
8. Harlem Yacht Club
9. Pelham Cemetery
10. Delmour Point
11. Trinity United Methodist Church
12. Focal Point Art Gallery
13. City Island Nautical Museum
14. Fordham Street Pier
15. 295 City Island Avenue
16. Hawkins Street Park
17. 284 City Island Avenue
18. City Island 9/11 Memorial Mural
19. 150 Carroll Street
20. The Boatyard Condominium
21. 31 Carroll Street
22. Starving Artist Art Gallery
23. 84–86 and 90 Schofield Street
24. Stuyvesant Yacht Club
25. PS 175
26. South Minneford Yacht Club
27. 95 Pell Place
28. City Island Yacht Club
29. 141 Pilot Street
30. Grace Episcopal Church
31. Morris Yacht and Beach Club
32. 175 Belden Street
33. Belden Point

1 • Just south of the City Island Bridge on the west side of City Island Avenue is Bridge Park. The Catherine Scott Walkway parallels the waterside of the City Island Channel separating the island from the mainland. The view across the water is the shoreline of Pelham Bay Park.

2 • Across the street on the east side of City Island Avenue is a frame house with a front porch and a tall mansard roof and a widow's walk that is the home of former Bronx borough president Adolfo Carrion Jr.

3 • Saint Mary Star of the Sea Roman Catholic Church on the east side of City Island Avenue at number 600 is made of brick and has a bas-relief statue of the Virgin Mary on the front of the steeple to the side of the church entrance. Although the building was erected in 1959, the parish dates from 1887. The parochial school is located behind the church at 595 Minnieford Avenue.

4 • The Samuel Pell House is just south of Saint Mary Star of the Sea Church, at 586 City Island Avenue. This imposing fifteen-room Second Empire style free-standing house was erected in 1876 for wealthy oysterman Samuel Pell, a descendant of the family that once owned the colonial manor of Pelham. Its elaborately detailed mansard roof retains its original polychrome slate shingles and its walls have the original clapboards. It is an official landmark of New York City.

5 • Jack's Bait and Tackle at 551 City Island Avenue on the west side of the street is a popular place for residents and visitors to obtain fishing supplies and to rent outboard motor boats to go fishing.

6 • The Touring Kayak Club of New York has its clubhouse at 205 Beach Street two blocks east of City Island Avenue. The club was founded in 1927 by a group of people who loved kayaking. This club building on Long Island Sound was purchased in 1946 and contains two boathouses for storing kayaks, lockers, showers, a kitchen, a large deck, a clubroom, and access to the beach.

7 • Temple Beth El of City Island at 480 City Island Avenue on the east side of the street serves the island's Jewish residents. While an active congregation organized in 1937, it was not until 1957 that this synagogue building was dedicated.

8 • The Harlem Yacht Club on 417 Hunter Avenue, between Bowne and Ditmars Streets two blocks west of City Island Avenue, is one of the oldest yacht clubs in the nation. It was founded in 1883, but opened its home on City Island in 1899. The current three-story clubhouse was erected after a fire destroyed the first one in 1915. The club's full-service restaurant and bar is open for lunch or dinner to visitors in proper attire Wednesday through Sunday from about mid-May to mid-October. Visit website: www.hyc.org/restaurant/ for details.

9 • Pelham Cemetery on King Avenue between Ditmars and Tier Streets two blocks east of City Island Avenue gets its name from the town of Pelham of which City Island once was a part. Gently sloping toward the water with occasional boats passing by, the quiet nautical background is a perfect setting for the final resting place of so many island residents, including veterans of the Civil War and subsequent conflicts.

10 • Delmour Point, 21 Tier Street at Eastchester Bay two blocks west of City Island Avenue, is a rare shingle-style seaside residence erected in 1896 by local builder Samuel H. Booth as a summer home for Lawrence Delmour, a highly placed Tammany Hall politician and real estate dealer. Its shingle surfaces, horizontal lines interrupted by the building's towers, and expansive porch are hallmarks of this architectural style. Because it evokes the New England houses of the era in which it was built, this building served as the set for the 1962 television film *Long Day's Journey into Night* starring Katharine Hepburn.

11 • Trinity United Methodist Church, 331 City Island Avenue (also 113 Bay Street on the west side of City Island Avenue) was established in 1854. This current structure, erected in 1892, is a white clapboard church with Gothic Revival elements. Its entrance is at the base of its steeple.

12 • Focal Point Art Gallery, 321 City Island Avenue on the west side of the street between Bay and Fordham Streets, specializes in displaying contemporary works produced by artists on the island and in the metropolitan area. The shows change monthly. Visitors can step in and browse Sunday through Thursday from 11:00 A.M. to 6:00 P.M. and on Friday and Saturday from 11:00 A.M. to 7:00 P.M. An open-house reception is held with the artists in attendance and free refreshments the first Friday of every month from 7:00 to 10:00 P.M.

13 • City Island Nautical Museum, 190 Fordham Street one and a half blocks east of City Island Avenue, occupies the ground floor of a building opened in 1898 as PS 102, then renumbered in 1903 as PS 17. Designed by New York City Board of Education's staff architect C.B.J. Snyder as a Georgian Revival red brick (now painted white) structure, the school closed in 1975. The museum occupied the ground floor almost immediately and contains an extensive collection relating to City Island's past and nautical heritage displayed in permanent and special exhibits. In 2000, the upstairs and the rear of the building were opened as sixteen condominium units. Hours are Saturday and Sunday 1:00 to 5:00 P.M. and by special appointment; free admission. Contacts: Telephone: 718-885-0008; website: cityislandmuseum.org; e-mail: cihs@cityislandmuseum.org.

14 • The Fordham Street Pier at the eastern end of Fordham Street two and a half blocks east of City Island Avenue has restricted access, but it can be viewed from its gated entrance. No one is permitted beyond the entrance gate without specific authorization of New York City's Department of Correction. Across the channel lies Hart Island, which has served as the city's potter's field since 1869. Those who die without anyone to claim the remains are interred on this island. Every Wednesday the burial detail is formed of volunteer prisoners sentenced for misdemeanors or other low-level offenses bused here under guard from the city's prison at Riker's Island and then ferried across the channel. They consider it a plum job since they spend the day outdoors in fresh air doing vigorous exercise. They are returned to their cells in the late afternoon.

15 • 295 City Island Avenue on the west side a short walk south of Fordham Street is one of the oldest buildings on the island dating from the 1840s or 1850s. Its frame structure is a simplified version of the Greek Revival style with a plain façade. This house is asymmetrical and built in two sections.

16 • Hawkins Street Park on the west side of City Island Avenue at Hawkins Street is a little park with seating, an oasis on a busy street.

Children can play on the two black sculptured seals and the sculpted black whale that carry through City Island's nautical theme on the grounds, while adults can sit on benches beneath trees. The park is named for Navy Seaman Second Class and City Island native Leonard Hillson Hawkins who died of spinal meningitis while serving on the USS *Delaware* in World War I. The granite monument and bronze plaque on the rear wall of the park honors Hawkins and 104 other City Island men who served in World War I.

17 • 284 City Island Avenue on the east side between Fordham and Hawkins Streets is an apartment house erected about 1898. It is five stories tall, including its attic, but it is very narrow, only twenty feet wide. When it was finished, it caused outrage among City Islanders for being so high. They feared that similar structures would dwarf their own single-family homes and change the character of the neighborhood. They pressed for a zoning change that forbade any future City Island structure from exceeding its height. Thus, it still is the tallest building on the island. It is City Island's skyscraper!

18 • City Island 9/11 Memorial Mural on the north side of Carroll Street just in from the east side of City Island Avenue commemorates the rescue effort of police, firefighters, and emergency medical workers who lost their lives during the attack on the World Trade Center on September 11, 2001. Many of the current residents of City Island are members of New York City's police and fire departments and were particularly affected by the event. This large mural was painted shortly afterward. It depicts the southern shoreline of Manhattan Island with the World Trade Center. The Statue of Liberty rises in the background. A large American flag with an American eagle fly to the left, while Uncle Sam doffs his hat in memoriam to the right. Below the flag are the images of a policeman, a fireman, and an ambulance.

19 • 150 Carroll Street on the south side of the street east of City Island Avenue is a residence erected in the mid-nineteenth century when the Greek Revival style of architecture was beginning to transition into something else. The Greek Revival elements include the attenuated pilasters at the corners in the Greek Doric style, the massive cornice they support, the triple-paneled door at the left flanked by sidelights, and the French doors to the right. The porch, however, has its turned posts linked by a jigsaw trellis-type decoration typical of Victorian eclectic design.

20 • The Boatyard Condominium, 210 Carroll Street, at the eastern end of the street two blocks east of City Island Avenue, was completed in 1986 on the site once occupied by a shipyard. This gated community of seventy wood-frame units fronting the waters of Long Island Sound boasts of docking facilities for residents' boats, a swimming pool, tennis courts, and a space for parties and gatherings. Judith Scheindlin (Judge Judy) was one of the first residents to move in. She occupied one of the ground floor units to the right beyond the gate.

21 • 31 Carroll Street on the north side of the street two and a half blocks west of City Island Avenue is a spectacular residence erected in the 1850s or 1860s showing a transition from the Greek Revival style of architecture to the Italianate style. Hallmarks of the Italianate are the square plan, overhanging eaves with double brackets, tall sash windows, and small square cupola atop the roof. Lingering are such traces of the Greek Revival style as the sidelights flanking the front door and the Greek Doric style porch posts. An unusual feature is the weathervane on top of the cupola. It is a carpenter's saw!

22 • The Starving Artist Art Gallery, 249 City Island Avenue on the west side of the street between Carroll and Schofield Streets, was opened in 1997 to feature the handmade jewelry of its owner, Elliot Glick, and fine art and craft work such as boxes, pottery, paintings, and photographs by local artisans. Since 2004, the gallery has also become a venue for music artists with performances by songwriters, blues musicians, and jazzmen with special celebrations for Chinese New Year and Mardi Gras. In addition, the gallery has a café offering sandwiches, salads, platters, desserts, and soft drinks. Performances are free, but music patrons must order something from the menu and are asked to contribute what they wish to a "music appreciation box." The tables feature small games patrons can play. For information about hours and events, telephone: 718-885-3779 or e-mail: elliott@starving artistonline.com.

23 • 84–86 and 90 Schofield Street on the south side of the street west of City Island Avenue are two interesting residential structures

dating from about 1875. Number 84–86 is only one story tall, but it has a grand mansard roof. The long porch has French doors, rather than windows, leading onto it. Number 90 next door, closer to City Island Avenue, has an abundance of Victorian gingerbread.

24 • Stuyvesant Yacht Club, 10 Centre Street at the western edge of the street on the north side of the street two blocks west of City Island Avenue, is a private member-owned yacht club with a restaurant and bar open for lunch on Saturday and Sunday and for dinner on Wednesday and Friday. Visits must be arranged in advance. Dress is casual, but bathing suits and bare feet are not permitted and shirts are required. Telephone the office at 718-885-1023 or the bar and restaurant at 718-885-2127 or visit the website: www.StuyvesantYC.org. The club was chartered in 1890 using the ferryboat named *Gerard Stuyvesant* as its clubhouse, beached along the East River at Port Morris on the southern coast of The Bronx. Membership growth led the club to move to Jack's Rock on Pelham Bay in Pelham Bay Park, but a short time later, in 1934, it was compelled to move when the bay was filled in to create Orchard Beach. The club then moved into a tent on what had been a coal yard at the end of Centre Street on City Island. Members pitched in to build a permanent home with improvements over the years. However, a fire in 1968 destroyed that clubhouse and the current one was erected on the site. The club sponsors and participates in several maritime events and races. Sailboats and motorboats fill the marina behind the club.

25 • PS 175, 200 City Island Avenue on the east side of the street across from Winters Street, is the elementary school that opened in 1975 to replace the first school building on the island. Although modern in design, on the angled wall leading to the front entrance below the name of the school is affixed a planter in the shape of a rowboat. It is another tribute to the nautical heritage of the island.

26 • South Minneford Yacht Club, 145 City Island Avenue on the east side of the street, is really a cooperative marina that opened in 1985 on the site of the old Minneford Shipyard. All slip owners own a share of the club, which is more low-key than most other yacht clubs, and their motorboats and sailboats fill the dry docks and the adjacent waters of the site.

27 • 95 Pell Place on the north side of the street west of City Island Avenue is a residence that prompts most visitors who see it for the first time to immediately assume it was designed by famed American architect Frank Lloyd Wright. In fact, it was designed by Sears, Roebuck and Company. It was built in 1930 from ready-made cut pieces ordered from a Sears Roebuck catalog for $8,500 and assembled on the site. It is a bungalow called the Osborne by the company. It is a low-lying structure with a steeply pitched roof with projecting horizontal members, clapboard siding, two stucco porches, broad windows and doors horizontally aligned, low transom bars, and multi-paned windows.

28 • City Island Yacht Club, 63 Pilot Street at the western edge of the street west of City Island Avenue, was formed in the winter of 1904–1905 and incorporated in 1907 to encourage yachting, yacht building and naval architecture, competitions, and naval science. It has occupied its current site on the north side of Pilot Street since 1921. The members participate in many events, including races and regattas. Visits to the site must be arranged in advance. Telephone: 718-885-2485.

29 • 141 Pilot Street at the east side of City Island Avenue is a small compact Italianate style farmhouse erected about 1862. It has a simple design with lath-turned porch posts and eyebrow windows.

30 • Grace Episcopal Church, 116 City Island Avenue on the east side of the street at the south side of Pilot Street, was first organized in 1849, but this structure was built by ship's carpenters from the David Carll shipyard in 1867 in the Carpenter Gothic style. It has a steeply pitched roof and narrow pointed arched windows. Wooden buttresses are outside the church. The steeple on the side with its polygonal roof is also the location of the church's entrance. If the church is open, see the stained-glass window called the Adoration of the Magi designed by William Bolton. It is the first known figurative stained-glass window made in America. The altar window, the Trial of Christ, was created by John Bolton. Hanging above the altar on either side are the metal outlines of two ships, one in a golden color and the other in silver color, to symbolize the nautical heritage of City Island and its shipping by both day and night. The church's rectory just south of the church structure was built in 1862 as a frame structure in the Italian Villa style. The Church Hall has been the venue for plays put on by the amateur members of the City Island Theater Group since 1998. For information about the group's performance schedule, telephone: 716-885-3066 or visit www.cityislandtheatergroup.com.

31 • Morris Yacht and Beach Club, 25 City Island Avenue on the west side of the street, is on five acres of land with a sand beach for swimming and sun bathing and a breathtaking view of Long Island Sound. Founded in 1899, the club participates in races and has facilities for fishing and cruising, in addition to docking facilities. Restaurant and banquet services are available to members and for outside group events.

32 • 175 Belden Street, one block east of City Island Avenue, can be found by walking down a single lane, dead-end street beyond the fence that marks the property line. It is a well-preserved picturesque cottage built about 1880, one of the few of such rural type cottages found within New York City. This structure, with a superb view of Long Island Sound, is distinguished by its jigsaw brackets, dormers, porches, and bays. It is an official New York City landmark.

33 • Belden Point at the southernmost end of City Island Avenue affords the public that same beautiful vista of Long Island Sound enjoyed by the members of the private Morris Yacht Club on one side and the residents of 175 Belden Street on the other. Named for William Belden, who opened an amusement park and resort in the area in 1887, it became a favorite recreation destination for New York wealthy merchants as Vincent Astor, J. P. Morgan, and William Randolph Hearst. During World War II, a long pier at this point was used by the Coast Guard. The far shoreline is the coast of New York City's borough of Queens and of Nassau County. In the water are several low-lying islands, one of which has a lighthouse. These islands, often a hazard to navigation, run through the East River and skirt the shores of the mainland beside Long Island Sound and are called the Stepping Stones. According to lore, the Devil was chased out of New Amsterdam by the Dutch (some would say it happened earlier by the American Indians) and fled across the water to safety. Everywhere he

stepped, one of these rocky outcroppings appeared. Thus, they were given the name of the Devil's Stepping Stones.

Return to the Pelham Bay station by taking the northbound Bx29 bus along City Island Avenue. Visitors may wish to combine a trip to City Island with a visit to Pelham Bay Park. See part I, "Pelham Bay Park: The Riviera of New York City." The Bx29 bus has two stops within the park after crossing the City Island Bridge. Those coming by automobile should cross the City Island Bridge, continue in the same direction after emerging from the traffic circle on the other side of the bridge to the traffic light at the end of the road. Turn left to cross the Pelham Bridge and continue along the road going beneath the Bruckner Expressway underpass to take the ramp to get onto the southbound expressway.

Belmont

NEW YORK'S REAL LITTLE ITALY

Walk along the streets of the Belmont neighborhood and see the real Little Italy. In this largely residential area, it is still possible to hear residents speaking Italian to one another. Here visitors can smell the aroma of delicately cooked Italian dishes, freshly baked Italian bread, salami hanging from the rafters, olive oil, fragrant Italian cheeses, fresh fish and shellfish wafting through the air from the many fine Italian restaurants, bakeries, and groceries that abound here. In Belmont, it is possible to witness pasta made by hand. Here a visitor can experience Italian culture in full flower.

DIRECTIONS

BY PUBLIC TRANSPORTATION: Take subway train letter D north to the Fordham Road station. Exit at the center of the platform and take the steps to the sidewalk on the west side of the Grand Concourse, north side of 188th Street. Do not cross the street. Walk along the Grand Concourse one short block north to the corner of Fordham Road. Transfer to the eastbound Bx12 local bus to the stop just before Arthur Avenue/Hoffman Street and Arthur Avenue. Walk down Arthur Avenue three blocks to 187th Street.

Alternatively, take the Metro-North Harlem Division railroad train from Grand Central Station to the Fordham Station. Then either take the eastbound Bx9, Bx12 local, Bx17, or Bx22 on Fordham Road to the stop just before Arthur Avenue/Hoffman Street and Arthur Avenue. Walk down Arthur Avenue three blocks to 187th Street.

BY CAR OR TAXI: Take the Major Deegan Expressway north to the Fordham Road exit. At the end of the ramp, turn right and proceed eastward on Fordham Road to Arthur Avenue. Then turn right and go down Arthur Avenue to 187th Street. Street parking, mostly with meters, is available; there is also a small metered parking lot on the right side of Arthur Avenue south of 186th Street accessed by an alleyway between the buildings marked by a decorative memorial mural on the wall along its entryway.

About Belmont

The Belmont neighborhood is named for the nineteenth-century estate of the Lorillard tobacco family who had a mansion on the hill where Saint Barnabas Hospital now stands overlooking today's Arthur Avenue at 184th Street. They called it Belle Mont, or beautiful mountain. This was corrupted to today's Belmont.

Starting in the 1890s, New York City began to cut streets through the old Belmont estate, but few people lived there. In the mid-1890s, the southern half of Bronx Park was leased to the New York Zoological Society (now the Wildlife Conservation Society) to create the Bronx Zoo. The zoo authorities wanted to landscape their grounds with Italian style gardens. Coincidentally, large numbers of Southern Italian landless farmers were beginning to immigrate to New York at the same time. They were hired to do the job. They took the Third Avenue Elevated rapid transit line to get to work. Soon, they decided it would be better to live within walking distance of their jobs, and they settled in Belmont. The neighborhood has had its Italian flavor ever since. Most of the residential structures in the neighborhood date from the end of the nineteenth to the beginning of the twentieth century. Soon, many Italian-owned shops opened to cater to the tastes of the residents.

Belmont remained a densely populated neighborhood south of Fordham Road extending from Southern Boulevard on the east to Third Avenue on the west for two generations. After World War II, many ethnic Italians of the third generation joined other Americans in moving to the suburbs. Around the edges of the neighborhood, Albanians, Puerto Ricans, and other Latinos moved in to take their place. The center of Belmont, however, remains proudly Italian.

Through the years, some who grew up in the neighborhood have had an impact in several fields. It was the home of the members of the

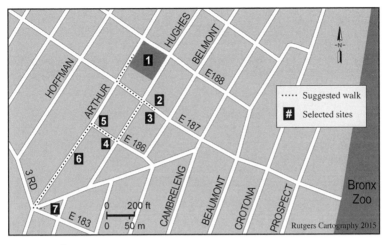

Map 4. Belmont

1. Ciccarone Playground
2. Our Lady of Mount Carmel Church
3. Borgatti's Ravioli and Egg Noodles
4. Enrico Fermi Cultural Center

5. Teitel Brothers' Grocery
6. Arthur Avenue Market
7. D'Auria-Murphy Square

doo-wop group Dion and the Belmonts and of the playwright and actor Chazz Palminteri.

The busy center of the neighborhood is where Arthur Avenue crosses 187th Street. While most of the fine Italian restaurants and businesses that attract visitors from throughout the world are found along Arthur Avenue, many others can be seen along other streets.

Walking Tour

1 • Ciccarone Playground on the east side of Arthur Avenue at 188th Street is a gathering spot for the neighborhood children, youth, and adults to play and for the elderly to sit. It honors Vincent Ciccarone, a Belmont resident, who served as a private in World War I. He was wounded in the Argonne Forest in 1918 and later died of his wounds.

2 • Our Lady of Mount Carmel Church on the north side of 187th Street at Belmont Avenue two blocks east of Arthur Avenue is the religious, cultural, and civic center of the Belmont community. It was established early in the twentieth century not to be a parish church,

but an ethnic church. The increasing number of Italian immigrants did not feel comfortable being served by an overwhelmingly Irish clergy. Italian priests serve there, Masses are celebrated in Italian, and Italian religious festivals take place at stated times during the year in the street in front of the church. Changes in the neighborhood can be seen in the number of Masses also scheduled in English and Spanish.

3 • Borgatti's Ravioli and Egg Noodles, 632 East 187th Street on the south side of the street between Belmont and Hughes Avenues, is a relatively small shop that makes its own pasta on site. Whether it is ravioli or linguini or any other type of pasta, it may be possible to witness the process by which it is freshly made. It is different from what dried pasta looks like coming out of a commercial box from the supermarket.

4 • The Enrico Fermi Cultural Center, also known as the Belmont branch of the New York Public Library, is a polished gray granite building erected in 1981 at 610 East 186th Street on the southwest corner of Hughes Avenue. Inside, there are changing art or historical exhibits. At a sunken square sitting area, patrons can read magazines and books in comfort. There, at one corner, is a large bust of Arturo Toscanini, the famed orchestra conductor who lived many years in The Bronx. There is also a smaller statue of Bishop Joseph Perniconi who served as the beloved spiritual leader of Belmont at Our Lady of Mount Carmel Church for many decades. On occasion, performances are held in this space. On the bookshelves is one full wall of books written in Italian. Lectures and talks are frequently given in a room upstairs.

5 • Teitel Brothers' Grocery, 2372 Arthur Avenue at the northeast corner of 186th Street, is an anomaly that is in some ways typical of the Belmont neighborhood. Established about the time of World War I by an Austrian Jewish family, and still operated by its fourth generation, this grocery is a magnet for Belmont residents and those of Italian descent from throughout the metropolitan area looking for high-quality fresh Italian cheeses, fish, produce, and canned goods selling at more than reasonable prices. Visitors can venture inside, breathe in the pungent aromas, and purchase whatever appeals to them. Note the hexagonal tiles at the floor outside the store's entrance. They form a Star of David. Teitel's is closed for business during the Jewish High Holy Days in autumn.

6 • The Arthur Avenue Market, 2344 Arthur Avenue on the east side of the street between 186th Street and Crescent Avenue, is a remnant of this Italian American community's early commercial past. In the first half of the twentieth century, many Italians established pushcart businesses selling fruit, vegetables, and other products from carts they pushed through the streets. Soon, they took permanent places in the street beside the curbs along Arthur Avenue where customers came along and selected what they required. In the 1930s, New York City mayor Fiorello LaGuardia wanted to eliminate the pushcart peddlers from the streets, but not to put them out of business. In 1940, the city erected the building called the Arthur Avenue Market and the pushcart peddlers were placed inside it. Today, the fruit and vegetable stands inside are located on wooden structures resembling the old pushcarts. However, there are more and different kinds of businesses there today. At the back are two Italian delicatessens. Mike's Deli on the right specializes in creating new and different kinds of delicious presentations and sandwiches from traditional ingredients. The other deli on the left sells pizza made in accord with the Old World recipes. Both have chairs and tables for patrons to sit and eat their snacks. Also in the market is a butcher shop, a place to purchase plates and other crockery, a shop selling graphic T-shirts and caps, a cigar store with hand-rolled cigars (a process that any visitor may witness), a plant shop, an indoor beer garden featuring Bronx-brewed beer, and other concerns. It is worthwhile to stop in and take a look.

7 • D'Auria-Murphy Square is a triangle with a park touching Arthur Avenue bounded by Crescent Avenue, 183rd Street, and Adams Place. It is named for two former residents of Belmont who were killed in World War I. John D'Auria arrived from Italy at the age of fifteen, became a stonecutter, and served as a machine gunner in the war when he died in 1918 at the age of twenty-nine. Henry J. Murphy was a post office clerk who also met his demise in 1918 at the age of twenty-seven. Inside the park is a carved bust of Christopher Columbus from the Bronx studio of the Piccirilli brothers, Italian immigrants known for carving such monumental figures as Abraham Lincoln in the Lincoln Memorial, the Library Lions outside the New York Public Library on Fifth Avenue at 42nd Street in Manhattan, and George Washington on the Washington Square Park Arch in Manhattan.

Dining

The restaurants and bakeries along Arthur Avenue and the other streets in Belmont should not be missed. The restaurants vary in menu and prices. Some specialize in southern Italian cuisine, and others in northern Italian. Be advised that Dominick's, 2335 Arthur Avenue on the west side of the street between 186th Street and Crescent Avenue, uses no printed menu, but has the bill of fare recited by its waiters without mentioning the price, and accepts only cash in payment. Nevertheless, just as with all the restaurants in the area, the food is exceptionally good. Local bakeries bake their own fresh Italian bread and pastry in ovens on the site. Stop in for a bite at a bakery or a complete meal in a restaurant and enjoy. Mangia!

Visitors might wish to combine their experience in Belmont with a visit to the Bronx Zoo by walking along 187th Street just eight short blocks east of Arthur Avenue to Southern Boulevard, crossing Southern Boulevard and turning right to walk to the Southern Boulevard entrance of the zoo across from 185th Street. See part I, "The Bronx Zoo."

The Enid A. Haupt Conservatory at the New York Botanical Garden

Lily pond at the New York Botanical Garden

Peacock at the Bronx Zoo Visitor Center

Face to face at the Congo Gorilla Forest

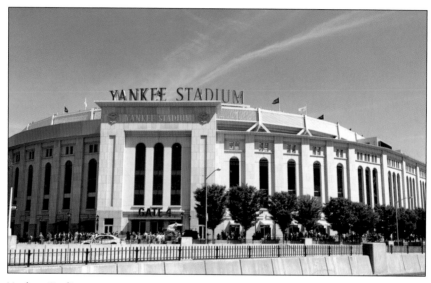

Yankee Stadium

Viewing the Hudson River and New Jersey Palisades from Wave Hill

Greyston, the mansion of William E. Dodge

The historic Van Cortlandt House in Van Cortlandt Park

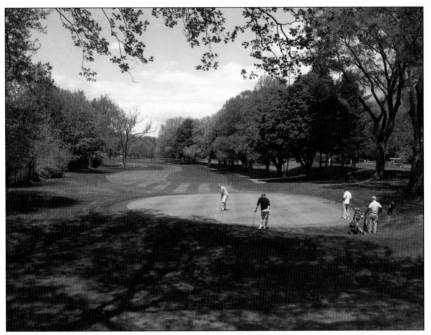

On the green at Van Cortlandt Golf Course, the first public course in America

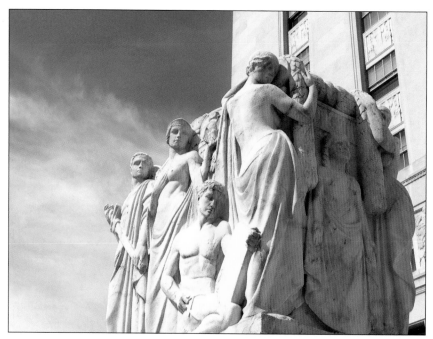

A high-relief sculpture at the 158th Street entrance to the Bronx County Building

The *Heinrich Heine–Lorelei Fountain* in Joyce Kilmer Park across from the Bronx County Building

The Edgar Allan Poe Cottage in Poe Park

Edgar Allan Poe's rocking chair inside his cottage

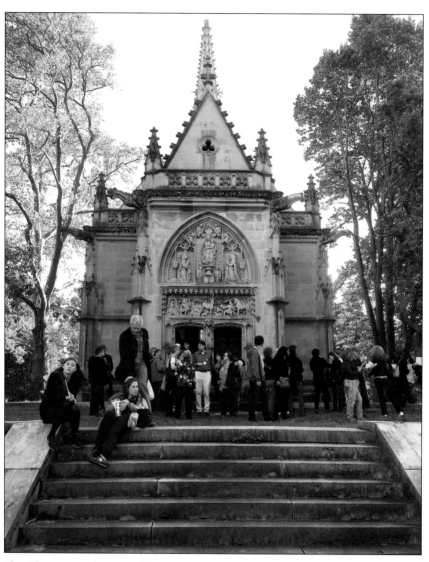

The Oliver Hazard Perry Belmont and Alva Smith Vanderbilt Belmont Mauso-leum in Woodlawn Cemetery

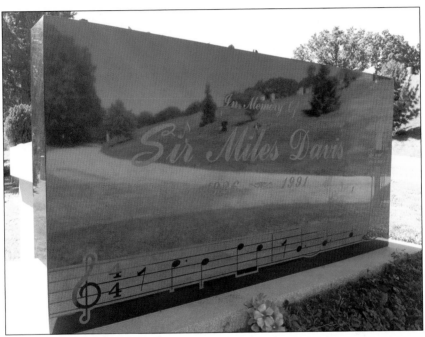
The highly polished gravestone of jazz great Miles Davis in Woodlawn Cemetery

The historic Valentine-Varian House, now the Museum of Bronx History

The Civil War Bronx River Soldier on the grounds of the Valentine-Varian House

A balmy day at Orchard Beach in Pelham Bay Park

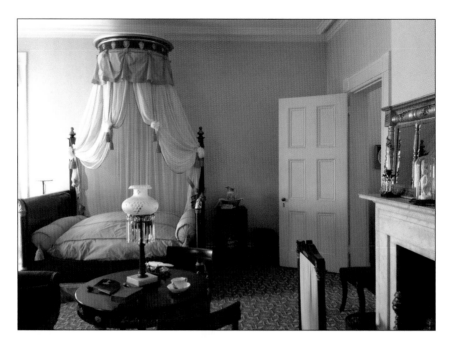

ABOVE: An elegant
bedroom in the Bartow-
Pell Mansion in Pelham
Bay Park

RIGHT: Looking up at
the spiral staircase in the
Bartow-Pell Mansion

ABOVE: The Hall of Fame for Great Americans on the Bronx Community College campus

LEFT: Portrait bust of Edgar Allan Poe sculpted by Daniel Chester French in the Hall of Fame for Great Americans

The Bronx Museum of the Arts

Absorbed in an exhibition in the Bronx Museum of the Arts

Boats anchored off the shore of City Island

Shops and residences on City Island Avenue, the local "skyscraper" to the left

Shopping for savory Italian goods at Teitel's on Arthur Avenue

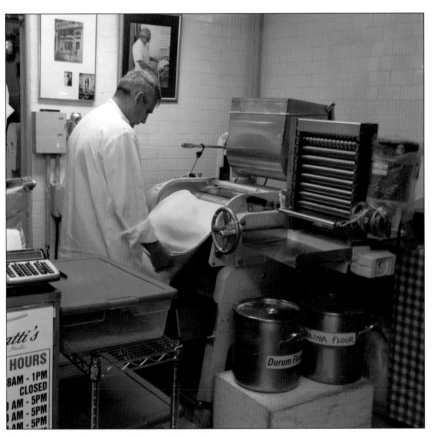

Making pasta at Borgatti's on 187th Street

The Art Deco Fish Building on the Grand Concourse

The elegant Andrew Freedman Home on the Grand Concourse

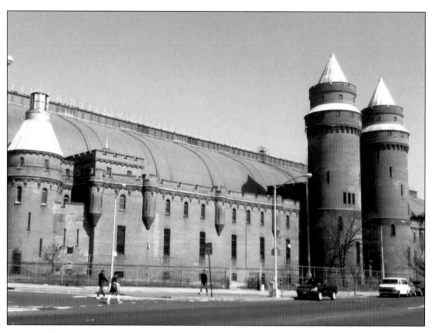

The medieval-style Kingsbridge Armory on Kingsbridge Road

The ultra-modern Apex on the Lehman College campus

The world comes shopping to Kingsbridge Road

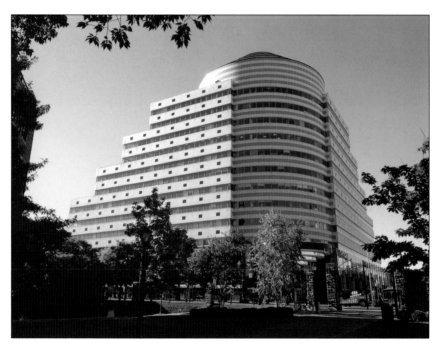

The Fordham Plaza office building on Fordham Road and Third Avenue

European elegance on the Bertine Block

Townhouses in the Mott Haven Historic District

The Grand Concourse Historic District

ART DECO DELIGHTS

The Grand Concourse is the elegant boulevard of The Bronx and the borough's answer to Manhattan's Park and Fifth Avenues. A walk along the Grand Concourse (officially, but never commonly called, the Grand Boulevard and Concourse) from 167th Street south to 149th Street is a pleasant stroll that brings a number of surprises and delights. In addition to the 182-foot-wide tree-lined thoroughfare, it includes elegant residential apartment houses, public art, monumental civic buildings, and parks. This self-guided walking tour begins on the Grand Concourse at 167th Street and ends on the Grand Concourse at 149th Street.

DIRECTIONS

BY PUBLIC TRANSPORTATION: Take the letter D subway train (letter B train in rush hours only) to 167th Street.

Alternatively, take the number 4 train to 167th Street and River Avenue and walk three blocks eastward (up the hill) to the Grand Concourse, or transfer to the eastbound Bx35 bus to the Grand Concourse.

BY CAR OR TAXI: Take the Major Deegan Expressway to eastbound Cross Bronx Expressway to the Jerome Avenue exit. At Jerome Avenue, make a short right turn to Mount Eden Parkway, then turn left again onto Mount Eden Parkway to the Grand Concourse. Turn right on the Grand Concourse to 167th Street. Street parking only.

About the Grand Concourse

As early as the 1880s, Louis A. Risse, an immigrant civil engineer from Alsace-Lorraine, envisioned the ridge between two valleys that then ran through farmland and the edges of suburban villages as a wide tree-lined multi-lane roadway modeled after the Champs Elysées in Paris. Work began in 1901 and was completed in 1909.

As projected the Grand Concourse began at 161st Street and went northward to Mosholu Parkway. It was meant to provide a parklike setting for people in Manhattan to ride over the Macombs Dam Bridge across the Harlem River in their carriages northward to connect with either Van Cortlandt or Bronx Parks. South of 161st Street was the much narrower Mott Avenue. Rapid urbanization, the coming of the automobile, and an increase in traffic led to the widening of Mott Avenue in 1927. In 1934, the Grand Concourse name was extended south of 161st Street, replacing the original Mott Avenue name.

Starting in the 1920s, elegant and sumptuous five- and six-story apartment houses were erected along the Grand Concourse. In the fashion of the time, they displayed details from several historic European architectural forms. These included Romanesque, Renaissance, Tudor, Spanish Colonial, and Moorish elements.

During the Great Depression of the 1930s, wealthy people desired to have a Grand Concourse address. It was a symbol of economic and social success and they boasted that they lived there. Private developers erected more elegant apartment houses in the then fashionable Art Deco style. Buildings in light yellow brick, often with contrasting abstract design elements in orange-colored brick, metal decorations specifically designed for each building, corner windows, and sunken living rooms appeared. Since few buildings were erected anywhere during those hard economic times, the Grand Concourse and its side streets today boast of having the largest collection of Art Deco style residences in the world.

From the 1920s to the 1960s, most families who resided along the Grand Concourse were Eastern European and German Jews, with an admixture of those of Irish and Italian heritage. Starting in the 1960s, increasing numbers of Blacks and Latinos arrived. They knew of the historic importance of the boulevard and petitioned the New York City Landmarks Preservation Commission to create a

Grand Concourse Historic District to preserve its elegant architecture. The area from the Grand Concourse from 167th Street south to 153rd Street and its adjacent side streets were declared such a district in 2011.

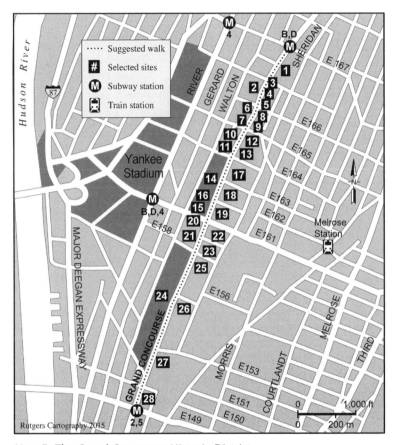

Map 5. The Grand Concourse Historic District

1. Art Deco buildings (incl. Fish Building)
2. Andrew Freedman Home
3. Bronx Works
4. Bronx Housing Courthouse
5. John Ericsson House
6. David Farragut House
7. Colonial Revival houses
8. Concourse Rehabilitation and Nursing Center
9. Bronx Museum of the Arts
10. Ginsbern House
11. Colonial Revival and Spanish Colonial buildings
12. Executive Towers
13. Sugarman & Berger Art Deco building
14. Joyce Kilmer Park
15. Heinrich Heine–Lorelei Fountain
16. Louis J. Heintz statue
17. Mediterranean Revival buildings
18. Ashley and Dillerwood Apartments
19. Concourse Plaza Hotel
20. Lou Gehrig Plaza
21. Bronx County Building
22. Roth and Kreymborg Art Deco buildings
23. Thomas Garden Apartments
24. Franz Sigel Park
25. 800 Grand Concourse/Renaissance Revival houses
26. Felson houses
27. Cardinal Hayes High School
28. Bronx General Post Office

Walking Tour

FROM 167TH STREET TO MCCLELLAN STREET — EAST SIDE OF THE CONCOURSE

1 • Here are four Art Deco style apartment houses in a row (one north of 167th Street and three south of it), all erected within one year of one another. Although all four have different designs, together they form a harmonious whole. Number 1212 on the northern corner was designed in 1936 by Horace Ginsbern and boasts of a slightly projecting cast-stone entrance with abstract design decoration. Number 1188 on the southern corner of 167th Street was designed in 1937 by Jacob M. Felson in a sawtooth design that enables residents to obtain the maximum sunlight in rooms with windows facing both west and south. Its neighbors on the block, numbers 1166 and 1150, were designed by Horace Ginsbern in 1936. A noted feature of number 1150 on the corner of McClellan Street is the colorful mosaic flanking the entrance. It depicts varieties of tropical fish that gave the structure the neighborhood name it has borne since it was built: the Fish House or the Fish Building. Its circular lobby inside sports a marble fireplace, a starburst terrazzo floor in gold, red, and green, and Art Deco style murals on the walls.

FROM MCCLELLAN STREET TO 166TH STREET — WEST SIDE OF THE CONCOURSE

2 • Behind a low wall, a fence, and some shrubbery is a three-story building sitting behind a vast block-long lawn that has the air of a French-style palace. Made of limestone and designed in 1924 with wings added in 1928 by Joseph H. Friedlander and Harry Allan Jacobs, it was erected according to the dictates of the will of Andrew Freedman.

Freedman was a contractor who helped build New York City's first subway line and once owned the New York Giants baseball team. As a result of a short, but very sharp, decline in values on the New York Stock Exchange in 1907 (called the Panic of 1907), many wealthy people lost their fortunes. Freedman did not, but he wondered what would have happened to him in his old age if he had. Then he thought of those who were once wealthy and now were destitute.

To help them, he provided in his will for the erection of an old folks home for people who were once rich but who had lost their money.

He also provided an endowment to pay for the staff that would cook for them, wait on them, and take care of their medical needs. A wood-paneled library, a billiard room, a barbershop, a beauty parlor, a dining room, and a lounge with overstuffed furniture and art were some of the public rooms. Residents could furnish their own rooms any way they wished and could travel off the property anytime they wanted. Among the residents who lived there were a former czarist general and a faded Edwardian actress.

By the 1960s, inflation led to an erosion of Freedman's endowment. The building was ultimately sold and now serves as offices for some local nonprofit groups, a Head Start program, an art exhibition space, and as a bed and breakfast.

It is possible to enter the building through the gate at the northern end of the property on the Grand Concourse near the entrance to the subway. If this gate is closed, try the gate around the corner on McClellan Street near the bottom of the hill. The original wood-paneled library remains intact and can be seen. Art exhibitions welcome the public.

FROM MCCLELLAN STREET TO 166TH STREET — EAST SIDE OF THE CONCOURSE

3 • Number 1130 on the northern corner opened in 1926 as the Bronx County Society for the Prevention of Cruelty to Children. In 1951, the building was converted for use by the Bronx YM/YWHA. In 1980, it became the home of the Girls Club of New York. In 1993, the Girls Club merged with the Citizens Advice Bureau to form Bronx Works, which now provides programs for children, youth, and families.

The building was designed in a Classical Revival style by the firm of Raldris and LaVelle. It features a double dogleg staircase leading to the main entrance marked by a portico with classical Corinthian columns. On the flat surface resting on the columns the words "Children's Shelter" can still be seen, testifying to the structure's original use.

4 • Next to it, number 1118 is the eleven-story contemporary-style Bronx Housing Courthouse, designed by noted architect Rafael Viñoly. Completed in 1999, it contains neo-Art Deco elements that help it fit in with the district's predominant architectural style. The use of alternating bands of textured brick and glass block helps evoke the era of the 1930s when such architectural details were popular.

5 • Number 1100, next to the court building and on the corner of 166th Street, is a Renaissance Revival style apartment house designed in 1927 by the architectural firm of Gronenberg & Leuchtag. The original owner was a Civil War naval buff who named the building after John Ericsson, the man who designed the *Monitor*, the Union ironclad ship often described as a cheesebox on a raft. A bas-relief portrait of Ericsson can be found on the panel on the south center portion of the front façade.

FROM 166TH STREET TO 165TH STREET — WEST SIDE OF THE CONCOURSE

6 • Number 1075 on the corner of 166th Street was designed in 1926, one year after the similar structure at number 1100 diagonally across the Grand Concourse. Designed by the same architects for the same owner, this apartment house is named after David Farragut, the hero of the Civil War naval battle of Mobile Bay and the nation's first admiral. A bas-relief portrait of Farragut can be found on the panel on the north center portion of the front façade. Note the original intricate heavy decorative ironwork on the front entrance doors that help protect the glass windows behind them.

7 • The two other apartment houses occupying the block (numbers 1055 and 1049) were also designed by the same architects as their northern neighbor, but for a different firm. Both are also a decade older. Number 1055 was designed in 1918 and number 1049 in 1917, both in the Colonial Revival style.

FROM 166TH STREET TO 165TH STREET — EAST SIDE OF THE CONCOURSE

8 • On the corner of 166th Street is number 1072, opened in 1974 as the Concourse Rehabilitation and Nursing Center. This institutional building of no particular architectural style was designed by Nelson H. Taday.

9 • The rest of the block is taken up by the Bronx Museum of the Arts. For details on this site turn to the chapter in part I, "The Bronx Museum of the Arts."

FROM 165TH STREET TO 164TH STREET — WEST SIDE OF THE CONCOURSE

10 • The apartment house, number 1035 on the corner of 165th Street, was designed in the Art Deco style by Horace Ginsbern in 1939. Unusually, it uses red brick rather than the light yellow brick of other Art Deco buildings. Note the curved entryway bearing geometrical forms. In the 1940s, one resident was Judge Peter J. Shmuck who refused anyone who petitioned for a change of name saying that if the judge could live with his name, the petitioner could live with his, too.

11 • In the middle of the block are two smaller buildings. The four-story apartment house at number 1027 was designed in 1922 by Emil Paulson in the Colonial Revival style. Next to it at number 1025 is a charming two-story structure originally used as a physician's office and residence. It was designed in 1922 by Thomas Dunn in the then popular Spanish Colonial style. Clad in white stucco with limestone trim, the structure's tiled roof and rounded arches rest on Tuscan columns. The original lettering, "Medical Offices," on the façade has been replaced by the words "Medicos Hispanos," which attests to the ethnic change in the neighborhood. The taller apartment house on the corner of 164th Street, number 1001, was designed by Horace Ginsbern and opened in 1941. Similar to his other Art Deco design on the 165th Street corner, Ginsbern uses red brick for this structure as well.

FROM 165TH STREET TO 164TH STREET — EAST SIDE OF THE CONCOURSE

12 • The massive twenty-story white-brick apartment house with terraces and a curved façade, number 1020 on the corner of 165th Street, is called the Executive Towers. It was designed by Philip Birnbaum in the Modern style and opened in 1963. A semicircular driveway and pedestrian walkway leads to the entrance pavilion with a sawtooth roof supported by green and white marble columns with a cantilevered arched marquee. Two statues, one male and one female, flank the entranceway. The height of this building guarantees that it dominates the skyline when cameras telecasting from the new Yankee Stadium scan beyond the bleachers.

13 • Number 1000 was considered by many people to be the epitome of gracious living on the Grand Concourse when it was erected in 1935. Designed in the Art Deco style by Sugarman & Berger, it is ten stories high and is topped by a penthouse, the ultimate symbol of luxury in the era. Its light yellow brick is decorated with raised and contrasting brick banding, and its entrance is made of cast stone.

FROM 164TH STREET TO 161ST STREET — WEST SIDE OF THE CONCOURSE

14 • Along the west side of the Grand Concourse is Joyce Kilmer Park. As originally designed by Louis A. Risse, this plot of land was shaped like a right triangle with one leg along the Concourse and the other along 161st Street. The hypotenuse of the triangle was formed by another roadway that connected 161st Street at Walton Avenue to the Concourse at 163rd Street. The triangular plot was designed to form a grand entrance to the beautiful boulevard. It was called the Concourse Plaza. In 1927, changes in traffic volume and flow led to a redesign. The entire plot of land was laid out as a rectangular park in the Beaux Arts style and renamed Joyce Kilmer Park in honor of the man who wrote the poem "Trees" and was also killed in World War I. The park has always been heavily used by local residents. When the neighborhood was largely Jewish, families promenaded in the park and sat on the benches during Jewish holidays, wearing their best, trying to see and be seen. People still sit on the benches beneath the shade trees, while others play team games on the center lawns. There are two significant sculptural pieces inside Joyce Kilmer Park at its southern end.

15 • The *Heinrich Heine–Lorelei Fountain*. For details of this site turn to part I, "The Bronx County Building: The Art of Democracy."

16 • Behind and slightly to the west of the fountain, standing on a granite base, is a statue of Louis J. Heintz. For details of this site turn to part I, "The Bronx County Building: The Art of Democracy."

FROM 164TH STREET TO 161ST STREET — EAST SIDE OF THE CONCOURSE

17 • On the block between 164th and 163rd Streets are two large six-story apartment houses designed in 1927 by Springsteen & Goldhammer in the Mediterranean Revival style. Both boast of a large garden courtyard leading to multiple entrances, terra-cotta tile decoration, and Spanish tile accents on the roofline. The main difference between the two is the color of the brick. Number 960 at the corner of 164th Street is made with beige brick, while number 940 on the corner of 163rd Street has red brick. An apartment in number 960 was the home of Joseph V. McKee, who became New York City's mayor after James J. Walker resigned that post in 1932. Since the city had no official residence for the mayor then, McKee lived in his Grand Concourse apartment throughout the span of his mayoralty.

18 • Between 163rd Street and 162nd Street are two Art Deco style apartment houses. Number 930 on the corner of 163rd Street is called the Ashley. Designed by H. Herbert Lilien in the waning years of World War II, it opened in 1948. The eleven-story structure has a cast-stone canopy over the entrance. Number 910 on the corner of 162nd Street, the Dillerwood Apartments, was designed in 1938 by Israel L. Crausman as an eight-story building topped by a penthouse. Its lobby has a surreal mural bearing a fragment of Joyce Kilmer's poem "Roofs."

19 • Between 162nd Street and 161st Street stands number 900, the building erected in 1923 as the Concourse Plaza Hotel. The eleven-story structure was designed by Maynicke & Franke in the Colonial Revival style. Its red brick is contrasted by masonry and terra-cotta decoration. The structure opened in October 1923, just in time for the first World Series played at nearby Yankee Stadium, with the ribbon cut by Governor Alfred E. Smith.

In 1924, the New York Yankees rented rooms to house the team and the visiting clubs. Only Babe Ruth and manager Miller Huggins were allowed to have private rooms, while the rest of the team members shared their living quarters with another teammate. By the 1930s, some team members, such as Joe DiMaggio and Lefty Gomez, preferred to live in the new Grand Concourse residences nearby and sublet apartments from the renters for the season. By the middle of the twentieth century, the Yankees' rooms were used to house rookies, such as Whitey Ford and Mickey Mantle, only for their first year.

The Concourse Plaza Hotel quickly became the social center of The Bronx. Important weddings, business meetings, religious services, and political conventions were held in its ballrooms. Franklin Delano Roosevelt, Harry S Truman, and John F. Kennedy all addressed events here.

With the construction of newer hotels and the social and economic troubles beginning to plague the South Bronx, the hotel lost patronage and closed in the 1960s. During that time, it served as the apartment house set for the original black-and-white version of the film *Gloria* starring Gena Rowlands. New York City purchased the building in 1975. After some interior renovations, it opened in 1982 as a residence for senior citizens. It still bears the grand name of Concourse Plaza.

FROM 161ST STREET TO 158TH STREET — WEST SIDE OF THE CONCOURSE

Have a bite to eat. There are several sandwich shops and fast-food restaurants on 161st Street on both sides of the Grand Concourse.

Along both sides of the Grand Concourse south of 161st Street are yellow and brown signs affixed to lampposts. Each bears the name of a person in the arts, literature, science, business, or government who lived in The Bronx and who achieved outstanding distinction in his or her field. The whole is called The Bronx Walk of Fame.

20 • On the west side of the Grand Concourse, the wide mall separating traffic flow on 161st Street is named Lou Gehrig Plaza in honor of the man who played first base for the New York Yankees and died of the disease named for him. The site is marked by a stanchion.

21 • The entire square block between the Grand Concourse and Walton Avenue south of 161st Street to 158th Street is filled by number 851, the massive ten-story Bronx County Building. For details of this site turn to part I, "The Bronx County Building: The Art of Democracy."

FROM 161ST STREET TO 158TH STREET — EAST SIDE OF THE CONCOURSE

22 • On the corner of 161st Street stands an Art Deco apartment house, number 888, designed in 1937 by the eminent New York architect Emery Roth. The façade at the intersection is rounded, and that is where the structure's entrance is located. The entrance court is concave and surmounted by a circular canopy with a terrazzo floor below. Its walls are covered by beige and gold mosaic tiles framed by black granite facing. Unusually, the building is entered through a revolving door.

Next door at the corner of 159th Street stands number 860. Its Art Deco design was drawn by Charles Kreymborg in 1940. The entranceway is framed by a pink marble portico with metal trim and the structure's façade boasts of contrasting orange terra-cotta bands.

23 • Between 159th Street and 158th Street is number 840, the Thomas Garden Apartments. It is named after the man who designed it in 1928, Andrew J. Thomas, for John D. Rockefeller Jr. as a means of providing new and decent housing for middle-class families, rather than always leaving them to the older castoffs of the wealthy. A simplified version of Renaissance Revival style, the five-story walkup building boasts of a sunken central courtyard with planting areas and concrete walkways, Japanese-inspired masonry lanterns, and a watercourse with charmingly arched bridges. Apartments in different sections of the building are entered through separate doorways off the central courtyard.

FROM 158TH STREET TO 153RD STREET — WEST SIDE OF THE CONCOURSE

24 • Franz Sigel Park runs the entire length from 158th Street south to 153rd Street between the Grand Concourse on the east and Walton Avenue on the west. It is the last remnant of the nineteenth-century estate of Gerard Walton Morris, called the Cedars. When New York City purchased the property for park use, it was originally called Cedar Park. Its facilities were happily used by the mostly German community that lived near it in the late nineteenth and early twentieth centuries. One nearby resident then was General Franz Sigel.

Sigel had been born in Germany, but was forced to flee to the United States in the wake of a failed revolution there in 1848. He settled in Missouri, and became a Union general after the outbreak of the Civil War. While he was not a great military hero, he performed yeoman service keeping the immigrant Germans loyal to the Union cause. Later, he moved to New York, owning and editing a German-language newspaper and spending his last years in a home in a German enclave south of Cedar Park. When he died in 1902, a long funeral cortege passed by the park on its way to his burial in Woodlawn Cemetery. Almost immediately residents urged the city to rename the park for the general. It has been Franz Sigel Park ever since.

Most of the park occupies a high rocky ridge about equal to the fourth floor of the nearby apartment houses. Its height can provide views of much of the surrounding neighborhood. Children use the slopes for sledding in winter, while many dog owners use it year round as a dog run. A baseball diamond on the flat area in the southernmost part of the park attracts local teams, while others can use the adjoining basketball courts.

FROM 158TH STREET TO 156TH STREET — EAST SIDE OF THE CONCOURSE

25 • Number 800, the apartment house at the corner of 158th Street, was designed in the Modern style by Hyman J. Feldman and opened in 1955. Like other buildings of the era, it has minimal architectural details. Its most outstanding feature is the long metal pavilion with octagonal columns that provides the entrance to the central courtyard.

Next to it are two apartment houses designed in the Renaissance Revival style in 1926 by Jacob M. Felson. Number 790 is called the Virginia, while number 780 bears the name of Franz Sigel. When built, they were touted as "a little bit of Park Avenue in The Bronx." Both have a central courtyard entranceway marked by plantings. They share a landscaped wide courtyard found between the two structures.

Number 760 on the corner of 156th Street is another Renaissance Revival style apartment house, this one designed in 1928 by Charles Kreymborg & Son. Here, there are several decorative features in colorful terra-cotta.

FROM 156TH STREET TO 153RD STREET — EAST SIDE OF THE CONCOURSE

26 • Most of the block south of 156th Street is occupied with three Art Deco style apartment houses. The first, number 750 on the corner of 156th Street, was designed in 1936 by Jacob M. Felson and opened in 1937. The main entry portico is made of marble and has rounded corners. The structure was built in conjunction with its neighbors on the block and they share several architectural features. This one, however, is larger and grander than the other two. Felson also designed the building next door, number 740, in 1939. It features an entry courtyard with plantings and vertical brick bands above the main entry. Number 730 next door to that was also designed by Felson in 1939 with similar features. These are the last residences in the Grand Concourse Historic District. The rest of the block is filled with industrial and commercial structures and are not part of the Landmark District itself. There are, however, significant sites to see just outside of the District's borders.

FROM 153RD STREET TO 149TH STREET — EAST SIDE OF THE CONCOURSE

27 • On the south side of 153rd Street occupying the corner with the Grand Concourse is Cardinal Hayes High School. Opened in 1941, the school is in the shape of a quarter circle, thus leaving a substantial lawn in front of it. It has an excellent academic reputation. Both Regis Philbin and Martin Scorsese graduated from there, and comedian George Carlin was very proud to have been thrown out of Cardinal Hayes.

Just to the south of the school is a deep railroad cut. It carries the tracks of the commuter Metro-North Hudson Division Line through it to meet with the Harlem Division Line going southward from the area in back of the school where they share the rails that take passengers to Grand Central Station. The rocky debris accumulated from the creation of the cut was used to fill in part of the site of the original Yankee Stadium.

28 • Between 150th Street and 149th Street stands the Bronx General Post Office. Designed in the Art Deco style by Thomas Harlen Ellett and supervised by Louis A. Simon, this was a project financed by a New Deal agency, the Public Works Administration, and opened in 1937. The gray brick walls bear tall arched windows. Two sculptures are affixed to the wall flanking the entrance, both of which carry the theme of delivering messages. On the north side is *Noah*, who can be seen as a massive giant standing atop a tiny Ark, receiving the dove he released to inform him that dry land had appeared. On the south side is *The Letter*, where a woman is reading newly received correspondence while her curious daughter stands by her eagerly awaiting the news it brings.

The lobby inside has been altered through the years, but it still displays the original Art Deco style chandeliers. More important are the murals that flank the walls. The government conducted a nationwide contest among the nation's artists to paint these murals. In the time of the Great Depression, almost all of the starving artists in the country entered the contest. The one who got the job was Ben Shahn, now recognized as one of the leading American artists, who was aided by his talented wife, Bernada Bryson. The panels he created exhibit the main themes of the Depression era. They show people happily working at agricultural and industrial jobs and the works they created. One panel shows the poet Walt Whitman instructing working men. Because the lobby is constantly used, these murals have been restored several times through the years. They can be seen during normal Post Office hours.

Standing on the corner of 149th Street and the Grand Concourse are the buildings of Hostos Community College of the City University of New York occupying both sides of the Grand Concourse across the street. Named for an important Puerto Rican educator, the two-year college specializes in multilingual courses and the health care field. On the corner diagonally across from the Post Office stands an orange brick structure erected in 1905 to service the subway lines below. Note the blue and white terra-cotta plaque below the roofline that bears the name Mott Avenue Station, thus perpetuating the original name of this section of the Grand Concourse.

Dining

Have a bite to eat at any of the restaurants nearby along the Grand Concourse and on 149th Street.

Visitors may return to Manhattan using the 149th Street/Grand Concourse subway station at the corner. Take the downtown number 4 train on the upper level to travel under Lexington Avenue to Grand Central Station and beyond. On the massive barrel-vaulted lower level, take the downtown number 5 train to the same location, or take the downtown number 2 train to travel under Broadway to Times Square and beyond. A visitor attending an event at Yankee Stadium can take the uptown number 4 train on the upper level to 161st Street. Those who wish to return to 167th Street where the tour began should take the uptown number Bx1, Bx1 Limited, or Bx2 bus from the bus stop in front of the Post Office along the Grand Concourse to 167th Street.

Valentine to Poe

A TOUR OF CULTURAL DISCOVERY

This is a self-guided walking tour that will take the visitor from the Valentine-Varian House, which was owned by Isaac Valentine in the eighteenth century, ending at the Edgar Allan Poe Cottage, which was owned by John Valentine in the nineteenth century. Along the route, the visitor will discover some of the cultural and educational offerings that abound in today's Bronx, but also see where The Bronx and its people have contributed to the cultural landscape of the entire country.

DIRECTIONS

BY PUBLIC TRANSPORTATION: Take subway train letter D to 205th Street station, exit at the middle of the station, and take the escalator up. Exit through the turnstiles, turn left, and climb up the steps to the street. On the street, turn around, walk to the corner, and turn right. Walk northward along Bainbridge Avenue just beyond Van Cortlandt Avenue East to the entrance of the Valentine-Varian House.

Alternatively, take the BxM4 Express bus on Madison Avenue to Van Cortlandt Avenue East and Rochambeau Avenue. (For schedule information and for pick-up and drop-off points, telephone 511 and say MTA, or visit website: www.mta.info/busco/schedules/.) Walk one block east to Bainbridge Avenue, turn left and walk half a block to the entrance of the Valentine-Varian House.

BY CAR OR TAXI: Take the Major Deegan Expressway to exit 13, East 233rd Street. Make a right at the end of the exit ramp onto Jerome Avenue and, bearing left, ride for approximately one mile to the second traffic light (where Jerome Avenue meets Bainbridge Avenue), then turn slightly left onto Bainbridge Avenue to 208th Street. The old stone Valentine-Varian House will be at your left. Street parking only.

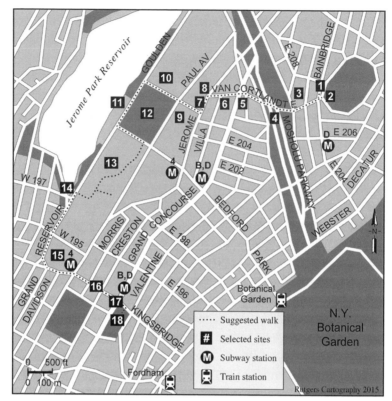

Map 6. Valentine to Poe

1. Valentine-Varian House
2. Williamsbridge Oval
3. PS/MS 80 ("The School the Stars Fell On")
4. Mosholu Parkway
5. Site of Negro Fort
6. Villa Avenue
7. Jerome Avenue
8. High Pumping Station
9. Subway Railroad Yard
10. Bronx High School of Science
11. Jerome Park Reservoir
12. Harris Park
13. Lehman College
14. Old Fort Number Four Park
15. Kingsbridge Armory
16. Kingsbridge Road
17. Kingsbridge Road–Grand Concourse Underpass
18. Edgar Allan Poe Cottage

Walking Tour

1 • The tour begins at the Valentine-Varian House. See part I, "The Valentine-Varian House: A Legacy of the Revolution," for what is to be seen in this house and on its grounds.

2 • Walk to the corner of Bainbridge Avenue and Van Cortlandt Avenue East. Behind the house and its grounds is a grassy dirt wall. At

the street, a stone archway leads walkers beneath the wall to Williams-bridge Oval, a park and playground inside. This structure was orig-inally built in 1888 as the Williamsbridge Reservoir, bringing water from the Kensico Reservoir in Valhalla in Westchester County to serve the needs of a growing New York City. By the 1930s, this res-ervoir was too small to meet those needs. Consequently, in 1937, the water was drained from it and the site was converted to park use. Today it serves as an attraction to all the people living in the neigh-borhood, young and old, who wish to partake in various individual and team sports, other forms of active recreation, and for quiet sitting under shady trees.

3 • Cross Bainbridge Avenue and walk west along Van Cortlandt Avenue East one block to the corner of Rochambeau Avenue. Note the white brick apartment house on the corner. It is in an apartment in this house that Calvin Klein, the famous clothing designer, grew up. Also see the red brick school building with limestone trim across Van Cortlandt Avenue East from that apartment house. The school is PS/MS 80, "The School the Stars Fell On." Attending and graduating from this school were Calvin Klein; his fellow clothing designer Ralph Lauren (who grew up in an apartment house on the other side of the school building); movie actors, producers and directors, brother and sister Garry Marshall and Penny Marshall; and the actor and comedian Robert Klein.

4 • Continue walking west along Van Cortlandt Avenue East one block to Mosholu Parkway. This wide, grassy, and tree-lined parkway was part of the original plan of John Mullaly for establishing parks on the mainland for New York City, which reached fruition in 1888. Park-ways were designed to connect the major parks so that people could ride in the carriages and bicycles from one park to another without leaving a parklike setting. Mosholu Parkway connects Van Cortlandt Park with Bronx Park. The name supposedly comes from the local American Indian name for Tibbett's Brook (part of which is in Van Cortlandt Park) meaning "smooth stones." Today, the parkway is a major traffic artery that also connects several highways and parkways with each other. Yet, it is also a neighborhood recreation area. Resi-dents often sunbathe or play football or volleyball games in the wide grassy area between the roadways or sit on the benches at its edges.

5 • Cross Mosholu Parkway and continue walking along Van Cortlandt Avenue East one block to the Grand Concourse. On the south side of the intersection, there is a hill traversed by a roadway called St. George's Crescent. In 1776, at the top of the hill, the British erected an earthen fortification with the help of Black people laboring for them. For this reason, it was called Negro Fort. It was a redoubt that guarded the approaches to larger and stronger forts overlooking the Harlem River farther to the west. Since it looked over the original Boston Post Road (now Van Cortlandt Avenue East) leading to those military objectives, several battles and skirmishes swirled around Negro Fort. It was destroyed once the Revolutionary War was over.

Across the Grand Concourse, on the northwest corner with Van Cortlandt Avenue East is a beige brick apartment house dating from the 1920s bearing terra-cotta trim with an elaborate entrance in the Moorish style. Garry Marshall and his sister Penny Marshall grew up in an apartment in this building. The small one-block street upon which it stands is named Risse Street in honor of Louis A. Risse, a civil engineer immigrant from Alsace-Lorraine who had the idea for, and planned, the wide Grand Concourse. To understand more about Risse and the importance of the Grand Concourse, see the introductory paragraphs of part II, "The Grand Concourse Historic District: Art Deco Delights."

6 • Continue walking west along Van Cortlandt Avenue East one block to the point where Villa Avenue comes into it from the south. Villa Avenue was first settled by immigrant Italians in the 1890s who took jobs constructing the nearby Jerome Park Reservoir, which will be seen later on this tour. It received its name from the Jerome Park Villa Site Company. The street remained heavily Italian for many decades. By the late 1960s, Puerto Ricans arrived to live here, and the residents of the street are now mostly Latino.

7 • Continue walking westward along Van Cortlandt Avenue East to Jerome Avenue. In 1866, Leonard W. Jerome, a wealthy stock speculator, built a racetrack running west of today's Jerome Avenue to Sedgwick Avenue and roughly south of today's Mosholu Parkway to about modern Kingsbridge Road. Then, trotting races were the most popular form of horse racing in the country. Jerome wanted to restore flat racing, with the jockey on the horse's back instead of in a sulky

behind the horse, to its old status as the "Sport of Kings." One strategy was to attract his wealthy friends to the park by building a road to connect their homes in upper New York City (today's midtown Manhattan) to his racetrack. That road is today Jerome Avenue. He persuaded the local towns in the area to issue bonds, to borrow the money, to pay the cost of construction. The townsmen did not want to pay any money back at all. Therefore, the date when these bonds become due for final payment is in 2041. In short, Jerome Avenue has not been paid for yet.

Another strategy Jerome devised for raising the status of horse racing was to name specific races for some of his wealthy friends. One of them was August Belmont. Thus, in 1867, the Belmont Stakes had its first run at Jerome Park. It was run there every year until 1890 when the track was taken by New York City to create the Jerome Park Reservoir. Today, the Belmont Stakes is the oldest and the longest race in the Triple Crown of racing that includes the Kentucky Derby and the Preakness.

Leonard W. Jerome had three daughters, one of whom, Jennie, was an international beauty. She married the third son of the Duke of Marlborough, Lord Randolph Churchill. Her son was Winston Churchill, who served as the British prime minister during World War II. Thus, Leonard W. Jerome, after whom Jerome Avenue is named, was Winston Churchill's maternal grandfather.

In 1907, in accordance with a local law passed by the New York City Board of Aldermen, each borough president was empowered to create a uniform house numbering system within his own borough. In The Bronx, Jerome Avenue, a geographical extension of Fifth Avenue in Manhattan, became the dividing line between east and west house numbers along east-west streets.

Ten years later, in 1917, the elevated subway tracks above Jerome Avenue opened. It carried (and still carries) subway trains of the Lexington Avenue Jerome-Woodlawn line (now known as the number 4 line). At that time, only areas of The Bronx that were densely populated and urbanized had subways run underground to avoid the racket created by the trains. This area at the time was sparsely populated with few houses anywhere nearby. Since erecting elevated structures was cheaper and faster than digging tunnels, and since no one was around to complain of loud noises, the subway tracks were elevated in this area. The presence of the subway, however, stimulated thousands of people to leave overcrowded Manhattan neighborhoods for the wide-open spaces of The Bronx. Thus, this elevated subway was a major cause for the development of the surrounding area.

8 • On the west side of Jerome Avenue just to the north of Van Cortlandt Avenue East is a long, narrow red brick building with a steeply gabled roof. This is the High Pumping Station, designed by architect George W. Birdsall. It was erected between 1901 and 1906 as part of the Jerome Park Reservoir complex to pump water from the reservoir to residents throughout The Bronx. It is built in Romanesque Revival style with a façade divided into a series of bays, each with two arched windows or doorways. This relatively simple structure is an outstanding example of industrial architecture.

9 • Walk southward on the west side of Jerome Avenue a short distance to West 205th Street, then turn right and walk west along West 205th Street on the viaduct between Jerome and Paul Avenues crossing the railroad yards below. These railroad yards are where the cars forming the subway letter D trains running under the Grand Concourse and Sixth Avenue are stored when they are not in use. Naturally, there are more cars in evidence here at night and on weekends and holidays. On the site of the yards, equivalent to ten blocks long, are facilities for inspection and repair of cars that need it.

10 • Continue walking west on West 205th Street past Paul Avenue to a point about three-quarters of the way along the block. The school structure to the right, on the north side of the street, is the Bronx High School of Science. The school was the idea of educator Dr. Morris Meister, who became its first principal. He believed that intellectually brilliant students were just as handicapped being placed in regular classes as those who were intellectually challenged. He felt that they were held back by having to follow the slower pace needed by average students, and thus had no opportunity to reach their full potential. He envisioned the institution as a school that would admit brilliant students identified by a citywide competitive examination. Here they could be challenged to the limit of their great abilities and exercise their capacity to think and their capability to create. The Bronx High School of Science began in 1937, but this building was erected for it in 1959. Since its founding, it boasts of more Ph.D.s among its alumni

than any other high school in the country, and of seven winners of the Nobel Prize, six in Physics and one in Medicine. The large mosaic decorating the wall seen through the glass along the main entrance illustrates the various sciences supported by the humanities.

11 • Continue walking west along West 205th Street and cross Goulden Avenue to the edge of the Jerome Park Reservoir. The reservoir holds water coming from New York City's Croton system originating in upper Westchester County. From here, water is distributed throughout the borough. The reservoir was originally planned to be more than twice its current size. What exists today was supposed to be only the western basin of the reservoir. The eastern basin was meant to occupy the area between Jerome and Goulden Avenues. However, a large amount of land in the Catskill Mountains became available that would provide much more water capacity for the same amount of money it would cost to build the eastern basin. The funds were then diverted to purchase the Catskill property, leaving the proposed eastern basin as forlorn empty lots. In the 1920s, civic activist and political leader Joseph S. Goulden campaigned to have the wasteland used for what would later be called an educational park. As a result of his efforts, the location became the site of DeWitt Clinton High School, the Bronx High School of Science, Hunter College in The Bronx (later Lehman College of the City University of New York), Walton High School, and an elementary school. For his effort, he is honored with the name of Goulden Avenue.

12 • Walk south along Goulden Avenue one block to Bedford Park Boulevard. On the eastern side of the street is Harris Park. It is laid out into several fields used by Little Leagues and other youth baseball and football sports organizations in The Bronx.

13 • At Bedford Park Boulevard, walk eastward along the south side of the street. To the south of the street is the campus of Lehman College of the City University of New York. While walking, note the building flanking the sidewalk. This is the athletic and physical education facility of the college called the Apex. It was designed in 1994 by noted architect Rafael Viñoly. Here, the basketball arena, the hall housing the Olympic-size pool, and the gymnasium with its running track all lie below ground level. This enabled the architect to rest the

leading edge of the convex roof almost directly on the ground. The façade facing the street is left as a plain two-story concrete structure paralleling the sidewalk, which contains offices and classrooms. From the campus side, almost the entire curved roof is revealed with only a few windows just above the ground to provide light for the athletic facilities inside. Just off center of the Apex is an opening to the campus from the street. Beyond the flanks of this opening are two different eccentric, but spectacular, entrances to the building.

Continue walking along the south sidewalk of Bedford Park Boulevard to the foot of Paul Avenue where is found the main entrance to the college. Turn right and walk onto the campus. Lehman College began in 1932 as Hunter College in The Bronx. Hunter College, a women's college, was located on Park Avenue and East 68th Street in Manhattan when much of it was destroyed by fire. It was initially decided to erect a new campus here, and in 1932, four buildings in the Tudor Gothic style designed by the firm of Thompson, Holmes & Converse were erected. During the course of the Great Depression, it was decided to rebuild at Park Avenue as well and for the college to have two campuses.

With the onset of World War II, the Bronx campus was taken over by the US government as a training facility for WAVEs, the women's division of the navy, and for SPARs, the women's division of the coast guard. Women from all over the country came here, marched in formation, attended classes, and learned to perform tasks useful for the war effort.

Once the war was over, the new United Nations began looking at sites in New York City for its permanent headquarters. Temporarily, the United Nations Security Council used this campus as a meeting place and offices from March to August 1946. It was at this time that the council made its first substantive decision, ordering Soviet troops out of northern Iran. When the Soviet Union complied, it gave the new peacekeeping organization credibility that its predecessor, the League of Nations, never had.

Hunter College, however, demanded the use of its campus back. At the time, hoards of veterans took advantage of the GI Bill that paid for their university education to apply to institutions of higher education in droves. If Hunter, a traditionally female college, were to take advantage of the circumstances, it would have to become a coeducational institution. Yet, it still wanted to provide a place for females who wanted to attend class only with other females. The solution was to admit males and females to the Bronx campus, while leaving the Park Avenue facility strictly female.

However, managing a two-campus college, many miles apart in two of the city's boroughs and each with a different mix of students, became increasingly difficult. In the 1970s, the decision was made to make Hunter College in The Bronx into Lehman College of the City University of New York. It was also decided that the new institution would specialize in teaching the visual and performing arts, while not neglecting all the other aspects of a superior higher education. Today, the various stages in the history of Lehman College can be seen by walking around the campus and examining its buildings and facilities.

After entering the main gate, walk along the sidewalk inside the campus. At the end of the sidewalk through the gate of the fence is an impressive concrete modern building that houses the large Concert Hall. Its box office is located inside. Turn right and walk up the slight slope. Here major international performers and groups present classical orchestra concerts, ballet, jazz, and popular music groups and stars. The Tudor Gothic building, originally called Student Hall but now called the Music Building, sports a modern concrete addition behind it that contains the smaller 200-seat Lovinger Theater. Here, plays performed by professional troupes and more intimate professional musical performances are presented. The box office here is located inside the building in the newer wing. In the basement of the new wing is a theater in the round where students produce plays and band concerts open to the public. There are other auditoriums upstairs in the older portion of the building where faculty present free chamber music concerts where the public is welcomed. Both the large Concert Hall and the new wing of the Music Building were designed by David Todd & Associates and Jan Hird Pokorny and were completed in 1980. Together they constitute The Lehman College Center for the Performing Arts. For information on performances, telephone 718-960-8833; or visit the website: www.lehmancenter.org/events.

Stand in front of the original Tudor Gothic style Music Building. Note the decoration carved in places around the entrance: the letter H, standing for Hunter College. In the space above the doorways there is placed a stained-glass window commemorating the presence of the WAVEs who trained on the campus during World War II.

From the front of the Music Building take the diagonal walkway that leads to the entrance of the newer style building at its end. That building is Shuster Hall. It was designed by the famous twentieth-century architectural firm of Marcel Breuer & Associates with Robert F. Gatje, associate, and opened in 1960. The entrance separates it into two wings. To the left, the windows are protected by a honeycomb-like sunscreen. It houses the college's major offices. The wing on the right houses the Lehman College Art Gallery. Its hours are Tuesday through Saturday 10:00 A.M. to 4:00 P.M.; closed Sunday and Monday. Contacts: Telephone: 718-960-8731; website: www.lehman.edu/vpadvance/artgallery/gallery.

The Lehman College Art Gallery can be entered through the main Shuster Hall doorways and turn right. The gallery specializes in changing exhibitions of works by contemporary artists in various media. Once inside the gallery space, note that the columns in the middle of the rooms splay out into funnel shapes near the ceiling. This is because the interior of the columns are hollow and act as downspouts for rainwater coming down on the roof.

On exiting Shuster Hall turn right and walk down the walkway paralleling it and turn left at the Tudor Gothic style building, called the Old Gymnasium Building, on the path that leads to the modern structure called the Leonard Lief Library. At a point in the front of the middle of the Old Gymnasium Building, right next to the pathway, is a metal ship's bell. This bell was used by the WAVEs as a signal when they trained on the campus during World War II.

Walk away from the Leonard Lief Library on the path beside the Old Gymnasium Building to the first pathway crossing it. Turn left and pass the Tudor Gothic style Davis Hall to the one-story plain Bookstore Building. Walk on the path between Davis Hall and the Bookstore Building to the parking lot behind the bookstore. On the left is Carman Hall, a large classroom building designed by the firm of DeYoung and Moskowitz and opened in 1970. In the subbasement of this building are the studios and office of BronxNet, the Bronx public access cable television channels. It not only provides access to anyone who wishes to put on a show, it teaches students all aspects of television production and, unusual for public access television channels across the country, even produces its own entertainment and other programming.

14 • Exit the Lehman College campus through the gate at the end of the parking lot and emerge onto Goulden Avenue. Turn left along sidewalk on the east side of Goulden Avenue. Across the street at the western side of Goulden Avenue, the Jerome Park Reservoir reaches its southern limit at Reservoir Avenue. Across from that limit, south of Reservoir Avenue, is a narrow, hilly park extending westward for several blocks that provides sitting areas and playgrounds for residents. It is called Old Fort Number Four Park. At the beginning of the American Revolution, in 1775 and 1776, the Americans erected a series of eight forts along the high ridge overlooking the Harlem River. Each fort was called by a number in the order of its location. At the western end of today's park was located Fort Number Four, which, although it no longer exists, gave the park its name.

15 • Continue walking south past Walton High School to Kingsbridge Road. Between West 195th Street and Kingsbridge Road and along the north side of Kingsbridge Road to Jerome Avenue is the massive red brick Kingsbridge Armory. Designed by the firm of Pilcher & Tachau and erected between 1912 and 1917, this is the largest armory in the world. Meant to house an artillery unit of the New York National Guard nicknamed the Washington Greys (because their forebears, wearing gray uniforms, guarded George Washington in 1789 at his presidential inauguration), the façade facing Kingsbridge Road is built like a medieval fortress with massive round towers and crenellated parapets. This is where the offices were located.

Behind, and linked to it, is the huge drill floor designed to look like a vast European train shed. It was possible to discharge a cannon at one end to hit a target at the other end, a range of four city blocks, and the arc of the cannonball's trajectory would not reach the height of the ceiling. Over the years, the drill floor was used for a variety of purposes, including the annual military ball when members of the unit would appear in their dress gray uniforms. Public use for the space ranged from bicycle races, the Bronx County Dog Show, school science fairs, and a boat show. AT&T once held their annual stockholders meeting here. In October 1944, President Franklin Delano Roosevelt arrived inside the drill floor in his open automobile to review and address the women training at the nearby Hunter College campus to become WAVEs or SPARs. The space was used also as a film set for the movie

I Am Legend starring Will Smith. There are levels below the drill floor used as truck garage spaces, an auditorium, and other purposes.

In the later twentieth century, New York governor George Pataki decided to close all the armories in the state. Because of the massive size of the Kingsbridge Armory, and because it is an official New York City landmark, the options for alternative uses were limited. The facility remained closed for many years until proposals could be offered and a decision made. In 2013, it was decided to sell the armory to a corporation that will convert the interior into several ice-skating rinks, including one that will be part of a 5,000-seat arena. This will provide space for year-round recreational ice skating, places to train hockey teams, athletes who compete in long and short track ice races, and figure skaters. Classes will be held to teach local children to ice skate, and rooms inside will be available for community meetings. When completed, this will be the first facility of its kind in the United States, and the armory will be renamed the Kingsbridge National Ice Center.

16 • Cross Kingsbridge Road to the southern sidewalk. Kingsbridge Road began as a narrow local American Indian trail leading to the crossing between the mainland and northern Manhattan. In colonial times, it was widened to become a cattle trail where local farmers would drive their cattle over the King's Bridge to Manhattan and the markets in New York City at the southern tip of the island. In the 1890s, it was widened still further and paved. The coming of the elevated subway along Jerome Avenue in 1917 enabled thousands of people to leave crowded Manhattan neighborhoods to newer housing in more open spaces here. Kingsbridge Road became a local shopping street, which it remains today, with shops, banks, and restaurants. It has become a bustling urban thoroughfare. The hip-hop music artist Kurtis Blow grew up in this area.

17 • Walk eastward along the south side of Kingsbridge Road to Creston Avenue. Here, in the middle of Kingsbridge Road, is the beginning of the Kingsbridge Road–Grand Concourse Underpass. When civil engineer Louis A. Risse was designing the Grand Concourse in the 1890s, he made an innovation. He knew that there would eventually arise traffic jams at major roads that intersected with the Grand Concourse. To avoid that trouble, he decided to create passes under the Grand Concourse at such major intersections. This kind of grade separation had been used earlier, but only inside such parks as Central Park in Manhattan. This is the first time it was used for an urban thoroughfare. Ramps on the side of the underpass would allow traffic to rise to go onto the Grand Concourse or to exit that roadway onto the cross street, while the underpass would allow traffic on the cross street to continue to go from one side of the Concourse to the other without interfering with the Concourse traffic. The innovation worked quite well. In fact, Risse's idea became the basis for the clover-leaf design used by all major post–World War II highways across the nation.

18 • Continue walking eastward along the south side of Kingsbridge Road. Cross the Grand Concourse to Poe Park. At the northern end of the park is the Edgar Allan Poe Cottage. See part I, "The Edgar Allan Poe Cottage: Poverty and Poetry" for information about it and what is to be seen inside.

Dining

Have a bite to eat at any of the diners, restaurants, and luncheonettes found along Kingsbridge Road or on the Grand Concourse south of Poe Park.

To return to Manhattan, take the subway letter D train on the corner of the Grand Concourse and Kingsbridge Road downtown.

To return to the starting point of this walking tour, walk southward along the east side of Poe Park one block and cross 192nd Street onto Valentine Avenue, walking southward along the west side of Valentine Avenue one more block to Fordham Road. There, board the Bx34 bus to Van Cortlandt Avenue East right in front of the Valentine-Varian House.

After your visit to the Edgar Allan Poe Cottage, you may wish to continue by taking the walking tour "In the Footsteps of Edgar Allan Poe."

In the Footsteps of Edgar Allan Poe

The famed nineteenth-century poet, author, and literary critic Edgar Allan Poe lived in the village of Fordham, now a part of The Bronx, from 1846 until his death in 1849. As a resident, he often walked from his home to the railroad station to visit friends in New York City on Manhattan Island, or, for intellectual stimulation, he ambled beyond it to the campus of the recently founded Saint John's College, now Fordham University. Here is a self-guided walking tour that will take the visitor to those sites on the same route in the footsteps of Edgar Allan Poe. In the process, it will be discovered what remains from his time and what has changed to create the Fordham neighborhood of today.

DIRECTIONS

BY PUBLIC TRANSPORTATION: Take subway train letter D to Kingsbridge Road, exit at the back of the station, and climb up the steps to the street.

Alternatively, take the BxM4 Express bus on Madison Avenue to Kingsbridge Road and the Grand Concourse. (For schedule information and for pick-up and drop-off points, telephone 511 and say MTA, or visit website: www.mta.info/busco/schedules/.) Cross Kingsbridge Road to Poe Park and Poe Cottage.

BY CAR OR TAXI: Take the Major Deegan Expressway northbound to the West 230th Street exit. At the end of the ramp, turn right onto West 230th Street, and then turn right onto Bailey Avenue to Kingsbridge Road. Turn left onto Kingsbridge Road to the Grand Concourse. Do not use the underpass. Street parking only.

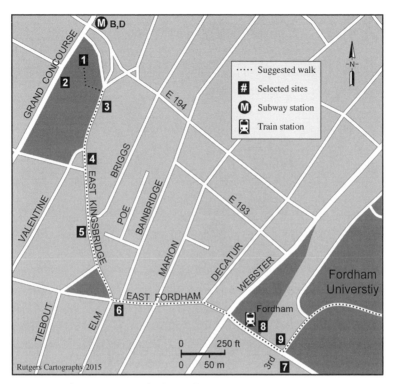

Map 7. In the Footsteps of Edgar Allan Poe

1. Edgar Allan Poe Cottage
2. Poe Park Visitor Center
3. Ethnic stores
4. Original location of Poe Cottage
5. Bronx Library Center
6. Fordham Road
7. Fordham Plaza office building
8. Fordham Station of Metro-North
9. Fordham University campus entrance

Walking Tour

1 • Start at the Edgar Allan Poe Cottage inside the northern end of Poe Park on the southeast corner of the Grand Concourse and Kingsbridge Road. For detailed information about the cottage and the opportunity to visit it, see part I, "The Edgar Allan Poe Cottage: Poverty and Poetry."

2 • Poe Park was created from what had been an apple orchard to preserve the Edgar Allan Poe Cottage. Here can be found the gray slate building that houses the Poe Park Visitor Center. Designed by architect Toshiko Mori, the black slate roof evokes the wings of a raven, the subject of one of Edgar Allan Poe's best-known poems. Since it

was erected in 2011, the center has hosted art exhibitions and events. Its hours are May to September, from Tuesday to Saturday 9:00 A.M. to 5:00 P.M.; October to April, Tuesday to Saturday from 8:00 A.M. to 4:00 P.M. Contacts: Telephone: 718-365-5516 or 718-365-5545; website: www.nygovparks.org/parks/x040.

At the southern end of the park is the Bandstand. Erected in the early twentieth century, this bandstand hosted some of the greatest ensembles of the Big Band era of jazz and swing music. From the 1920s to the 1950s, local residents and visitors came on a summer's night, elegantly dressed, to listen and to dance. Rosemary Clooney, the singer and aunt of actor George Clooney, had her first professional engagement here performing with her sister in front of a band. Recently, there are occasional daytime performances by rock, Latin, and hip-hop musical groups.

In 1939, a recent graduate of DeWitt Clinton High School who lived nearby sat with a friend, Bill Finger, on one of the benches in Poe Park. Holding a sketchbook in his hand, he drew some cartoon characters. His friend urged him to present the idea behind one of them to a publisher of comic books. He did so, and the character he created appeared as a cover story in *Detective Comics* later that year. The character became so popular that it quickly earned a comic book all its own. The artist was Bob Kane, and the character he created on the bench in Poe Park was Batman.

3 • Walk to the eastern edge of Poe Park on the sidewalk paralleling it beside Kingsbridge Road. Across the street from Poe Park, notice the signs identifying the shops at the street level of the apartment houses. The proprietors appeal to the many different ethnic groups that today inhabit the Fordham neighborhood. They range from Latino to West Indian to Cambodian to Bangladeshi. It speaks volumes about the diversity of the people who reside in today's Bronx and the harmony in which they live next to each other as neighbors.

4 • Walk along the sidewalk to the southern end of Poe Park at 192nd Street. Look across Kingsbridge Road at the light yellow-colored brick Art Deco style apartment house. Note that at the northern end of that apartment house the bend in Kingsbridge Road had forced the architect to design a slight bend in the building marked by a straight line in the brickwork from the ground to the roof. At the curb, there is a

street lamp and a fire hydrant. Exactly at the location of the bend in the apartment house behind the street lamp and the hydrant is the original location of the Edgar Allan Poe Cottage. It was moved to Poe Park and its current location to save it from destruction by debris falling from the older apartment houses now abutting the Art Deco building when those houses were under construction.

5 • Cross 192nd Street walking along Kingsbridge Road to the Bronx Library Center at 310 East Kingsbridge Road. Opened in 2006, designed by Dattner Architects, this five-story structure is the largest public library in The Bronx and was the first municipally built green building in New York City. In 2007, it won the Green Builder's Council Silver Award for Leadership in Energy and Environmental Design (LEED). The glass curtain wall fills the library with daylight aided by custom light shelves and translucent shades. Sensors located throughout the building turn off electric lights when rooms are unoccupied. The roof reflects solar heat, reducing the need for cooling. Many of the structural and cosmetic details are derived from recycled materials.

The lobby entrance is designed to give the visitor the feeling of entering a modern bookstore. Here is found the Circulation Department, the Adult Library, and a Teen Center with computers, books, DVDs, and music CDs and where teen programs are held.

Below, on the Concourse level, is a 150-seat auditorium where performances, lectures, films, and forums are presented. In addition, there is space for instructional workshops, as well as a computer lab, an adult literacy program, and English as a Second Language classes.

Children's programs and services are centered on the library's second floor. This includes a story hour room and a puppet theater.

The adult department on the third floor is where adults may read or use computers or audio or digital books. Here is also an outdoor reading terrace accessible on days with fine weather.

On the fourth floor is the reference department with its reference collection in both English and Spanish and an electronic database collection. It also has collections of Puerto Rican / Latin Heritage, of Bronx history, and of Edgar Allan Poe's works.

The fifth floor houses the career and education information service for job searching and résumé creation, editing, and posting. One-on-one educational and job counseling services are provided by appointment. The center's hours are Monday through Saturday

9:00 A.M. to 9:00 P.M.; Sunday noon to 6:00 P.M. Contact: Telephone: 718-579-4257.

6 • Walk back to 192nd Street and cross Kingsbridge Road. Turn right and walk down toward Fordham Road. Kingsbridge Road and this section of Fordham Road leading to it began as an American Indian trail, just wide enough to be a footpath. In the colonial period, it was a cattle trail where cows and bulls were herded to market in New York City at the southern tip of Manhattan Island via the King's Bridge. It was a rural path when Edgar Allan Poe resided here in the 1840s. Rapid urbanization starting in the 1890s led to Kingsbridge Road's widening and paving. Fordham Road from Third Avenue to this point was part of that old Indian trail and colonial cattle trail.

Today, Fordham Road is the premier shopping street in The Bronx. There are over 300 specialty stores ranging from locally owned shops to national chains. Sales on apparel, sportswear, electronics, appliances, jewelry, food, pharmaceuticals, optical services, and more abound. Amid this bustling commerce, there are green spaces, parks, and plazas.

7 • Walk eastward (left) along the northern sidewalk of Fordham Road and cross Webster Avenue to the northeast corner of the intersection. Across Fordham Road is a striking twelve-story office building of yellow brick, glass block, black marble, and polished chrome in the neo–Art Deco style with a rounded façade facing the intersection. This is the Fordham Plaza office building. Designed by the major New York architectural firm of Skidmore, Owings & Merrrill, it opened in 1986 and instantly became the premier office building in The Bronx, the one against which all others are measured.

8 • Walk a few steps along the north sidewalk of Fordham Road just past the intersection with Webster Avenue and the park to the Fordham Station of Metro-North. The railroad that services the passengers who use this station was first built in 1841 as the New York and Harlem River Railroad. The Fordham station was the first one the railroad opened on the mainland, and it remains a major station in the system today with both the Harlem and New Haven divisions of the Metro-North commuter railroad stopping here. The village of Fordham began to grow around this station and Edgar Allan Poe came here in 1846 using this railroad. He also came to this station to take a train to New York City on Manhattan Island whenever he wished to visit his friends or his publishers. In Poe's time, there was only one track to the line and it was at surface level. Increased usage led to a second track's being laid in 1852. In 1891 when the area began to urbanize, the number of tracks rose to four and were depressed below grade level to prevent accidents.

9 • Walk a few steps along the north sidewalk of Fordham Road beyond the railroad station to the gate that leads to the campus of Fordham University. The university was founded in 1841 by Bishop (later raised to Archbishop) John Hughes of the New York diocese (later archdiocese) to provide a Catholic-based education for the growing Catholic population in his see. He soon turned the task of running the institution, first called Saint John's College, over to a group of French Jesuits from Kentucky. The college attained university status in 1907, taking its new name from the Fordham area in which it is located. Today, it is an independent institution under a lay board of trustees, but it is still described as operating in the Jesuit tradition.

When he lived in his cottage in Fordham from 1846 to 1849, Edgar Allan Poe frequently visited this campus. Here he found intellectual stimulation conversing with the Jesuit faculty, who also gave him free use of the library. After his wife died, Poe entered into a period of severe melancholy. When he came to the campus at that time, he would often sit motionless, staring blankly into space until, when the library closed for the evening, one of the Jesuit faculty would nudge the poet's elbow and say quietly that it was time to go home. Poe then rose and slowly left the campus. It is often stated that when Poe wrote his poem "The Bells" while he was living in Fordham that he was inspired, in part at least, by the ringing of the bell in the campus church. Later, students dubbed the bell "Old Edgar" in honor of Poe. Today that bell is stored in the attic of the new Walsh Library on the campus.

The many noted graduates of Fordham University include actors Alan Alda and Denzel Washington, Bob Keeshan (Captain Kangaroo), radio and television commentator Charles Osgood, sportscasters Vin Scully and Michael Kay, Hall of Fame baseball player Frankie Frisch (the "Fordham Flash"), Hall of Fame football coach Vince Lombardi, author Mary Higgins Clark, and the first woman vice presidential candidate, Geraldine Ferraro.

Go through the gate onto the campus grounds. If questioned by the security guard at the gate, inform him that you wish to see the museum, and he will admit you. The museum is in the Walsh Library to the right just beyond the entrance gate.

The Walsh Library is one of the newest buildings on the campus, but it is sheathed in a stone façade to make it blend in with the older buildings on the grounds. Inside is the Fordham Museum of Greek, Etruscan, and Roman Art donated from the private collection of William D. Walsh, a successful graduate who provided half the cost of building the structure and after whom the library is named. The museum is filled with more than 200 artifacts from classical antiquity, and is the largest collection of its kind in the New York Metropolitan Area. The hours at which the library is open vary with the academic calendar. During regular session: Monday to Thursday 8:30 A.M. to 2:00 A.M., Friday 8:30 A.M. to 9:00 P.M., Saturday 9:00 A.M. to 10:00 P.M., and Sunday noon to 2:00 A.M. During summer session: Monday to Thursday 8:30 A.M. to 11:00 P.M., Friday 9:00 A.M. to 5:00 P.M., Saturday and Sunday closed. Library hours during intersession: Monday to Friday 9:00 A.M. to 5:00 P.M., Saturday and Sunday closed. For information as to hours, telephone 718-817-3595.

On exiting the library, walk along the winding road leading up a gentle slope to the right until you reach the Administration Building at the flat area at the top of the gentle hill. It consists of an older center portion made of stone flanked by two newer additions in red brick. The center portion was the Rose Hill Manor House, erected in 1838 of rough stone in the Greek Revival style. The portico features marble Greek columns. The oldest building on the campus, it precedes the creation of the institution by three years. Facing the entrance is a statue of Bishop (later Archbishop) John Hughes who founded the original Saint John's College here.

Continue walking along the road past the Administration Building and turn left at the first crosswalk. Walk just past the massive, columned, dull orange brick-and-limestone-trim building, bearing to the right where the University Church (officially Our Lady, Mediatrix of All Graces) appears. It was designed by William Rodrigue, John Hughes's brother-in-law, in 1845, and was one of the first buildings erected by the college on the campus grounds. The transept, chancel, crossing, and lantern, however, were added in 1929. Inside there are beautiful stained-glass windows donated by King Louis Philippe of

France. Made at a workshop in Sèvres, each depicts one of the Apostles identified by the French form of his name (Saint Pierre, Saint Luc, Saint Marc, etc.). The church also contains the altar from the Old Saint Patrick's Cathedral in Manhattan.

On exiting from the University Church, notice the quadrangle and the U-shaped building to the right. Also designed by William Rodrigue in 1845, this structure is now the Saint John's Residence Hall, the oldest dormitory for students on the campus. When it was originally completed, it was also used for classroom instruction.

Turn back to the walkway. On your left, note the massive bronze bust of Orestes Brownson, a nineteenth-century theologian and philosopher. He had converted to Catholicism, but often clashed intellectually with John Hughes. Fordham's students say that the statue of Hughes in front of the Administration Building faces away from the bust of Brownson and Brownson shows his back to Hughes because of their many arguments and disagreements in life.

Walk back to the Administration Building. Go past it along its side until you come to a large lawn enclosed by an iron-pipe fence. Walk around the large lawn to get to its east side. There is found the large Keating Hall, designed in 1936 by Robert J. Reilly. It is marked by a tall, massive tower on its roof. Walk up the flight of stone steps leading to the main entrance of the building that faces the large lawn. Note there is inscribed on several of the steps the names of presidents and prime ministers of various countries who have visited Fordham's campus and the date of their visits. Most of them headed Latin American or other countries with large Catholic populations. However, President Franklin Delano Roosevelt is included among them for his visit in 1940. At the topmost step, the name of George Washington is incised. He came to the site where you entered the campus as general in the Continental Army in 1781 to secure the services of nineteen-year-old Andrew Corsa to guide him and the combined American and French armies down to the southern part of what is today The Bronx to survey British fortifications on Manhattan Island with a view to a possible invasion. The campus was then the Corsa family farm.

Inside Keating Hall are not only a large number of classrooms, but also the studios of radio station WFUV, a National Public Radio station with a 50,000-watt capacity. This is the only radio station headquartered in The Bronx, and it affords programming of music, news, public affairs, and sports for its 40,000 listeners every week.

Walk south on the path in front of Keating Hall with the building on your left and the lawn on your right. At the first intersection with another footpath, turn right, keeping the lawn on your right, and stop at a small, cube-like nondescript structure on your left clad in the same stone as the academic buildings. This building was erected in 1924 to house the William Spain Seismic Observatory, named for a student who died in 1922 whose father donated the funds to build it. The seismograph inside has measured much of the world's earthquakes and China's first atomic explosion in 1964. This one at Fordham is part of a network of similar machines that monitor earthquake activity in the northeastern United States and supplies data to the Advanced National Seismic System operated by the United States Geological Survey.

Continue walking along the footpath keeping the lawn on your right. At the western edge of the lawn, there is another intersecting footpath. Turn left on that path and walk southward to the gate at the end of the campus. Walk through that gate and continue walking along the short block to Fordham Road. There is a bus stop at the corner. Note the massive school building across Fordham Road and slightly to your right. This was erected as Theodore Roosevelt High School, now housing several high schools and called the Theodore Roosevelt Campus. Attending this school in the 1930s were two people who became successful in Hollywood films in the 1940s, John Garfield and June Allyson.

This is where the tour ends. To return to your starting point at the Grand Concourse and Kingsbridge Road, take the westbound bus number Bx9 at the bus stop.

Dining

You may also wish to partake of a delicious meal of Italian fare at any one of the fine restaurants along nearby Arthur Avenue. To do so, cross Fordham Road and turn left. Walk east for three short blocks to Arthur Avenue and turn right. For further information, consult part II, "Belmont: New York's Real Little Italy."

Marvelous Mott Haven

Mott Haven today exhibits a record of all of the eras of its past, each existing cheek-by-jowl with the other. To walk through it is a journey of discovery not only of its development from a rural countryside to a throbbing urban area but of such aspects of American history as the colonial and revolutionary periods, the coming of the Irish, German, Jewish, Black, and Latino ethnic groups, industrialization and urbanization. While it is true Mott Haven is part of the poorest urban congressional district in the country, it does not appear to be so to the casual observer. The residents are friendly, and pleasant surprises abound. Who would believe that it is the final resting place of two of the nation's Founding Fathers? Who would conceive that three declared historic districts lie within the neighborhood's boundaries? Who would think that there are busy shops selling goods to the residents? Who would suppose that some wealthy people have discovered the treasures of the neighborhood and have moved in next to their poorer neighbors? Take a walk and discover the true wonders of marvelous Mott Haven.

DIRECTIONS

This self-guided walking tour of the Mott Haven neighborhood begins on 138th Street and Lincoln Avenue on the southeast corner where it converges with Third Avenue and ends on 138th Street and Alexander Avenue.

BY PUBLIC TRANSPORTATION: Take the number 6 subway train to the Third Avenue station. Use the exit that leads to 138th Street and Third Avenue.

BY CAR OR TAXI: Take the Major Deegan Expressway to the 138th Street exit and turn right. On exiting the ramp proceed eastward to Third Avenue.

Alternatively, take Madison Avenue to the Madison Avenue Bridge and proceed straight ahead eastward along 138th Street to Third Avenue. Street parking only.

About Mott Haven

Mott Haven's written history began in 1639 with the arrival of Jonas Bronck, a Swede who became a merchant sea captain in the Netherlands. He, along with his wife and indentured servants, were the first European settlers. They felled several trees, planted crops, and grazed livestock. Bronck's stone house with a tile roof was used as the site of peace negotiations between the Dutch authorities of New Netherland and a local tribe of American Indians.

Bronck died in 1643, and his land eventually came into possession of the Morris family, originally from Monmouthshire in Great Britain, but arriving here from the West Indian island of Barbados. They owned the southwest quarter of the modern Bronx that they erected into the manor of Morrisania. In 1776, Lewis Morris signed the Declaration of Independence. In 1787, his half brother, Gouverneur Morris, became a principal framer of the Constitution of the United States and the man to whom was given the responsibility to write its text in literary form, thus becoming the "Penman of the Constitution."

By the 1840s, it was clear that wealth came from the new industries being established and no longer from the possession of land. Gouverneur Morris II began to sell portions of Morrisania. In 1841, the extreme southwestern corner was sold to Jordan L. Mott, an iron founder who was also the inventor of the coal-burning stove. He immediately named his property Mott Haven. Mott envisioned attracting more factories to Mott Haven in what would be called today an industrial park. He established his iron foundry there and expanded it through the years until it was forced to move in 1906 for lack of space to expand further.

The coming of industry coincided with the onset of a mass of Irish immigrants fleeing from the poverty and famine of Ireland. They got jobs in the new factories and settled near them. Through the years, several grew to be wealthy. For many decades Mott Haven was a heavily Irish neighborhood.

In the middle of the nineteenth century, a failed revolution in Germany and a severe drought caused large numbers of German immigrants to arrive. They erected townhouse residences and shops and also established piano factories, since many of them were trained in the piano manufacturing crafts. By the end of the nineteenth century, The Bronx in general, and Mott Haven in particular, was the piano manufacturing capital of the United States.

By the 1890s, an increasing number of Eastern European Jews fleeing from persecution in Imperial Russia arrived in Mott Haven. They used the recently expanded Third Avenue Elevated rapid transit line, and later the new subway to travel to their new homes. They lived in new apartment houses erected in the area and opened up their own shops and factories as well.

In 1943, in the midst of World War II, Blacks and Puerto Ricans began moving in from Harlem and East Harlem in Manhattan. Mott Haven residents welcomed them by electing Black and Puerto Rican parents to the executive board of the local Parent-Teacher Association, finding jobs for them and teaching them skills they might not otherwise have. In this way, Mott Haven was peacefully integrated.

After the war, there was great interest in establishing decent housing for the poor. The city took land filled with older structures, condemned them, and erected high-rise low-income housing projects. The theory behind them was the "tower in the park." The tall buildings could accommodate the same number of people as in the old structures, but the high-rise buildings also created open land for grass, trees, playgrounds, and benches. No schools or shops were planned in order to encourage resident children to attend local schools and adults to shop in the surrounding neighborhood, while local children also had access to the new projects' playgrounds.

The construction of the Triborough Bridge in 1936 and the Major Deegan Expressway's extension up the west bank of the Harlem River in the 1950s, combined with the great prosperity after World War II, encouraged the older ethnic groups to leave for suburban locations. Thus, Mott Haven became increasingly Black and Puerto Rican in population. Most recently, large numbers of Dominicans and Mexicans have moved into the area, and the southernmost portion of Mott Haven has attracted artists to set up residences and studios in old factory buildings. A new antiques district has opened up and some wealthier people have moved in to add to the population mix.

Walking Tour

1 • Start at the southeast corner of 138th Street and Lincoln Avenue. A few steps away is the exit from the Lexington Avenue local subway (number 6) line, which was completed in 1920. The fact that the station is underground indicates that when it was built the neighborhood it serves was already densely populated and highly urbanized. The more rural and suburban areas of The Bronx at the time were served by elevated sections of the subway since it was believed that the racket it caused would not disturb too many people. Here, the noise would have disturbed too many nearby residents and trains had to travel underground.

2 • The John Purroy Mitchel Houses extending south from 138th Street to 135th Street along Lincoln Avenue is a major high-rise low-income housing project designed and erected in the years after World War II when the Irish were the major ethnic group in the neighborhood. It is named for John Purroy Mitchel, a Bronx native of Irish background. He became a lawyer and political reformer and was elected New York City's mayor in 1913. After his term was over in 1917, the nation had entered World War I. He joined the new Army Air Corps and suddenly died in an accident while on a training mission.

3 • Walk south along Lincoln Avenue to 137th Street. At the southern end of the triangular-shaped park across Lincoln Avenue is a pink granite shaft topped by a ball. This is the only memorial in The Bronx to those who died during the Spanish-American War in 1898. It was designed by Albert Eggerton Davis, an architect whose office was on part of the site now occupied by the John Purroy Mitchel Houses.

4 • Cross Lincoln Avenue to the park north of 137th Street. South of 137th Street is a white building in terra-cotta in a Neo-Classical style. The building, opened in 1912 with its cornerstone on the corner of 137th Street and Lincoln Avenue put in place by New York City's mayor William J. Gaynor, was originally constructed for the North Side (later The Bronx) Board of Trade, the borough's first business organization. On the Lincoln Avenue and Third Avenue sides of the building, just below the roof line, are incised the fields in which businessmen were engaged. Today, the space upstairs is used as a business

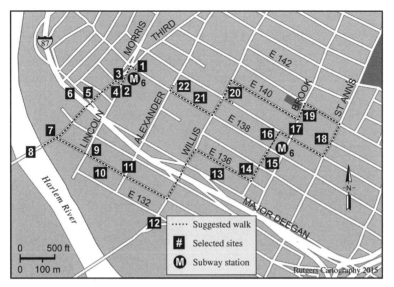

Map 8. Marvelous Mott Haven

1. 138th Street Subway Station
2. John Purroy Mitchel Houses
3. Spanish-American War Memorial
4. Old Bronx Board of Trade Building
5. Underground Railroad route
6. Major Deegan Expressway
7. J. L. Mott Iron Works
8. Third Avenue Bridge
9. Clock Tower Building
10. Site of Jonas Bronck's house
11. Bronx Antiques District

12. Willis Avenue Bridge
13. Bertine Block Historic District
14. Brown Place
15. Site of Teatro de Puerto Rico
16. Plaza Borinquen
17. Brook Avenue
18. Saint Ann's Church
19. Esai Morales's neighborhood
20. Mott Haven East Historic District
21. Site of Third Avenue Elevated Station
22. Mott Haven Historic District

incubator where enterprises just beginning can find inexpensive space and share machines, supplies, and facilities until each can branch off on its own and be replaced by another business startup.

5 • Walk along Third Avenue to 136th Street and cross Third Avenue to its west side. Continue walking south along Third Avenue to its end. In the years before the Civil War, Third Avenue, connected to Manhattan by a wooden bridge lying close to the water (now replaced by a more modern bridge), was a route of the Underground Railroad. Escaped slaves were taken along the route, stopping at several "stations" on their way up to New England and freedom via the Boston Road.

6 • The overpass crossing Third Avenue between 135th and 134th Streets carries a portion of the Major Deegan Expressway from the

Triborough Bridge westward and northward. It was designed in the mid-1930s as an approach road to the planned bridge. It is named after William Francis Deegan, an architectural engineer from The Bronx who was an active captain in the local National Guard unit. In World War I, he was tasked by the US Army to design and erect barracks for the troops in upstate New York and left the service with the rank of major. After the war, he took a leading role in organizing the war's veterans into the American Legion and became its New York State commander. Under the mayoral administration of his friend, James J. Walker, Deegan was named New York City's tenement house commissioner, but he was never touched by the scandals of the mayor's government. In the early 1930s, he was elected the president of the Bronx Chamber of Commerce, but died soon after undergoing an operation for appendicitis. At that time, the highway was being planned and a demand arose to name it after him, a request that was granted. Today, the Major Deegan Expressway is an important automobile and truck artery linking upstate New York with The Bronx and with both Manhattan and Long Island.

7 • Walk along the west side of Third Avenue to its end. Stop at the end of the street under the approach to the Third Avenue Bridge. Do not go up the steps. The complex of red brick buildings along the west side of Third Avenue was erected for the J. L. Mott Iron Works. It is believed that the single-story buildings with pitched roofs inside the property beyond the fence were the original foundry structures. Look up at the façade of the brick building nearest the streets facing the Harlem River and note the name "J. L. Mott Iron Works" laid out in brick just below the roofline. The building complex is now divided and used by many different businesses.

8 • The Third Avenue Bridge and its approach overhead were built in 1899. The first span on this site was a low wooden structure called the Harlem Bridge erected in 1797. That bridge was replaced by an iron span produced in 1862 by the American Bridge Company, a subsidiary of the J. L. Mott Iron Works. That one, in turn, was replaced by the current steel structure to connect The Bronx with Manhattan.

9 • Walk back northward to the first street coming into Third Avenue from the east, Bruckner Boulevard, and continue walking along

the sidewalk on its north side one block to Lincoln Avenue. On the northeast corner of the intersection is a structure now called the Clock Tower Building. It was erected in 1885 as a factory for the Estay Piano Company, one of several such concerns, such as Krakauer and Kroeger, that later set up business nearby. They employed the resident immigrant Germans who had attained skills in piano manufacturing in Germany. The nexus of such factories here made The Bronx the piano manufacturing capital of the United States. Then, a piano in the home was a popular method of family entertainment. As the twentieth century progressed, however, the introduction of the phonograph, radio, and television rapidly eroded the piano market. The Estay factory was later converted into spaces occupied by several manufacturing concerns. In the 1990s, however, rising prices for artists' studios and residential spaces in Manhattan caused New York–based artists to look to Mott Haven as a reasonably priced alternative. The factory was converted into artists' lofts where they could live and work. This, in turn, led to the beginning of the neighborhood's gentrification. Other old factories were renovated into similar residences, and new apartment houses were built. New shops and restaurants catering to the new clientele began occupying the storefronts along Bruckner Boulevard.

10 • Walk along the north side of Bruckner Boulevard. In the middle of the block on the south side of the street is the site of the farmhouse of Jonas Bronck, the first European settler who ultimately gave The Bronx its name. Born in Sweden in 1600, he moved to Amsterdam and became a merchant sea captain. He married in 1638 and arrived here in 1639 with some indentured servants. He erected his stone farmhouse with a tile roof and windows of imported panes of glass. He owned the largest library recorded in the New Netherland colony. His house was used as the site for peace negotiations between the colony's Dutch government and the local Indians. Bronck died in 1643, and his farm was eventually sold, but his name lives on in the Bronx River, and later in the borough of The Bronx and in the county of Bronx.

11 • Walk to the intersection of Bruckner Boulevard and Alexander Avenue. This is the site of the Bronx Antiques District. It was established in 1983 when an observant entrepreneur noted that many of the cars passing by on Bruckner Boulevard to the Third Avenue Bridge bore Connecticut license plates. Believing the drivers were wealthy

enough to collect antiques, he opened an antique shop. His success attracted other antique dealers to the site. Visitors should feel free to drop in and browse. It is possible to find a treasure at a bargain price.

12 • Continue on the northern sidewalk of Bruckner Boulevard to the Willis Avenue Bridge approach over the street. The bridge was erected in 1901 to connect the rapidly growing mainland to Manhattan. The resulting traffic caused varied shops to open to make it a major local shopping street. The bridge forms part of the route of the New York City Marathon every November. It is the spot for what runners call "the wall." At this point the racer's bodily reserves of food and oxygen suddenly run out and the runner must draw upon his or her emotional resources to continue to race to the finish line.

13 • Pass beneath the Willis Avenue Bridge approach and turn left to walk north along the sidewalk on the east side of Willis Avenue. Willis Avenue was named for Edward Willis, a nineteenth-century real estate dealer who developed this area. Cross over the Major Deegan Expressway below and continue to 136th Street. Cross 136th Street and turn right. Walk along the north sidewalk of 136th Street to the middle of the block. The visitor is now in the middle of the Bertine Block Historic District. Across the street on the south side, note the townhouses numbered 404 to 412. They were designed in 1871 in the neo-Grecian style by Rogers and Browne. Further urbanization of the area had to wait until after the 1880s when the Third Avenue Elevated rapid transit line opened nearby connecting the mainland with the Manhattan business districts.

Developer Edward Bertine hired Manhattan architect George Keister to erect from 1891 to 1895 the Queen Anne style low-stooped, narrow row houses featuring yellow brick, brownstone trim, and a vast array of window openings and roof lines. This outstanding grouping bearing house numbers 414 to 432 is reminiscent of homes found in German and other northern European cities and were meant to attract the German population of the area. Bertine, himself, lived in number 416. Note that some of these houses bear a house number in stained glass just above the entry door, but a different number is found elsewhere on the front. When these structures were erected, the dividing line to calculate house numbers was the distance east or west of the Harlem River. In 1907, the dividing line changed to Jerome Avenue.

Therefore the difference in house numbers here reflects the change made at that time.

After his success with his initial row houses, Bertine turned to the north side of the street and from 1892 to 1893 erected the Romanesque Revival single-family homes at numbers 415 to 425 designed by John Hauser. He then in 1895 constructed the two-family neo-Renaissance houses designed by Adolph Balchun Jr. on the south side of the street at numbers 434 to 440.

After these buildings were completed, the increasing numbers of people arriving to live in the area made it possible to erect apartment houses for them. The eight apartment houses in the district were built between 1897 and 1899 and were designed by Bronx architect Harry T. Howell.

14 • Walk east on the north side of 136th Street to Brown Place. With the coming of large numbers of eastern European Jews fleeing persecution in Imperial Russia in the 1890s, the Baron de Hirsch Fund built workshops and barracks here to teach these poor immigrants from rural areas the industrial skills they needed to survive in a machine-based urban economy. This spot was the first location where eastern European Jews settled in The Bronx. Many Jewish families lived in the area until the years after World War II.

15 • At Brown Place, turn left and walk along the west side of the street to the corner of 138th Street. Across Brown Place at the corner is a church for a Spanish-speaking congregation in a structure that began its existence as a movie theater. It still bears a marquee over the entrance on 138th Street. In the 1950s, with increasing numbers of Puerto Ricans settling in the neighborhood, it became the Teatro de Puerto Rico, a center for live appearances by Spanish-speaking performers, singers, and musicians. The great Mexican comedian Cantinflas once played here. However, the facility could not survive the increasing competition from television and other electronic media and from nightclubs catering to Spanish-speaking audiences that opened elsewhere in The Bronx. That is why it serves as a church today.

16 • Cross 138th Street. Along the sidewalk on the north side of the street right where the crossing is located is a three-story complex faced with large red brown bricks called Plaza Borinquen. Borinquen is the

name for Puerto Rico used by the native Taino people of the island, and this complex, designed in 1974 by Ciardullo-Ehmann, is meant to replicate the ambience of living in Puerto Rico. Walk inside the complex through the entryway in the middle of the brick façade. Be careful in walking. There are scattered steps with low risers that might trip the unwary. Inside, see triplex attached row houses all grouped around a quiet interior courtyard where children can play and neighbors can greet each other.

17 • Walk through the courtyard of Plaza Borinquen to exit through the entryway leading to 139th Street. On exiting, turn right and walk along the south side of 139th Street to Brook Avenue. The street gets its name from the Mill Brook that used to meander along this route and powered a mill at about 137th Street in colonial times. During the American Revolution, the British settled refugee Tories, Americans who supported their cause, in log cabins grouped on either side of the brook. In the first half of the twentieth century, Brook Avenue was a heavily Jewish area with families residing in the apartment houses erected in that era still standing today. Now the population is largely Latino.

18 • Cross Brook Avenue and continue to walk east to St. Ann's Avenue. Turn left at St. Ann's Avenue and walk north along the west side of the street to the ornamental iron fence in the middle of the block. This is the site of Saint Ann's Protestant Episcopal Church. If the wide southern gate is open, go inside and walk to the front of the church. Otherwise go to the northern end of the fence and take the steps outside up to the church and stand in front of it.

Saint Ann's Church was built in 1841 by Gouverneur Morris II. His father, Gouverneur Morris, was a principal framer of the Constitution of the United States, ambassador to France during the French Revolution's Reign of Terror, US senator from New York, member of the committee that approved the grid pattern of streets for New York City, and the first chairman of the Erie Canal Commission. His mother was Ann Carey Randolph of Virginia, a distant cousin of Thomas Jefferson's.

By 1841, it had become clear that the path to wealth was no longer the ownership of land, but the ownership of industry. Gouverneur Morris II began the process of selling off parts of the vast family estate called Morrisania. First, however, he wanted to be sure that the members of his illustrious family would have a burial spot that could never be touched in the future. For this reason, he erected this church and reinterred his long-dead ancestors in its crypt and churchyard.

Today, this building is the oldest church structure in The Bronx, although it is not the oldest parish. Its construction came before the city's street grid pattern was imposed; thus it lies slightly askew in relation to the neighboring streets. It is a simple church made of fieldstone with Gothic windows and a Greek Revival steeple.

Access to the interior of the church is often difficult to attain unless a service or event is taking place. But if the church is open, on the rear wall facing the altar is a large bronze plaque bearing the names, along with a short description of each of their accomplishments, of the distinguished members of the Morris family from colonial to Civil War times who are interred there. The list includes Lewis Morris, the first native-born chief justice of the colony of New York and the first royal governor of the colony of New Jersey; his grandson, also named Lewis Morris, who signed the Declaration of Independence; and Gouverneur Morris, another grandson. Another person interred in the crypt who was not a member of the Morris family, and thus not on the plaque, but who served as the church's vestryman in the nineteenth century, is Colonel Richard March Hoe, the inventor of the rotary printing press. Several of the stained-glass windows honor nineteenth-century members of the Morris family and were donated by relatives.

Saint Ann's Church today is active in providing facilities for the education of neighborhood children, youth recreation, and feeding the area's poor.

19 • On exiting the grounds of Saint Ann's Church, turn left to 141st Street and turn left. Walk westward along the south side of 141st Street to Brook Avenue. This is the area where the actor Esai Morales grew up.

20 • On 141st Street, cross Brook Avenue and walk one block south to 140th Street, turn right on 140th Street, and walk westward on the north side of 140th Street. The visitor has entered the Mott Haven East Historic District. The residences here reflect the influx of population caused by the spread of mass transit facilities in the late nineteenth and early twentieth centuries. Apartment houses erected in the early twentieth century for working-class and middle-class families were

designed by two of the most prolific architects of apartment houses in New York City—numbers 481 to 465 by Neville & Bagge from 1901 to 1902 and numbers 461 to 441 by George Pelham from 1902 to 1903.

In the middle of the block is the Second Saint Peter's Lutheran Church at number 435. This neo-Gothic structure was designed in 1911 by Louis Allmendinger who was commissioned to do so by the many German parishioners living in the area. Today it is a reminder of the era when the German ethnic group was among the largest in the neighborhood.

Just to the west of the Second Saint Peter's Lutheran Church along the north side of 140th Street, numbers 412 to 409, are row houses built by William O'Gorman with picturesque façades by William Hornum from 1897 to 1900. They are designed in the Romanesque Revival and Renaissance Revival styles with echoes of Dutch and Flemish architecture, especially the roofs. Across the street, on the south side of 140th Street is another set of row houses, numbers 450 to 406, in the neo-Grecian style that were also erected by architect and builder William O'Gorman, from 1897 to 1902. As increasing numbers of people came into this district, O'Gorman, again assisted by Hornum, erected the apartment house on the north side of the street at number 407.

Walk westward to Willis Avenue and turn left and walk one block south to 139th Street, then walk eastward on 139th Street. Here on both sides of the street, numbers 403 to 445 on the north and numbers 408 to 450 on the south, are two-and-a-half-story red brick neo-Grecian style row houses with cast-iron railings on the stoops, erected from 1887 to 1892 by William O'Gorman.

21 • Cross Willis Avenue, turn left and walk southward on the west side of the street to 138th Street. Then turn right and walk westward along the north side of the street. The shops at street level here constitute a local neighborhood shopping area. Some of them are decorated in red, white, and green, the colors of the Mexican flag, indicating the presence of the newest immigrants into Mott Haven.

Near the center of the block, there is a break in the solid façades of the adjoining buildings. There is a parking lot on the site. At first glance, it appears that a building was once on the property, but that it was torn down to make way for the parking lot. A closer look reveals a different tale. The blank walls on either side of the parking lot are smooth, showing no trace of brick shards or clumps of dried mortar remaining from a destroyed structure. This indicates that no edifice was ever on the site to begin with. Indeed, looking at the long vista behind and in front of the parking lot, not a single building interrupts the unending view. That is because this was the route of the Third Avenue Elevated rapid transit line from the 1880s until 1955. Because the southern end of Third Avenue in The Bronx did not coordinate with the northern end of Third Avenue in Manhattan, the line had to build its own right-of-way through the narrow backyards of apartment houses from the point when it crossed the Harlem River until the point it met Third Avenue in The Bronx at 145th Street. There was a station at 138th Street just over the site of the parking lot entrance. Because the space for it was so narrow, there was a single central platform with the uptown tracks on one side and the downtown tracks on the other.

22 • Continue walking westward to Alexander Avenue. Here the visitor enters the Mott Haven Historic District. In the late nineteenth and early twentieth centuries, Alexander Avenue was considered the Irish Fifth Avenue. Physicians of Irish background lived here and opened their offices on this street. They lined Alexander Avenue with well-designed townhouses and, later, apartment houses. Here also are two churches, an important public library, and the local police stationhouse. To walk along Alexander Avenue is an experience that brings the visitor back to the elegant Bronx of that era.

On the southeast corner of Alexander Avenue at 138th Street is Saint Jerome's Roman Catholic Church. Wealthy parishioners of the time paid for its design by Delhi & Howard in 1898, its construction, and its elaborate decoration. It has two unequal towers at the ends; the one at the corner is taller and more ornate than the other. Although the first parishioners were almost all Irish, the architecture incorporates several elements of Spanish Colonial and Mediterranean styles, which fit in with the largely Puerto Rican and Mexican population of today's Mott Haven. A seated statue of Saint Jerome is placed at the corner facing the intersection. If it is possible to enter, look up at the painted pair of eyes in the ceiling. Originally, the irises were painted the color blue, which accorded with the way many of the Irish residents looked. During a recent restoration of the church, at the request of the current Latino parishioners, the irises of the eyes were repainted brown to fit in with the newer population.

Walk northward along the east side of Alexander Avenue to the block between 139th and 140th Streets. Here are the first, and still the oldest, townhouses in The Bronx. They were erected between 1863 and 1865 in the midst of the Civil War. The real estate developer, Edward Willis, after whom Willis Avenue is named, lived here at number 280.

Continue walking northward on the east side of Alexander Avenue to number 322 at the southeast corner of 141st Street. This ecclesiastical structure designed by Ward & Davis was erected in 1902 as the Alexander Avenue Baptist Church. As the sign above its entrance now proclaims, it is today the Tercera Iglesia Bautista, or Third Baptist Church, and serves a predominantly Spanish-speaking population.

Cross Alexander Avenue and turn left to walk southward along the west side of Alexander Avenue. On the northwest corner of Alexander Avenue and 141st Street (with its entrance at 321 East 141st Street) is the Mott Haven Branch of the New York Public Library. Funded personally by Andrew Carnegie, it was designed by the firm of Babb, Cook & Willard and opened in 1905. This was the first branch of the New York Public Library ever erected in The Bronx. The architectural firm's design using dark red brick with limestone trim echoes the same firm's 1901 design for Carnegie's own mansion on Fifth Avenue and 91st Street in Manhattan, now the Cooper-Hewitt Museum.

Continue walking southward on the west side of Alexander Avenue. Between 140th Street and 139th Street are twelve row houses designed in 1881 by Charles Romeyn. The one at the northwest corner of Alexander Avenue at 139th Street was owned by James L. Wells. Wells was a born Bronxite and engaged in real estate, but he also took an active part in the political life of The Bronx. He served in the New York State Legislature, on the New York City Board of Aldermen, and as New York state treasurer. He actively campaigned for improving the government and the physical infrastructure of New York City, especially of The Bronx. He was a good friend of Theodore Roosevelt. When Roosevelt bolted the Republican Party and tried to run for a third presidential term in 1912 on the Progressive (or Bull Moose) ticket, he came to this townhouse to enlist the support of Wells. Wells, however, remained loyal to the Republican Party and its candidate. Roosevelt never spoke to Wells again.

Continue walking southward on the west side of Alexander Avenue to 138th Street. On the northwest corner at 257 Alexander Avenue is the stationhouse of the 40th Precinct of the New York City Police Department. The building dates from 1924 and was designed by Thomas O'Brien.

To return to Manhattan, take subway train number 6 downtown to Grand Central Station and beyond. The subway entrance is on 138th Street just around the corner to the west of Alexander Avenue.

PART III

Places to Go, Things to See

Museums in The Bronx

The Bronx is the home of a wide variety of museums. Objects on exhibit range from ancient to contemporary art and sculpture, historic photographs, engravings, illustrations, artifacts, objects and furnishings, and exotic animals and plants. Together, they form a cultural treasure trove to be admired, studied, and savored.

The Bartow-Pell Mansion

For details, consult part I, "Pelham Bay Park: The Riviera of New York City."

The Bronx Museum of the Arts

For details, consult part I, "The Bronx Museum of the Arts."

The Bronx Zoo

For details, consult part I, "The Bronx Zoo."

City Island Nautical Museum

For details, consult part II, "City Island: New England in The Bronx," no. 13.

Derfner Judaica Museum

INFORMATION

5961 Palisade Avenue (in the Jacob Reingold Pavilion on the grounds of the Hebrew Home in Riverdale), Bronx, NY 10471

HOURS: Sunday to Thursday, 10:30 A.M. to 4:40 P.M.; closed on federal and Jewish holidays.

ADMISSION: Free.

CONTACTS: Telephone: 718-581-1787; e-mail: JudaicaMuseum@hebrew home.org; website: www.hebrewhome.org.

DIRECTIONS

BY PUBLIC TRANSPORTATION: Take subway train number 1 northbound to 231st Street. Transfer to westbound and northbound bus either Bx7 or Bx10 at West 231st Street and Broadway near the Chase Bank to West 261st Street and Riverdale Avenue. Cross Riverdale Avenue and walk west to Palisade Avenue. Turn left on Palisade Avenue a short distance to the entrance to the grounds of the Hebrew Home. A photo ID is required for entrance to the grounds. Ask the security guard to direct you to the Jacob Reingold Pavilion and the museum.

Alternatively, take the BxM1 express bus on Third Avenue or the BxM2 bus on Sixth Avenue to West 261st Street and Riverdale Avenue. (For schedule information and for pick-up and drop-off points, telephone 511 and say MTA, or visit website: www.mta.info/busco/schedules/.) Cross Riverdale Avenue and walk west to Palisade Avenue. Turn left on Palisade Avenue a short distance to the entrance to the grounds of the Hebrew Home.

BY CAR OR TAXI: Take the Henry Hudson Parkway northbound to 246th Street exit. Continue north on Henry Hudson Parkway East. After passing West 252nd Street, take the left fork and continue northward on Riverdale Avenue to West 261st Street. Turn left on West 261st Street to Palisade Avenue. Turn left on Palisade Avenue and then right into the entrance to the parking lot of the Hebrew Home.

Established in 1982 and occupying its current 5,000-square foot exhibition space since 2009, the Derfner Judaica Museum offers permanent and changing displays of objects relating to Jewish practice, including a set of eighteenth-century German Torah scrolls, a velvet fish-scale embroidered matzah cover from turn-of-the-twentieth-century Jerusalem, and some 800 other gold, silver, brass, pewter, ivory, and wood artifacts, books, and rare embroidered textiles.

Nearby attraction: part I, "Wave Hill and the Mansions of Riverdale."

The Edgar Allan Poe Cottage

For details, consult part I, "The Edgar Allan Poe Cottage: Poverty and Poetry."

The Hall of Fame for Great Americans

For details, consult part I, "The Hall of Fame for Great Americans."

Hebrew Home at Riverdale Museum

INFORMATION

5961 Palisade Avenue (in the Gilbert Pavilion and outdoor sculpture garden on the grounds of the Hebrew Home in Riverdale), Bronx, NY 10471

HOURS: Daily, 10:30 A.M. to 4:40 P.M.

ADMISSION: Free.

CONTACTS: Telephone: 718-581-1596; website: www.hebrewhome.org.

DIRECTIONS

BY PUBLIC TRANSPORTATION: Take subway train number 1 northbound to 231st Street. Transfer to westbound and northbound bus either Bx7 or Bx10 at West 231st Street and Broadway near the Chase Bank to West 261st Street and Riverdale Avenue. Cross Riverdale Avenue and walk west to Palisade Avenue. Turn left on Palisade Avenue a short distance to the entrance to the grounds of the Hebrew Home. A photo ID is required for entrance to the grounds. Ask the security guard to direct you to the Gilbert Pavilion and the museum.

Alternatively, take the BxM1 express bus on Third Avenue or the BxM2 bus on Sixth Avenue to West 261st Street and Riverdale Avenue. Cross Riverdale Avenue and walk west to Palisade Avenue. Turn left on Palisade Avenue a short distance to the entrance to the grounds of the Hebrew Home.

BY CAR OR TAXI: Take the Henry Hudson Parkway northbound to 246th Street exit. Continue north on Henry Hudson Parkway East. After passing West 252nd Street, take the left fork and continue northward on Riverdale Avenue to West 261st Street. Turn left on West 261st Street to Palisade Avenue. Turn left on Palisade Avenue and then right into the entrance to the parking lot of the Hebrew Home.

This museum's permanent collection consists of over 5,000 sculptures, drawings, photographs, prints, decorative arts, and objects from around the world. It includes works by Marc Chagall, Louise Nevelson, Pablo Picasso, Ben Shahn, and Andy Warhol. Displays appealing to children of all ages may be found throughout the halls. Changing exhibitions of works by emerging artists are mounted throughout the year. The broad lawn overlooking a spectacular view of the Hudson River and the New Jersey Palisades beyond form a sculpture garden filled with modern works by noted artists.

Nearby attraction: part I, "Wave Hill and the Mansions of Riverdale."

The Fordham Museum of Greek, Etruscan, and Roman Art

For details, consult part II, "In the Footsteps of Edgar Allan Poe," no. 9.

Maritime Industry Museum

INFORMATION

The Maritime College of the State University of New York, The Maritime Industry Museum at Fort Schuyler, 6 Pennyfield Avenue, Bronx, NY 10465

HOURS: Monday to Saturday, 9:00 A.M. to 4:00 P.M.

ADMISSION: Free.

CONTACTS: Telephone: 718-409-7218; website: www.sunymaritime.edu/ Maritime%20Museum/.

DIRECTIONS

BY PUBLIC TRANSPORTATION: Take subway train number 6 northbound to the Westchester Square station. Transfer on Tremont Avenue at the corner of Westchester Avenue to eastbound bus Bx40 with the destination "Fort Schuyler" to the last stop, the gate of the college. Ask the security guard at the gate for directions to Fort Schuyler and the Maritime Museum.

Alternatively, take the BxM9 express bus on Madison Avenue to the intersection of Pennyfield and Harding Avenue. Walk eastward on Pennyfield Avenue a half mile to the entrance of the college, or transfer to the Bx40 bus with the destination "Fort Schuyler" to the last stop, the gate of the college.

BY CAR OR TAXI: Take the Bruckner Expressway north and follow the signs to the Throgs Neck Bridge. On the approach to the toll plaza, stay in the extreme right lane and exit to the right at the Harding Avenue / Fort Schuyler exit, the last exit before the toll. Make a left at the foot of the ramp, then a quick right onto Harding Avenue to the stop sign at Pennyfield Avenue. Turn left at the stop sign to the end of Pennyfield Avenue and the entrance to the college. There is free parking at the fort.

Located inside Fort Schuyler, a granite fort completed in 1845 to protect the backdoor approaches to New York City on the tip of the Throggs Neck peninsula thrusting into Long Island Sound, the Maritime Industry Museum is the premier museum of its kind in the country. Visitors enter through the fort's sally port to Saint Mary's pentagon, with a flagpole in its center, across to the entrance at the middle of the opposite side. The museum, founded in 1986, has one of the largest maritime history collections in the nation, chronicling the history of seafaring from the time of the Phoenicians to the days of steamship companies and passenger ships. Displayed are paintings, photographs, models of early sailing vessels, clipper ships, and modern vessels, and historic and modern tools and navigation instruments. Portions of the museum are devoted to exhibits illustrating the growth of the port of New York and New Jersey and of several steamship companies.

The Museum of Bronx History

For details, consult part I, "The Valentine-Varian House: A Legacy of the Revolution."

The New York Botanical Garden

For details, consult part I, "The New York Botanical Garden."

New York Yankees Museum

For details, consult part I, "Yankee Stadium."

The Van Cortlandt House Museum

For details, consult part I, "Van Cortlandt Park and the Van Cortlandt House."

Wave Hill

For details, consult part I, "Wave Hill and the Mansions of Riverdale."

Art Galleries in The Bronx

The Bronx is blessed with art galleries that can be found in several of its neighborhoods. Many are intimate galleries; others are larger. Their exhibits vary throughout the year. It is strongly suggested that the visitor contact the art gallery in advance to find out what is currently on exhibit. Listed here are some of the more prominent galleries in the borough.

Bronx Documentary Center

INFORMATION

614 Courtlandt Avenue (at 151st Street), Bronx, NY 10455

HOURS: Thursday and Friday 3:00 P.M. to 7:00 P.M.; Saturday and Sunday 1:00 P.M. to 5:00 P.M.

CONTACTS: Telephone: 716-993-3512; website: bronxdoc.org.

DIRECTIONS

BY PUBLIC TRANSPORTATION: Take subway train number 2 or 5 to the Third Avenue station. Walk along the north side of 149th Street west two blocks to Courtlandt Avenue. Turn right two blocks to 151st Street.

BY CAR OR TAXI: Take the Major Deegan Expressway to the Third Avenue exit. Turn north to 149th Street. Turn left to Courtlandt Avenue and continue to 151st Street. Street parking only.

The Bronx Documentary Center, established in 2011, is located on the ground floor of a landmarked brick building erected in 1882 as a three-story townhouse with a mansard roof. The gallery specializes in exhibitions of documentary photographs, photojournalism, and multimedia presentations. Two or three times a month there are documentary film screenings followed by discussions.

Nearby walking tours: part II, "The Grand Concourse Historic District: Art Deco Delights"; "Marvelous Mott Haven."

Bronx River Art Center Gallery

INFORMATION

TEMPORARY LOCATION DURING RENOVATIONS: 305 East 140th Street (west of Alexander Avenue), Bronx, NY 10454. Permanent location reopens during 2015: 1087 East Tremont Avenue (at West Farms Square east of Boston Road), Bronx, NY 10460.

HOURS: During exhibitions only, Wednesday to Friday 3:00 P.M. to 6:30 P.M.; Saturday 10:00 A.M. to 5:00 P.M.

CONTACTS: Telephone: 718-689-5819; website: www.bronxriverart.org.

DIRECTIONS

BY PUBLIC TRANSPORTATION, TO THE TEMPORARY LOCATION: Take the northbound number 6 subway train to the Third Avenue station at 138th Street. Get off at the Alexander Avenue exit. Walk north on Alexander Avenue for two blocks. Then turn left to the gallery.

BY CAR OR TAXI: Take the Major Deegan Expressway to Third Avenue. Turn right on Third Avenue to 138th Street. Turn left on Alexander Avenue to 140th Street. Turn left on 140th Street to the gallery on your left. Street parking only.

BY PUBLIC TRANSPORTATION, TO THE PERMANENT LOCATION: Take the northbound number 2 or 5 subway train to Tremont Avenue/West Farms Square station. Walk east along the north side of Tremont Avenue to the gallery.

BY CAR OR TAXI: Take the Bruckner Expressway north to exit 49, the Sheridan Expressway (I-95) north to the 177th Street exit. Turn left on 177th Street to Tremont Avenue. Turn left on Tremont Avenue to the gallery on your right. Street parking only.

The Bronx River Art Center Gallery exhibits the work of contemporary artists from around the world.

Nearby attractions: to the temporary location: walking tour in part II, "Marvelous Mott Haven"; to the permanent location: part I, "The Bronx Zoo," West Farms Gate.

Elisa Contemporary Art

INFORMATION

5622 Mosholu Avenue (at the foot of Liebig Avenue), Bronx, NY 10471. Mailing address: 130 Seventh Avenue, Suite 353, New York, NY 10011.

HOURS: Saturday, 11:00 A.M. to 5:00 P.M., and by appointment.

CONTACTS: Telephone: 212-729-4974; e-mail: Lisa@ElisaArt.com.

DIRECTIONS

BY PUBLIC TRANSPORTATION: Take the northbound number 1 subway train to 231st Street. Transfer to either the number Bx7 or Bx10 westbound and northbound bus on 231st Street and Broadway at the side of the Chase Bank. Get off at West 256th Street and Riverdale Avenue. Walk east along West 256th Street one block to Mosholu Avenue. Cross Mosholu Avenue, turn left, and walk one block to the gallery on your right.

Alternatively, take the BxM1 express bus on Madison Avenue or BxM2 express bus on Sixth Avenue to West 256th Street and Riverdale Avenue. (For schedule information and for pick-up and drop-off points, telephone 511 and say MTA, or visit website: www.mta.info/busco/schedules/.) Walk east along West 256th Street one block to Mosholu Avenue. Cross Mosholu Avenue, turn left and walk one block to the gallery on your right.

BY CAR OR TAXI: Take the Henry Hudson Parkway northbound to exit 21, the West 246th Street/250th Street exit. Continue on Henry Hudson Parkway East. At the fork in the road, take the left fork and continue on Riverdale Avenue to West 256th Street. At West 256th Street, turn right one block to Mosholu Avenue. Then turn left along Mosholu Avenue one block to the gallery. Street parking only.

This intimate gallery specializes in exhibitions of works by contemporary artists.

Nearby attraction: part I, "Wave Hill and the Mansions of Riverdale."

Focal Point Art Gallery

For information, consult part II, "City Island: New England in The Bronx," no. 12.

Glyndor Art Gallery

For information, consult part I, "Wave Hill and the Mansions of Riverdale."

Haven Arts Gallery

INFORMATION

50 Bruckner Boulevard (just west of Willis Avenue), Building A, Bronx, NY 10454

HOURS: Every day, noon to 6:00 P.M.

CONTACTS: Telephone: 718-585-5763; website: www.havenarts.org.

DIRECTIONS

BY PUBLIC TRANSPORTATION: Take the northbound number 6 subway train to the Third Avenue station at 138th Street. Get off at the Alexander Avenue exit. Walk south on Alexander Avenue beneath the overpass of the elevated Major Deegan Expressway to Bruckner Boulevard. Turn left to the gallery.

BY CAR OR TAXI: Take the Major Deegan Expressway to Third Avenue. Turn south at Third Avenue. Bear right and do not go up the ramp. Turn left beneath the ramp onto Bruckner Boulevard to the gallery. Street parking only.

Founded in 2004, the Haven Arts Gallery exhibits primarily the works of local artists in this newly established artists' neighborhood.

Nearby walking tour: part II, "Marvelous Mott Haven."

Krasdale Art Gallery

INFORMATION

400 Food Center Drive, Bronx, NY 10474

HOURS: By appointment only.

CONTACTS: Telephone: 718-585-5763; website: www.havenarts.org.

DIRECTIONS

BY PUBLIC TRANSPORTATION: Take uptown number 6 subway train to Hunts Point Avenue. Transfer to the eastbound Bx6 bus on Hunts Point

Avenue at the corner of Bruckner Boulevard. Ask the bus driver to let you off at the closest point on Food Center Drive to Krasdale Foods at 400 Food Center Drive. Then walk a short distance to the entrance.

BY CAR OR TAXI: Take the Bruckner Expressway northbound and merge onto Bruckner Boulevard. Continue north on Bruckner Boulevard beneath the elevated Bruckner Expressway for one to two miles to Hunts Point Avenue. Turn right onto Hunts Point Avenue to the intersection with Halleck Street and Food Center Drive. Make a slight right onto Halleck Street to Ryawa Avenue. Turn left at Ryawa Avenue onto Food Center Drive to 400 Food Center Drive. Turn right to the parking lot on the site.

Established in 1986, the Krasdale Art Gallery is located in the corporate offices of a food distribution company. It specializes in exhibits of modern and contemporary art in all media by artists from all geographical areas. Each exhibit is designed around a theme, a collection, or a geographical area where the artists live and work.

Lehman College Art Gallery

For information, consult part II, "Valentine to Poe: A Tour of Cultural Discovery," no. 13.

Longwood Art Gallery

INFORMATION

Hostos Community College, 450 Grand Concourse (at 149th Street), Bronx, NY 10451

HOURS: Monday, Tuesday, Thursday, and Friday 10:00 A.M. to 5:00 P.M.; closed Wednesday, Saturday, and Sunday.

CONTACTS: Telephone: 718-518-6728; e-mail: longwood@bronxarts.org.

DIRECTIONS

BY PUBLIC TRANSPORTATION: Take subway train number 2, 4, or 5 to the 149th Street/Grand Concourse station. The gallery is on the southeast corner of the intersection.

BY CAR OR TAXI: Take the Major Deegan Expressway to the Grand Concourse exit. Continue north on the Grand Concourse to 149th Street. Street parking only.

The Longwood Art Gallery presents solo and group exhibitions mostly by Bronx or Bronx-based artists in various media who address a variety of contemporary issues. It also hosts programs of open dialogue on arts and culture.

Nearby walking tour: part II, "The Grand Concourse Historic District: Art Deco Delights."

Poe Park Visitor Center Gallery

For details, consult part II, "In the Footsteps of Edgar Allan Poe," no. 2.

Nearby attraction: part I, "The Edgar Allan Poe Cottage: Poverty and Poetry."

Starving Artist Art Gallery

For information, consult part II, "City Island: New England in The Bronx," no. 22.

Professional Musical and Theatrical Performance Venues

The Bronx has venues for theatrical plays, musicals, opera, classical and popular music concerts, ballet and modern dance, some performed by internationally renowned artists and ensembles. It is strongly suggested that the visitor contact the theater in advance to discover the current performance schedule and the availability and the price of tickets.

The Lehman College Center for the Performing Arts

For details, consult part II, "Valentine to Poe: A Tour of Cultural Discovery," no. 13.

Live from the Edge Theater

INFORMATION

The Point Community Development Corporation, 940 Garrison Avenue, Bronx, NY 10474

CONTACTS: Telephone: 718-542-4139; website: www.thepoint.org.

DIRECTIONS

BY PUBLIC TRANSPORTATION: Take subway train number 6 northbound to Hunts Point Avenue. On Hunts Point Avenue, walk eastward beneath the Bruckner Expressway overpass one block beyond to Garrison Avenue. Turn right on Garrison Avenue and walk one block to Manida Street. Turn left on Manida Street. The entrance to The Point and the theater is a few steps in from Garrison Avenue on Manida Street.

BY CAR OR TAXI: Take Bruckner Expressway northbound and merge onto Bruckner Boulevard. Continue north on Bruckner Boulevard beneath the elevated Bruckner Expressway for one to two miles to Barretto Street. Turn right onto Barretto Street for one block to Garrison Avenue. The entrance to The Point and the theater is a few steps in from Garrison Avenue on Manida Street. Street parking only.

Performances in this 100-seat black box theater have won Obie and Bessie awards for edgy musical, dance, and theatrical works for audiences of all ages.

Pregones Theater

INFORMATION

571 Walton Avenue (just north of 149th Street), Bronx, NY 10451
CONTACTS: Telephone: 718-585-1202; e-mail: info@pregones.org.

DIRECTIONS

BY PUBLIC TRANSPORTATION: Take subway train number 2, 4, or 5 to the 149th Street/Grand Concourse station. Walk one short block west to Walton Avenue. Turn right to the Pregones Theater.

BY CAR OR TAXI: Take the Major Deegan Expressway to the Grand Concourse exit. Continue north on the Grand Concourse to 149th Street. Turn left to Walton Avenue. Walk to the theater. Street parking only.

The Pregones Theater specializes in presenting new plays performed in either English or Spanish.

Nearby walking tour: part II, "The Grand Concourse Historic District: Art Deco Delights."

Wave Hill Armor Hall

The Gothic Revival style wing of the Wave Hill mansion known as Armor Hall provides the setting for chamber music concerts.

For details, consult part I, "Wave Hill and the Mansions of Riverdale."

Woolworth Chapel of Woodlawn Cemetery

The Woolworth Chapel near Woodlawn Cemetery's Jerome Avenue entrance is the venue for varied concerts ranging from jazz to popular songs to classical usually connected to the composers interred in the cemetery.

For details, consult part I, "Woodlawn Cemetery: Beauty for Eternity."

Tours and Events

Visitors to The Bronx can enjoy special events throughout the year. These range from displays of ethnic pride such as in the Bronx Puerto Rican Day Parade, Bronx Dominican Day Parade, or the Bronx Saint Patrick's Day Parade; to street fairs offering merchandise, food, and hip-hop music; to local theatrical performances; to ethnic festivals that vary from Greek to Irish to Italian to Hispanic; to special tours by foot, bicycle, or trolley featuring art sites, restaurants, historic neighborhoods, or the natural world; to athletic events such as track meets and tennis tournaments.

These events are scheduled at specific dates all year round. Perhaps the largest single concentration of Bronx events occurs in May during Bronx Week, a celebration of the borough's ethnic diversity, commerce, visual and performing arts, and legacy to the wider world. A highlight is the induction into the Bronx Walk of Fame at the Bronx County Building of selected Bronx residents whose national and global achievements encompass entertainment, science, literature, and other fields. This is followed by a massive parade of varied groups from all over The Bronx held on Mosholu Parkway.

Visitors coming to The Bronx at other times still have a large number of events they can attend to savor the cultures of the people who are proud to call The Bronx their home. The precise dates when the events and tours are scheduled vary from year to year. Check the following sources of information to discover when and where these events are programmed.

The Bronx Tourism Council

CONTACTS: Telephone: 718-590-3518; website: www.ilovethebronx.com.

The Bronx Tourism Council maintains a calendar of events occurring throughout the borough ranging from Bronx Week, the Tour de Bronx bicycle tour, the Bronx Salsa Fest, bus and trolley tours, and more. Its website is the most comprehensive for event information.

The Bronx Council on the Arts

CONTACTS: Telephone: 718-931-9500; website: www.bronxarts.org.

The Bronx Council on the Arts provides information about arts and culture tours by the Bronx trolley, art exhibits, and a calendar of events relating to the visual and performing arts.

The Bronx County Historical Society

CONTACTS: Telephone: 718-881-8900; website: www.bronxhistoricalsociety .org.

The Bronx County Historical Society conducts neighborhood walking tours, exhibits, and special events throughout the year.

The New York City Department of Parks and Recreation

CONTACTS: Telephone: 212-447-2029; website: www.nycgovparks.org.

The city's Parks Department has information about free and low-cost outdoor concerts, athletic events, exhibits, and bird-watching and nature tours occurring in parks throughout The Bronx.

Where to Stay

There are an increasing number of hotels opening in The Bronx. Why stay in one of them?

First, Bronx hotels are less expensive than those in Manhattan. Then, too, staying in The Bronx places the visitor nearer to many of the family-friendly attractions, including Yankee Stadium, the Bronx Zoo, the New York Botanical Garden, and the other fascinating points of interest found in this guide. Attractions in nearby Manhattan are only minutes away via efficient subway connections.

Andrew Freedman Home

INFORMATION

1125 Grand Concourse (near 167th Street), Bronx, NY 10452

AVERAGE RATES: $130.00 to $250.00 per night.

CONTACT: Telephone: 718-588-8200.

DIRECTIONS

BY PUBLIC TRANSPORTATION: Take subway train letter D (B in rush hours only) to 167th Street. Get off at the McClellan Street exit. The building is on the west side of the Grand Concourse at the south side of McClellan Street.

BY CAR OR TAXI: Take the Major Deegan Expressway to the eastbound Cross Bronx Expressway to the Jerome Avenue exit. At Jerome Avenue, make a short right turn to Mount Eden Parkway, then turn left again onto Mount Eden Parkway to the Grand Concourse. Turn right on the Grand Concourse to McClellan Street. Street parking only.

ACCOMMODATIONS AND FACILITIES

A portion of this landmarked building has been converted into a ten-room hotel with flat-screen TVs in the rooms and a grand piano in the lobby. Be sure to call in advance to check if accommodations are available.

Nearby attractions: part I, "The Bronx Museum of the Arts"; "The Bronx County Building: The Art of Democracy"; walking tour, part II, "The Grand Concourse Historic District: Art Deco Delights."

The Bronx Opera House Hotel

INFORMATION

436 East 149th Street (between Third and Brook Avenues), Bronx, NY 10455

AVERAGE RATES: $100.00 to $140.00 per night.

CONTACTS: Telephone: 718-407-2800 or 718-407-2100; e-mail: reservations@operahousehotel.com.

DIRECTIONS

BY PUBLIC TRANSPORTATION: Take subway train number 2 or 5 to the Third Avenue and 149th Street station. Walk one block east.

BY CAR OR TAXI: Take the Major Deegan Expressway to Third Avenue exit. Turn north onto Third Avenue to its junction with 147th Street and Bergen Avenue. Make a gentle right turn onto Bergen Avenue to 149th Street. Turn right on 149th Street to the hotel. Limited free parking is available on a first-come, first-served basis. Nearby parking lots charge $10.00 per night.

ACCOMMODATIONS AND FACILITIES

This new, luxury boutique hotel is in the spot where Harry Houdini, the Marx Brothers, John and Lionel Barrymore, George Burns, and others performed before the venue's recent conversion to a hotel. The hotel's décor includes historic paintings, playbills, and memorabilia from the original Bronx Opera House. Guests receive a complimentary breakfast and afternoon tea and coffee, complimentary Crunch Gym Fitness, free wi-fi and newspapers.

Nearby walking tours: part II, "The Grand Concourse Historic District: Art Deco Delights"; "Marvelous Mott Haven."

Howard Johnson Inn Yankee Stadium

INFORMATION

1300 Sedgwick Avenue (at 167th Street), Bronx, NY 10452

AVERAGE RATES: $179.00 per night. Children age sixteen and under stay free with an adult.

CONTACT: Telephone: 1-800-221-5801 or 718-293-1100.

DIRECTIONS

BY PUBLIC TRANSPORTATION: Take subway train number 4 or letter D (letter B in rush hours only) to the 161st Street/Yankee Stadium station. Transfer to the east- and northbound Bx13 bus to Ogden Avenue at 167th Street. Walk west one long block to Sedgwick Avenue.

BY CAR OR TAXI: Take the Major Deegan Expressway to exit 5 at 157th Street. Continue straight northward toward 161st Street. Turn right toward Sedgwick Avenue and continue straight onto Sedgwick Avenue, keeping the expressway on your left, to the inn at 167th Street. Free parking.

ACCOMMODATIONS AND FACILITIES

This newly refurbished inn offers free wi-fi, rooms equipped with refrigerators, a microwave oven in the lobby, and free continental breakfast.

Nearby attraction: part I, "Yankee Stadium."

Howard Johnson Express Inn Bronx

INFORMATION

1922 Boston Road (just south of Tremont Avenue), Bronx, NY 10460

AVERAGE RATES: $155.00 per night. Children age seventeen and under stay free with an adult.

CONTACT: Telephone: 1-800-221-5801 or 718-589-2222.

DIRECTIONS

BY PUBLIC TRANSPORTATION: Take subway train number 2 or 5 to the Tremont Avenue/West Farms Square station. Take a short walk to the junction of Tremont Avenue and Boston Road, then another short walk south on Boston Road to the inn.

BY CAR OR TAXI: Take the Bruckner Expressway north to exit 49, the Sheridan Expressway (I-95), north to the 177th Street exit. Turn left on

177th Street to Tremont Avenue. Turn left on Tremont Avenue to Boston Road. Turn left on Boston Road and then make a quick right to continue on Boston Road to the inn. Free parking.

ACCOMMODATIONS AND FACILITIES

Rooms are equipped with refrigerators and microwave ovens. There is free wi-fi and free continental breakfast.

Nearby attraction: part I, "The Bronx Zoo," West Farms Gate.

Ramada Bronx

INFORMATION

1000 Baychester Avenue (near Coop City Boulevard and Interstate 95, the Bruckner Expressway/New England Thruway), Bronx, NY 10475

AVERAGE RATES: $160.00 per night. Children age seventeen and under stay free with an accompanying adult.

CONTACT: Telephone: 718-862-2000.

DIRECTIONS

BY PUBLIC TRANSPORTATION: Take subway train number 5 to the Gunhill Road station. Transfer to eastbound Bx38 bus to nearest stop at the corner of Coop City Boulevard and Baychester Avenue.

Alternatively, take BxM7 express bus on Madison Avenue to Coop City Boulevard at Carver Loop (For schedule information and for pick-up and drop-off points, telephone 511 and say MTA, or visit website: www.mta .info/busco/schedules/.) Walk west to the corner of Coop City Boulevard and Baychester Avenue, and turn right to the inn.

BY CAR OR TAXI: Take I 95 (Bruckner Expressway/New England Thruway) north to exit 13, Connor Street. Turn right to Tillotson Avenue. Turn right onto Tillotson Avenue and continue about a half mile to Coop City Boule-vard and make a U-turn to the inn on your right. Free parking.

ACCOMMODATIONS AND FACILITIES

Free continental breakfast, free access to nearby gym, free wi-fi, and refrigerators in rooms.

Nearby attractions: part I, "Pelham Bay Park: The Riviera of New York City"; walking tour, part II, "City Island: New England in The Bronx."

Index

31 Carroll Street, 106
40th Precinct Stationhouse, 167
84–86 Schofield Street, 106
90 Schofield Street, 106
95 Pell Place, 108
135th Street, 156
136th Street, 160–161
137th Street, 156, 162
138th Street, 156, 161, 164, 166
139th Street, 162, 164, 166
140th Street, 163–164, 166
141 Pilot Street, 108
141st Street, 163, 166
149th Street, 117, 129–130, 137, 181, 184, 189
150 Carroll Street, 105
150th Street, 129
153rd Street, 127–129
156th Street, 128
158th Street, 47, 126–128
159th Street, 126–127
161st Street, 42, 46, 124–126
163rd Street, 124–125
164th Street, 123–125
165th Street, 93, 122–123
166th Street, 120–122
167th Street, 117, 119–120, 168, 190
175 Belden Street, 109
183rd Street, 115
186th Street, 114
187th Street, 114, 116
284 City Island Avenue, 105
295 City Island Avenue, 104

Acconci, Vito, 93
Adams, Herbert, 82
Adams, John, 61, 81
Adams, John Quincy, 82
Adams Place, 115
Addams, Jane, 84
Agassiz, Louis, 80
Aileen B. Ryan Recreational Complex, 71
Aitkin, Robert, 81
Albanians, 112
Alda, Alan, 149
Alderbrook, 30
Alderbrook Road, 30
Alexander Avenue, 159, 165–167, 178
Alexander Avenue Baptist Church, 166
Allen Shandler Recreation Area, 36
Allmendinger, Louis, 164
Allyson, June, 152
Altschul House, 88
American Boy (sculpture), 72
American Bridge Company 158
American Indians, 10, 32, 39, 66, 98, 109, 154. *See also* Stockbridge Indians
American Revolution, 1, 33, 39, 41, 48, 59, 60, 66, 71, 98–99, 141
America's Cup, 88–89, 99
Andrews, William Loring, 91
Anna Bliss Titanic Memorial, 57
Andrew Freedman Home, 120, 188–189
Anthony Campagna Estate, 27–28
Anthony, Susan B., 84
Appleton, Thomas H., 25
Archipenko, Alexander, 54
architecture, 57, 105–106, 108, 119, 136, 164–165. *See also specific architectural styles*
Armour, Herman Ossian, 59

Arquitectonica, 93
art, 25–27, 41, 42, 46, 90, 92–94, 114,
	117, 120–121, 121, 129–130, 137, 150,
	172, 173—174, 186. *See also* murals;
	sculpture
Art Deco, 14, 42–43, 45–47, 70, 118,
	120–121, 123–129, 146–147
art galleries, 100, 103–104, 106, 121, 140,
	145–146, 177–182
Arthur Avenue, 17, 112–116, 162
Arthur Avenue Market, 115
Art Nouveau, 54
Ashley, the, 125
Astor, Vincent, 109
Audubon, John James, 79
Awakenings (film), 100

Babb, Cook & Willard, 166
Bainbridge Avenue, 34, 37, 61, 132–133
Baker, Bryant, 80, 83
Baltrop, Alvin, 93
Bancroft, George, 86
Bangladeshis, 146
barbecuing, 41, 75. *See also* dining;
	picnicking; restaurants
Baron de Hirsch Fund, 161
Barrymore, John, 189
Barrymore, Lionel, 189
Barthe, Richmond, 81
Bartók, Béla, 24
Barton, Clara, 87
Bartow-Pell Mansion, 53, 64, 67, 69, 74;
	Carriage House, 64, 74
baseball, 1, 18–21, 31, 34, 36, 67, 72, 120,
	128, 137, 149
basketball, 137
basketball courts, 36, 67, 72, 128
Batman, 146
Baum, Dwight James, 26, 28
Bayes, Nora, 54
Bay Street, 103
Beach, Chester, 79–80, 84
Beach Street, 102
Bedford Park Boulevard, 137–138
Beecher, Henry Ward, 85
Belden, William, 109
Belden Point, 109
Bell, Alexander Graham, 79
Beller, William C., 61

Beller, William F., 61
Belmont, 111–116
Belmont, Alva Smith Vanderbilt, 85
Belmont, August, 135
Belmont Avenue, 113–114
Belmont Stakes, 135
Benedict XVI (pope), 20
Berlin, Irving, 4
Berra, Yogi, 19
Bertine, Edward, 160–161
Bertine Block Historic District, 160–161
bicycling, 36, 67, 186–187
Bingham, Emma S., 80
Birdsall, George W., 136
bird-watching, 5, 7, 31, 37, 68, 72, 187
Birnbaum, Philip, 123
bison, 12, 14, 16
Blacks, 19, 118, 134, 156
Blow, Kurtis, 142
Bly, Nelly. *See* Seaman, Elizabeth
	Cochran
Board of Trade building, 156
boating, 70, 97–98, 102–103, 106–107
Boatyard Condominium (City Island),
	106
bocce courts, 36
Bolton, John, 108
Bolton, William, 108
Boone, Daniel, 83
Booth, Edwin 84
Booth, Samuel H., 103
Borgatti's Ravioli and Egg Noodles, 114
botanical gardens, 5–11, 25–26, 64, 175
Bowne Street, 103
boxing, 19, 21
Brandeis, Louis Dembits, 87
Brescia, Bernardo Fort, 93
Breuer, Marcel, 88–89, 140
Brewster, George T., 83
British, 25, 33, 38, 41, 48, 60, 66, 71,
	88–89, 99, 134–135, 151, 162. *See also*
	English
Britton, Nathaniel Lord, 7
Bronck, Jonas, 48, 154, 159
Bronx Antiques District, 155, 159–160
Bronx borough president, 44, 65, 102,
	135
Bronx Chamber of Commerce, 158
Bronx Civic Center, 42

Bronx Community College 76, 79, 87–91; Bergrisch Lecture Hall, 88–89; Butler Hall, 88; cannon, 89; Colston Hall, 88; Community Hall, 88; flagpole, 88–89; Gould Memorial Library, 78, 87; Hall of Languages, 77; Hall of Philosophy, 77–78; Mac-Cracken Hall, 90–91; Meister Hall, 89; North Hall and Library, 90; South Hall, 89; Technology II, 89

Bronx Council on the Arts, 187

Bronx County Building, 42–48, 93, 126, 186

Bronx county clerk, 45

Bronx County Historical Society, 50, 61–62, 69, 187

Bronx County Society for the Prevention of Cruelty to Children, 121

Bronx County Supreme Court, 42, 45, 48

Bronx Documentary Center, 177–178

Bronx Dominican Day Parade, 186

Bronx Equestrian Center, 69–70

Bronx General Post Office, 129–130

Bronx High School of Science, 89, 136–137

Bronx Housing Courthouse, 121

Bronx Library Center, 147–148

Bronx Museum of the Arts, 92–94, 122, 171

BronxNet, 140

Bronx Opera House Hotel, 189

Bronx Park, 6–7, 14, 34, 112, 118, 133

Bronx public administrator, 45

Bronx Puerto Rican Day Parade, 186

Bronx River, 5–7, 12, 62, 159

Bronx River Art Center Gallery, 178

Bronx River Soldier (sculpture), 62

Bronx Saint Patrick's Day Parade, 186

Bronx Salsa Fest, 187

Bronx surrogate, 45

Bronx Tourism Council, 187

Bronx Victory Garden, 72

Bronx Walk of Fame, 126, 186

Bronx Week, 186–187

Bronx Works, 121

Bronx YM-YWHA, 121

Bronx Zoo, 12–17, 73, 112, 171; African Plains, 16; Astor Court, 14; Baboon Reserve, 16; Bear Den, 16; Butterfly Zone, 17; camel ride, 15; Children's Zoo, 16; Congo Gorilla Forest, 12, 15; Himalayan Highlands, 16; Jungle World, 16; Madagascar!, 12, 16; Mouse House, 17; Rainey Gate, 14; Rare Animal Range, 16; Reptile House, 16; Sea Lion Pool, 16; Tiger Mountain, 12, 15; Wild Asia, 12, 15; World of Birds, 16; Zucker Bug Carousel, 15

Brook Avenue, 162–163

Brooks, Phillips, 85

Brown Place, 161

Brownson, Orestes, 151

Bruckner Boulevard, 72–73, 158–160, 180

Brutalism, 88–89

Bryant, William Cullen, 86

Bulova, Arde, 55

Bunche, Ralph, 55

Burbank, Luther, 87

Burns, George, 189

business incubator, 156–157

Calder, A. Stirling, 79, 82

Cambodians, 146

Campagna, Anthony, 27–28

canoeing, 70

Cantinflas, 161

Carey, Harry, 54, 100

Cardinal Hayes High School, 129

Carlin, George, 129

Carll, David, 99, 108

Carnegie, Andrew, 7, 87, 166

Carrière & Hastings, 54

Carrion, Adolfo Jr., 102

Carroll Street, 105–106

Carter, Granville W., 72

Carver, George Washington, 81

Caryl Field, 36

Cass Gallagher Nature Trail, 37

Castro-Blanco, Piscioneri & Feder, 93

Cat Briar Island, 70

Catherine Scott Walkway (City Island), 102

Catlett, Elizabeth, 93

Catt, Carrie Chapman, 55

Cedars, the, 127

Centre Street, 107

Ceracchi, Giussepi, 82
Chagall, Marc, 174
Chandler, Elizabeth Gordon, 81
Channing, William Ellery, 85
Charles Kreymborg & Son, 128
Choate, Rufus, 82
Christ Church, Riverdale, 27
Churchill, Winston, 135
Ciardullo-Ehmann, 162
Ciccarone, Vincent, 113
Ciccarone Playground, 113
Citizens Advice Bureau, 121
City Island, 75, 97–110
City Island (film), 100
City Island Avenue, 100–110
City Island Bridge, 102
City Island Channel, 102
City Island Circle, 71
City Island Memorial Mural, 105
City Island Nautical Museum, 104, 171
City Island Road, 69
City Island shipyards, 99, 106, 107, 108
City Island's skyscraper, 105
City Island Theater Group, 109
City Island Yacht Club, 108
Civic Fame (sculpture), 46
Civic Government (sculpture), 46
Civil War, 47, 54, 62, 83, 85, 99, 103, 122,
    127, 157, 163, 166
Clamdiggers, 100
Claremont Park, 34
Classical Revival style, 121
Clark, Allan, 86
Clark, Mary Higgins, 149
Clark, William A., 57
Classic Playground (Van Cortlandt
    Park), 37, 39
Clay, Henry, 81
Clemens, Samuel Langhorne, 86. See also
    Twain, Mark
Cleveland, Grover, 82
Clock Tower Building, 159
Clooney, George, 146
Clooney, Rosemary, 146
Cohan, George M., 54
Colonial Revival style, 122–123, 125
Columbus, Christopher, 115
concerts, 5, 10, 20–21, 26, 29, 41, 59, 64,
    74, 139, 183–185, 187

Concourse Plaza, 42, 44, 124
Concourse Plaza Hotel, 125–126
Concourse Rehabilitation and Nursing
    Center, 122
Cooper, James Fenimore, 85
Cooper, Peter, 84
Coronet Blue (television series), 100
Corsa, Andrew, 151
Crausman, Israel L., 125
Crescent Street, 115
cricket fields, 31, 36
Crimi Road, 72
cross-country race course, 35, 39
Croton Aqueduct, 33–34, 38, 137
Croton Woods, 38
Crotona Park, 34
Crotona Parkway, 34
Cruz, Celia, 54
Cullen, Countee, 54
Cushman, Charlotte Saunders, 84

dance performances, 5, 10, 26, 183–184
Darwin, Charles, 25
Dattner Architects, 147
D'Auria, John, 115
D'Auria-Murphy Square, 115
David Farragut building, 122
Davidson, Jo, 83
David Todd & Associates, 139
Davis, Miles, 54
Day, Clarence, 57
Dean, Bashford, 26
Deegan, William Francis, 158
Delhi & Howard, 165
Delmour, Lawrence, 103
Delmour Point, 103
De Niro, Robert, 100
Derfner Judaica Museum, 172
DeWitt Clinton High School, 137, 146
DeYoung and Moskowitz, 140
Dillerwood Apartments, 127
Dillon, Sidney, 55
DiMaggio, Joe, 19, 125
dining, 11, 17, 22, 27, 41, 69, 75, 116, 130,
    143, 152. See also barbecuing; picnick-
    ing; restaurants
Dion and the Belmonts, 113
Ditmars Street, 103
Dodge, Cleveland, 29–30

Dodge Grace, 29
Dodge, William E., 29, 55
Dominicans, 155, 186
Dominick's restaurant, 116
Dowling, Andrew Jackson, 30
Downey, Juan, 93
Dunn, Thomas, 123
Dunne, Finley Peter, 64
Durant, William, 57
Dutch, 98, 109, 154, 159, 164

Eads, James Buchanan, 80
Eastchester Bay, 68, 103
East River, 56, 99, 107, 109
Eden, Anthony, 26
Ederle, Gertrude, 54
Edgar Allan Poe Cottage, 50–53, 131, 143, 145, 147, 149, 173
Edison, Thomas Alva, 81
Edwards, Gus, 54
Edwards, Jonathan, 85
Effect of Good Administration (sculpture), 47
Egyptian Revival style, 54
Elisa Contemporary Art, 179
Elizabeth, empress of Austria, 42–43
Elizabeth, Queen Mother, 26
Ellett, Thomas Harlen, 129
Ellington, Duke, 54
Emerson, Ralph Waldo, 86
English 57, 98. *See also* British
Enrico Fermi Cultural Center, 114
Estay Piano Company, 159
Evans, Rudolph, 82, 86
events, 5, 7, 10, 15 , 21, 26, 36, 48, 58, 62, 64, 68–69, 72, 93, 107–109, 125, 139, 146, 186–187
Executive Towers, 123

Fahlstöm, Oyvind, 93
Farragut, David, 54, 56, 122
Feldman, Hyman J., 128
Felson, Jacob M., 120, 128
Ferraro, Geraldine, 149
Finger, Bill, 146
Fish Building, 120
fishing, 36–37, 66, 68, 98–99, 102, 109
Fjelde, Paul, 81

Flagg, James Montgomery, 54
Flanagan, John, 80
Flemish style, 164
Focal Point Art Gallery, 103–104, 179
Foch, Ferdinand, 89
football, 20–21, 37, 73, 133, 137, 149
Ford, Whitey, 125
Fordham, Orrin, 99
Fordham Museum of Greek, Etruscan, and Roman Art, 150, 174
Fordham Plaza, 148
Fordham Road, 14, 91, 148, 152
Fordham Station, 52, 91, 148–149
Fordham Street, 103–105; Fordham Street Pier, 104
Fordham University, 52, 144, 149–152; Keating Hall, 151–152; Saint John's Residence Hall, 151; University Church, 150–151; Walsh Library, 149–150; William Spain Seismic Observatory, 152
Foster, Stephen Collins, 83
Fort Number Eight, 89
Fort Schuyler, 174–175
Frank Kelly Field (Van Cortlandt Park), 36
Franklin, Benjamin, 81
Franz Sigel Park, 127–128
Fraser, James Earl, 78, 83–84
Fraser, Laura Gardin, 84
Freedman, Andrew, 120
French, 45, 60, 89, 151
French, Daniel Chester, 64, 78, 85, 87
French style, 86, 105, 107, 120, 149
Friedlander, Joseph H., 45, 120
Frisch, Frankie, 54, 149
Fulton, Robert, 80

Garfield, John, 152
Gates, John Wayne "Bet a Million," 55
Gatje, Robert F., 88, 140
Gaynor, William J., 156
Gehrig, Lou, 19, 27, 126
Georgian style, 26, 59, 104
Gerard Stuyvesant (ferryboat), 107
Germans, 44, 127, 159. *See also* Hessians
Gibbs, Josiah Willard, 80
Ginsbern, Horace, 120, 123
Girls Club of New York, 121

Glick, Elliot, 106
Glinsky, Vincent, 81
Gloria (film), 126
Glover, Colonel John, 66, 71
Glover's Rock, 68
Glyndor Art Gallery, 25, 180
Glyndor II, 26
golf courses, 31, 34, 37–38, 64, 66, 68–69
Gomez, Lefty, 125
Goose Creek Marsh, 69
Gorgas, William Crawford, 80
Gothic Revival style, 29, 30, 103, 184
Gould, Jay, 55, 78
Gould, Helen, 78
Goulden, Joseph S., 137
Goulden Avenue, 137, 141
Grace Episcopal Church, 108; Adoration
    of the Magi window, 108; Trial of
    Christ window, 108
Grafly, Charles, 80–81, 85
Graham, Billy, 20
Grand Concourse, 44, 46–47, 72, 93,
    117–130, 134, 136, 142–143, 145, 181,
    188
Grant, Ulysses Simpson, 56, 83
Grignola, John, 62
Grimes, Frances, 67, 85
Gray, Asa, 80
Greek Revival style, 54, 74, 104–106,
    150, 163
Greeks, 150, 174, 186
Greyston, 29
Gronenberg & Leuchtag, 122
Gruppe, Karl H., 83
Guastavino tiles, 78, 90

Hall of Fame for Great Americans,
    76–87, 90, 173
Hall of Fame Terrace, 90
Hamilton, Alexander, 82
Hampton, Lionel, 54
Hancock, Walter Kirtland, 82–83
handball courts, 34, 37, 69
Handy, W. C., 54
Harlem Bridge, 158
Harlem River, 19, 77–76, 88–89, 116,
    134, 141, 155, 158, 165
Harlem Yacht Club, 103
Harris Park, 137

Hart Island, 104
Hartland Schist, 70
Hauben, David, 90
Hauser, John, 161
Hausle, Max, 45
Havana Café, 75
Haven Arts Gallery, 180
Hawkins, Leonard Hillson, 105
Hawkins Street, 104
Hawkins Street Park, 104–105
Hawthorne, Nathaniel, 86
Hearst, William Randolph, 109
Hebrew Home at Riverdale Museum,
    173–174
Heinrich Heine–Lorelei Fountain, 43, 124
Heins and LaFarge, 15
Heintz, Louis J., statue of, 44, 124
Hell Gate, 99
Henry, Joseph, 80
Henry, Patrick, 82
Hepburn, Katharine, 100, 103
Herbert, Victor, 54
Heritage Field, 21
Herter, Christian Archibald, 55
Herter, Ernst, 43
Hessians, 33, 38, 60. *See also* Germans
Hewlett, James Monroe, 48
High Pumping Station, 136
hiking trails, 31, 34, 37–38, 69
hockey, 21, 142
Hoe, Richard March, 163
Hoerbst, Hans, 85
Hoffman, Malvina, 61, 83
Holmes, Oliver Wendell, 86
Holmes, Oliver Wendell Jr., 83
Hopkins, Mark, 85
Hornaday, William, 14
Hornum, William, 164
horseback riding, 31, 35, 38, 64, 69
Hostos Community College, 130
Houdon, Jean-Antoine, 80–81
Howard, Cecil, 80
Howard Johnson Express Inn Bronx,
    190–191
Howard Johnson Inn Yankee Stadium,
    190
Howe, Elias, 79
Howe, Sir William, 33, 41
Howell, Harry T., 161

Hudnut, Richard, 55
Hudson River, 23, 25, 27–28, 174
Huggins, Miller, 125
Hughes Avenue, 114
Humphreys, Albert, 86
Hunter College in The Bronx, 137–139, 141
Hunter Island, 69–70
Hunter Island Marine Zoology and Geology Sanctuary, 70
Huntington, Anna Hyatt, 14, 54, 80
Huntington, Archer Milton, 72–73
Huntington, Collis P., 55
Huntington Woods, 72–73
Hutchinson River, 68, 71
Huxley, Thomas, 25

I Am Legend (film), 142
ice skating, 31, 35, 39, 142
Indian Field (Van Cortlandt Park), 33, 38
Irish, 24, 34, 42, 114, 118, 153–154, 156, 165, 169, 186
Irving, Washington, 86
Italianate style, 106, 108
Italians, 28, 36, 100, 111–116, 118, 134, 186
Italian Villa style, 108–109

Jack's Bait and Tackle, 98, 102
Jackson, Andrew, 82
Jackson, Thomas Jonathan "Stonewall," 83
Jack's Rock, 107
Jacobs, Harry Allan, 120
Jefferson, Thomas, 81, 162
Jehovah's Witnesses, 20
Jennewien, C. Paul, 83
Jerome, Jennie, 135
Jerome, Leonard W., 134–135
Jerome Avenue, 34, 36–37, 39–41, 58, 134–137, 142, 160, 185
Jerome Park Reservoir, 134–137, 141
Jerome Park Villa Site Company, 34
Jerome-Woodlawn line, 135, 142
Jeter, Derek, 19
Jewish War Veterans, 63
Jews, 19, 43–44, 118, 155, 161
J. L. Mott Iron Works, 158
John Ericsson building, 122
John Kieran Trail, 37

John Muir Trail, 37–38
John Paul II (pope), 20
John Purroy Mitchel Houses, 156
Jolie, Angelina, 100
Jones, John Paul, 83
Jones, Thomas Hudson, 83
Joyce Kilmer Park, 42–44, 124
Judge Judy. *See* Scheindlin, Judith
Juilliard, August, 57
Julius Silver Residence Center and Cafeteria, 88

Kane, Bob, 146
kayaking, 70, 102
Kay, Michael, 149
Kazan, Lainie, 100
Kazimiroff Nature Trail, 69
Keck, Charles, 46, 79, 81–62
Keeshan, Bob, 149
Keister, George, 160
Kennedy, John F., 24, 27, 125
Kennedy, Joseph P., 24, 27
Kennedy House, 24, 27
Kent, James, 82
Kepler Field (Van Cortlandt Park), 36
keystone of the bridge at Chateau Thierry, 45
King's Bridge, 59–60, 142, 148
Kingsbridge Armory, 141–142
Kingsbridge National Ice Center, 142
Kingsbridge Road, 51–52, 134, 141–143, 145–148
Kinney, Belle, 72, 82
Kiselewski, Joseph, 46, 85
Klein, Calvin, 133
Klein, Robert, 133
Kliegl, Anton, 57
Krakauer piano company, 159
Krasdale Art Gallery, 180–181
Kreisler, Fritz, 54
Kreymborg, Charles, 126
Kroeger piano company, 159

LaGuardia, Fiorello, 27, 55, 115
Lanier, Sidney, 85
Lauren, Ralph, 133
Law and Order: Criminal Intent (television series), 100
Lazzeri, John B., 62

Lee, Canada, 54
Lee, Robert Edward, 83
Lehman College, 137–140; the Apex, 137–138; Carman Hall, 140; Concert Hall, 139; Davis Hall, 140; Leonard Lief Library, 140; Music Building, 139; Old Gymnasium Building, 140; Shuster Hall, 140; Student Hall, 139
Lehman College Art Gallery, 140, 181
Lehman College Center for the Performing Arts, 139, 163
Leslie, Frank, 57
Letter, The (sculpture), 129
Lilien, H. Herbert, 125
Lincoln, Abraham, 48, 78, 81, 115
Lincoln Avenue, 156, 159
Lipton, Sir Thomas, 88–90
Live from the Edge Theater, 183–184
Lober, Georg, 82
Lombardi, Vince, 149
Long Day's Journey into Night (film), 100, 103
Longfellow, Henry Wadsworth, 86
Long Island Sound, 51, 64, 67–68, 70–71, 97, 99, 102, 106, 109, 175
Longman, Evelyn, 85
Longwood Art Gallery, 181–182
Lord and Burnham Company, 8
Lorillard family, 6, 117
Lou Gehrig Plaza, 126
Louis, Joe, 19
Louis Philippe, king of France, 150–151
Love Is All There Is (film), 100
Lovinger Theater, 139
Lowell, James Russell, 86
Loyalty, Valor, and Sacrifice (sculpture), 46
Lyon, Mary, 84

MacCracken, Henry Mitchell, 77–78
MacDowell, Edward Alexander, 83
MacMonnies, Frederick, 78, 80, 84, 86
MacNeil, Hermon A., 82, 85–86
Macombs Dam Bridge, 118
Madison, James, 81
Majesty of the Law (sculpture), 46
Major Deegan Expressway, 35, 37, 155, 157–158, 160
Mali, Henri W. T., 88

Mann, Horace, 85
Manship, Paul, 114
Mantle, Mickey, 19
Maris, Roger, 19
Marshall, John, 82
Marshall, Garry, 133–134
Marshall, Penny, 133–134
Martineau, Stanley, 79–80
Marx Brothers, 189
Masterson, William "Bat," 57
Maury, Matthew Fontaine, 80
Maynicke & Franke, 125
McAdoo, William, 55
McCartan, Edward, 86
McClellan Street, 120–121
McKee, Joseph V., 125
McKim, Mead & White, 54
McManus, George, 54
Mears, Helen Farnsworth, 80
Mediterranean Revival style, 124–125
Meister, Morris, 89–90, 135
Melville, Herman, 54
Memorial Grove (Pelham Bay Park), 72
Metro-North Harlem Division, 51, 128, 148
Metro-North Hudson Division, 129
Metro-North New Haven Division, 148
Mexicans, 156, 161, 164–165
Michelson, Albert Abraham, 81
Middletown Road, 72
Mike's Deli, 115
Mill Brook, 162
Miniwitz, 98
Minneford, 98
Minneford Shipyard, 107
Minnieford Avenue, 102
Mitchell, Maria, 80
model train show, 8–9
Monroe, James, 82
Monument Park, 21–22
Moorish style, 118, 134
Morales, Esai, 163
Moral Law (sculpture), 47
Morgan, J. P., 7, 26, 109
Mori, Toshiko, 145
Morrisania, 62, 154, 162
Morris, Gerard Walton, 127, 154
Morris, Gouverneur, 154, 162–163
Morris, Gouverneur II, 154, 162

Morris, Lewis, 154, 163
Morris Yacht and Beach Club, 109
Morse, Samuel Finley Breese, 79
Morton, William Thomas Green, 80
Moses, Robert, 34–35, 70
Mosholu, 32
Mosholu Avenue, 24, 35, 37–38
Mosholu Golf Course, 34
Mosholu Parkway, 34, 118, 133–134, 179, 186
motion picture production, 20, 46, 100, 103, 126, 141–142
Motley, John Lathrop, 86
Mott, Jordan L., 154
Mott Avenue, 118, 130
Mott Haven, 153–167
Mott Haven Branch of the New York Public Library, 166
Mott Haven East Historic District, 163–164
Mott Haven Historic District, 165–167
Mullaly, John, 34, 133
Munson, Thurman, 19
murals, 48, 90, 105, 120, 125, 129–130
Murphy, Henry J., 115
Museum of Bronx History, 62, 175
Musselsuckers, 100

Nadelman, Elie, 30
Nast, Thomas, 54
Naumkeag, 29–30
Negro Fort, 134
neo-Art Deco style, 121, 148
neo-Classical style, 42–43, 45, 156
neo-Gothic style, 164
neo-Grecian style, 160, 164
neo-Renaissance style, 161
Nevelson, Louise, 174
Neville & Bagge, 164
Newcomb, Simon, 80
New York and Harlem River Railroad, 91, 148
New York Botanical Garden, 5–11, 175, 188; Azalea Garden, 9; Benenson Ornamental Conifer Collection, 9; Cherry Valley, 9; Daffodil Hill, 9; Enid A. Haupt Conservatory, 8–9; Everett Children's Adventure Garden, 10; Herbarium, 7; Magnolia Way, 9;

Native Plant Garden, 9–10; Peggy Rockefeller Rose Garden, 10; Rock Garden, 5, 9; Ruth Rea Howell Family Garden, 10; T. A. Havemeyer Lilac Collection, 9; Thain Family Forest, 10
New York Central Railroad, 34–35, 38
New York City Department of Parks and Recreation, 187
New York City Marathon, 160
New York Yankees, 18–19, 21, 125–136
New York Yankees Museum, 21–22, 175
New York Zoological Society. See Wildlife Conservation Society
Noah (sculpture), 129
Northeast Forest, 38

O'Brien, Thomas, 167
O'Gorman, William, 164
Old Croton Aqueduct Trail, 38
"Old Edgar" (bell), 149
Old Fort Number Four Park, 141
Orchard Beach, 64, 67–71, 75, 107
Orchard Beach Nature Center, 70
Orchard Beach Playground, 71
Orchid Show, 8
Ortiz, Raphael Montañez, 93
Osgood, Charles, 149
Our Lady of Mount Carmel Church, 113–114
outdoor fitness equipment, 35, 39

Paine, Thomas, 81
Palmer, Alice Freeman, 85
Palmer, Benjamin, 99
Palminteri, Chazz, 113
parades, 186
Paramino, John Francis, 81
Parkman, Francis, 86
Pataki, George, 142
Paul Avenue, 136, 138
Paul VI (pope), 20
Paulson, Emil, 123
Peabody, George, 84
Pelham, George, 164
Pelham, manor of, 66, 98
Pelham, town of, 98–99, 103
Pelham Bay Nature Center, 73
Pelham Bay Park, 34, 48, 53, 64–75, 102, 107

Pelham Bridge, 69
Pelham Cemetery, 103
Pelham Golf Course, 68–70, 74
Pelham Parkway, 34
Pelham Track and Field, 72–73
Pelican Bay Playground, 71
Pell, John, 48
Pell, Samuel, 102
Pell, Thomas, 66, 98
Pell's Point, Battle of, 48, 66, 71
Penn, William, 82
Penney, James Cash, 55
Perkins, George Walbridge, 26
Perkins-Freeman family, 26
Perniconi, Bishop Joseph, 114
Perry, Antoinette, 57
Peters, Rev. Absalem, 56
Phelps-Dodge Copper Company, 29
Philbin, Regis, 129
Philipse, Frederick, 33
piano manufacturing, 155, 159
Picasso, Pablo, 174
Piccirilli brothers, 115
picnicking, 7, 11, 17, 27, 31, 41, 56, 58, 64,
    73, 75. See also barbecuing; dining;
    restaurants
Pilcher & Tachau, 141
Pilot Street, 108
Platt, Eleanor, 84
Playground for All Children (Pelham
    Bay Park), 72–73
playgrounds, 36–37, 39, 64, 67, 71–73,
    113, 133, 141, 155
Plaza Borinquen, 161–162
Poe, Edgar Allan, 1, 50–52, 86, 148–149.
    See also Edgar Allan Poe Cottage
Poe Park, 52, 143, 144–146
Poe Park Bandstand, 146
Poe Park Visitor Center, 145
Poe Park Visitor Center Gallery, 145–
    146, 182
Pokorny, Jan Hird, 139
Polasek, Albin, 83
Pope, John Russell, 54
Port Morris, 107
Potter's Field, 104
Pregones Theater, 184
Protection of Law (sculpture), 47
PS 17, 104

PS/MS 80, 133
PS 102, 104
PS 175, 107
Public Works Administration, 129
Puerto Ricans, 122, 130, 134, 147, 155, 161,
    165, 186
Pulitzer, Joseph, 55
Punishment of Law (sculpture), 46
Putnam, Brenda, 86
Putnam Division, 35, 38
Putnam Trail, 35, 38
Pyne, Percy, 30

Quattrocchi, Edmondo, 80
Queen Anne style, 160
Quinn, Edmond T., 52, 82, 84, 86

Raldris and LaVelle, 121
Ramada Bronx, 191
Reed, Walter, 80
Reilly, Robert J., 151
religious gatherings, 20
Renaissance Revival style, 122, 127–128,
    164
Renwick, James Jr., 129
restaurants, 17, 24, 69, 75, 97, 99–100,
    103, 107, 109, 111, 113, 116, 126, 130,
    142–143, 152, 159, 186. See also barbe-
    cuing; dining; picnicking
Revere, Paul, 60
Revolutionary War, 1, 33, 38–39, 41,
    47–48, 59–60, 66, 71, 89, 99, 134, 141,
    153, 162
Rhind, Massey, 85
Rice, Grantland, 54
Richard, Tex, 54
Riker's Island, 104
Risse, Louis A., 42, 44, 118, 124, 134,
    142–143
Risse Street, 134
Riverdale, 23–24, 27–29, 172–173, 179
Riverdale Country School, 27
Riverdale Equestrian Center, 38
Riverdale Presbyterian Church, 28
Rochambeau, comte de, 60
Rochambeau Avenue, 133
Rockefeller, John D. Jr., 127
Rockne, Knute, 20
Rodman's Neck, 66, 71, 75

Rodrigue, William, 150–151
Rogers and Browne, 160
Romanesque Revival style, 54, 136, 161, 164
Romeyn, Charles, 166
Roosevelt, Franklin Delano, 83, 125, 141, 151
Roosevelt, Theodore, 14, 25–26, 82, 166
Rose Hill Manor House, 150
Roth, Emery, 126
Rowlands, Gena, 126
running tracks, 35, 39, 72–73, 137
Runyon, Damon, 54
Russians, 24
Ruth, Babe, 19, 125

Sachkerah Woods Playground (Van Cortlandt Park), 39
Sacks, Oliver, 100
Saint Ann's Protestant Episcopal Church, 162–163
Saint Barnabas Hospital, 112
Saint-Gaudens, Augustus, 81, 83–84
Saint Jerome's Roman Catholic Church 165
Saint Mary Star of the Sea, 102
Salvatore, Victor, 85
Samuel Pell House, 102
Sanford, Edward F., 46
Scheindlin, Judith, 100, 106
Schmeling, Max, 19
Schuler, Hans, 84–85
Schwab, Gustav, 89
Scorsese, Martin, 129
Scully, Vin, 149
sculpture, 14–15, 26, 42, 44–47, 54, 62, 72–73, 79–87, 88, 93, 102, 105, 114, 123–124, 129, 150–151, 165, 171, 173–174
Seaman, Elizabeth Cochran, 54
Sears, Roebuck and Company, 108
Second Saint Peter's Lutheran Church, 164
Sedgwick Avenue, 134, 190
Sense of Place, A (murals), 90
Shahn, Ben, 129, 174
Shamrock IV (yacht), 88–89
Sherman, William Tecumseh, 83
Sheridan, John H., 72
Sherry, Louis, 55

Shmuck, Peter J., 123
Shore Road, 69
Sievers, F. William, 80
Sigel, Franz, 54, 127–128
Simon, Louis A., 129
Sinatra, Frank, 29
Siwanoy Indians, 64, 66, 68
Siwanoy Trail, 69
Skidmore, Owings & Merrrill, 148
Smith, Alfred E., 125
Smith, Hamilton, 89
Smith, Will, 142
Snowden, George, 46
Snyder, C.B.J., 104
soccer, 20–21, 31, 34, 39
softball, 31
Sousa, John Philip, 83
South Asians, 31, 36
Southern Boulevard, 112
South Minneford Yacht Club, 107
Southwest Playground (Van Cortlandt Park), 39
Spanish-American War (sculpture), 47
Spanish-American War memorial, 156
Spanish Colonial style, 123, 165
Spar, Laurenda, 93
SPARs, 138, 141
Spencer, Herbert, 25
Spirit of Progress (sculpture), 46
Split Rock, 69, 71
Split Rock Golf Course, 68–69, 74
Split Rock Trail, 69
Springsteen & Goldhammer, 124
stained-glass windows, 54, 88, 108, 139, 150–151, 160, 163
St. Ann's Avenue, 162
Stanton, Elizabeth Cady, 55
Starving Artist Art Gallery, 106, 182
Stella, Joseph, 57
Stepping Stones, 109–110
Stern, Robert A. M., 90
St. George's Crescent, 134
St. Lanne, Louis, 72
St. Mary's Park, 34
Stockbridge Indians, 33, 38
Stonehenge of The Bronx, 34–35, 38
Stone Mill, 5, 7, 9
Story, Joseph, 82
Stowe, Harriet Beecher, 86

Straus, Isidor, 55
street fairs, 186
Stuart, Gilbert Charles, 84
Stuyvesant Yacht Club, 107
subway railroad yards, 136
Sugarman & Berger, 124
Sweetgum Playground (Pelham Bay
    Park), 73
swimming, 31, 35, 39–40, 70–71, 106,
    109

Taday, Nelson H., 122
Taft, Lorado, 84
Taylor, Laurette, 57
Teatro de Puerto Rico, 161
Teitel Brothers' Grocery, 114
television films and series, 29, 100. 103
Temple Beth El, 102
tennis, 31, 40, 71, 73, 75, 106, 186
Tercera Iglesia Bautista, 166
Thackeray, William Makepeace, 25
Thayer, Sylvanus, 84–85
Theodore Roosevelt High School, 152
Third Avenue, 112, 148, 155–158, 165
Third Avenue Bridge, 157–159
Third Avenue Elevated, 112, 160, 165
Third Baptist Church, 166
Thomas, Andrew J., 127
Thomas Garden Apartments, 127
Thomas Pell Wildlife Sanctuary, 69
Thompson, Holmes & Converse, 138
Thoreau, Henry David, 83
Throggs Neck, 175
Tibbett's Brook, 32–33, 37, 135
Tier Street, 103
Titanic (ship), 57
Topping, Dan, 54
Toscanini, Arturo, 25–26, 114
Tour de Bronx, 187
Touring Kayak Club, 102
tours, 7–8, 10, 15, 21–22, 26, 40, 57–58,
    64, 74, 186–187
Triborough Bridge, 155, 158
Trinity United Methodist Church, 103
Triumph of Civic Administration (sculp-
    ture), 47
Triumph of Good Government (sculp-
    ture), 46–47
Truman, Harry S, 125

Tudor Gothic style, 138–140
Turtle Cove, 66
Turtle Cove Golf Center, 69
Twain, Mark, 25–26. See also Clemens,
    Samuel Langhorne
Twin Islands, 70
Two Trees Island, 70
Tyndall, John, 25

Underground Railroad route, 157
United Nations, 24–25, 138; Security
    Council, 138
University Heights, 77, 79
Upjohn, Richard M., 28
Urban Park Ranger free programs, 31, 35,
    40, 64, 72–73
U Thant, 24

Valentine, Isaac, 59–61, 131
Valentine, John, 131
Valentine family, 51
Valentine-Varian House, 59–63, 131–132
Van Cortlandt, Augustus, 33
Van Cortlandt, Frederick, 33
Van Cortlandt, Jacobus, 33
Van Cortlandt Avenue East, 59, 61, 132–
    134, 136
Van Cortlandt Golf Course, 34, 37–38
Van Cortlandt House, 31, 33–35, 37,
    39–41, 48
Van Cortlandt Lake, 31, 35–36
Van Cortlandt Park, 31–41, 118, 133
Van Cortlandt Park Nature Center,
    37, 40
Van Cortlandt Park Stadium, 36–37
Vanderbilt, Cornelius, 7
Varian, Isaac, 61
Varian, Isaac Leggett, 61
Varian, Jesse Huestis, 61
Vault Hill, 33, 35
Veterans' Memorial Hall, 47–48, 93
Victory, Peace, and Love of Country
    (sculpture), 46–47
Villa Avenue, 134
Viñoly, Rafael, 121, 137
Virginia, the, 128

Wald, Lillian D., 84
Walker, James J., 125, 158

Walker, Madam C. J., 55
Walsh, William D., 150
Walton Avenue, 44, 46–47, 124, 126–127, 184
Walton High School, 137, 141
Ward & Davis, 166
Warhol, Andy, 174
Washington, Booker T., 85
Washington, Denzel, 149
Washington, George, 31, 33, 41, 48, 60–61, 66, 71, 81, 84, 115, 141, 151
Washington Greys, 141
Wave Hill, 23, 25–28, 176; Aquatic Garden, 26; Armor Hall, 26, 185; Marco Polo Stufano Conservatory, 26; Monocot Garden, 26; Wild Garden, 26
WAVEs, 138–141
Webb, William 47
Webster, Daniel, 81
Webster Avenue, 57–58, 148
Weckquasgeek Indians, 66
Weinman, Adolph, 46, 85
Wells, James L., 166
West Indians, 31, 36, 146
West 205th Street, 136–137
West 247th Street, 29–30
West 248th Street, 30
West 249th Street, 27, 29
West 252nd Street, 24, 27
West 256th Street, 24, 35
Westinghouse, George, 80
WFUV (radio station), 151
Whistler, James Abbott McNeill, 84
White, Stanford, 77, 87, 90
Whitman, Walt, 85, 129

Whitney, Eli, 79
Whittier, John Greenleaf, 86
Wildlife Conservation Society, 12, 14, 112. See also Bronx Zoo
Wilkinson Avenue,, 73
Willard, Emma, 85
Willard, Frances Elizabeth, 84
Williams, Bert, 54, 57
Williams, Robin, 100
Williams, Roger, 85
Williamsbridge Oval, 133
Williamsbridge Reservoir, 133
Willis, Edward, 160, 166
Willis Avenue, 160, 164, 166
Willis Avenue Bridge, 160
Wilson, Big, 100
Wilson, Woodrow, 30, 48, 82
Winged Victory (sculpture), 72
Wisdom of the Law (sculpture), 46
The Wizard of Oz (film), 79
Wong, Martin, 94
Woodlawn Cemetery, 54–58, 62, 73, 127, 185; Woolworth Chapel, 185
Woodlawn Playground (Van Cortlandt Park), 39
Woolworth, F. W., 55
World War I, 30, 42, 45, 47, 99, 105, 109, 113–115, 124, 156, 158
World War II, 24, 26, 63, 72, 83, 89, 99, 109, 112, 125, 135, 138–140, 155–156, 161
Wright, Orville and Wilbur, 81

Yankee Stadium, 18–22, 123, 125, 129
Young Israel of the Concourse, 93

Zelnick, Simon H., 93

About the Authors

Lloyd Ultan was born in The Bronx in 1938 and has lived there his entire life. He is a professor of history at Fairleigh Dickinson University in Hackensack, New Jersey. In 1996, he was appointed to the government position of Bronx Borough Historian. He is the author of over one thousand articles on aspects of the history of The Bronx, the author or coauthor of ten other books in the field, and is considered by many to lead the best walking tours in New York City.

Shelley Olson was born in Sacramento, California, and moved at an early age to Massachusetts. This began her exploration of over thirty countries. She holds a doctorate in education from the University of Houston. She moved to The Bronx in 2007 and began her discovery of the natural and constructed beauty of that borough of New York City. Frustration that there was no guidebook to interesting sites in The Bronx inspired her to collaborate on this book.